# Spanish Cuisine

# Spanish Cuisine
## The Gourmet's Companion

*Matt A. Casado*

**JOHN WILEY & SONS, INC.**

New York   Chichester   Weinheim   Brisbane   Singapore   Toronto

This publication is designed to provide accurate and
authoritative information in regard to the subject
matter covered. It is sold with the understanding that
the publisher is not engaged in rendering legal, accounting,
or other professional services. If legal advice or other
expert assistance is required, the services of a competent
professional person should be sought.

*Library of Congress Cataloging-in-Publication Data*

Casado, Matt A., 1937-
    Spanish cuisine : the gourmet's companion / Matt A. Casado.
        p.    cm.
    Includes bibliographical references (p.    ).
    ISBN 0-471-13722-7 (paper : alk. paper)
    1. Cookery. Spanish.  2. Cookery—Spain.
    3. Cookery, Spanish—terminology.    I. Title.
    TX723.5.S7C3567    1997
    641.5946—dc20                                96-15478

Printed in the United States of America

10 9 8 7 6 5 4 3 2 1

# Contents

## INTRODUCTION     ix

The Cuisine of Spain: A Regional Overview     ix

The Cuisine of Andalusia     ix

The Cuisine of the Basque Country     x

The Cuisine of Castile     xi

The Cuisine of Catalonia     xi

The Cuisine of Extremadura     xii

The Cuisine of Galicia     xiii

The Cuisine of the Islands     xiii

The Cuisine of La Mancha     xiv

The Cuisine of León     xiv

The Cuisine of the Levant     xv

The Cuisine of Portugal     xv

The Cuisine of Rioja/Aragon     xvi

## PART I — Spanish and Portuguese Dishes, by Course   1

Tapas — Snacks     3

Entremeses — Appetizers     5

Ensaladas — Salads     8

Sopas — Soups     11

Pescados y Mariscos — Seafood     15

Huevos — Eggs     22

Arroz — Rice     26

Pastas — Pasta     29

Legumbres y Verduras — Vegetables     31

Guisos, Ollas, Potajes, y Pucheros — Stews 38

Aves — Poultry 44

Carnes — Meats 48

Caza — Game 53

Postres, Frutas, y Nueces — Desserts, Fruits and Nuts 57

Quesos — Cheese 61

Pan y Pastelería — Breads and Pastry 63

Salsas — Sauces 65

Condimentos, Hierbas, y Especias — Condiments, Herbs and Spices 68

Vinos — Wines 69

Bebidas y Refrescos — Beverages and Refreshments 71

## PART II — Spanish Food and Beverage Vocabulary 73

Spanish Pronunciation Key 75

# Culinary Regions
# of Spain

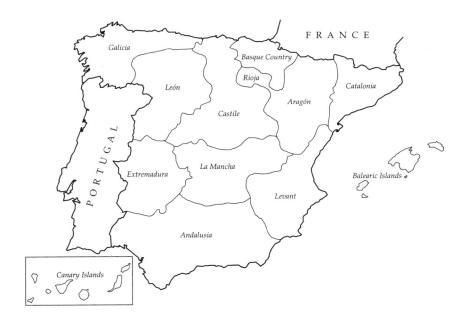

FRANCE

Galicia

Basque Country

Rioja

León

Catalonia

Aragón

Castile

La Mancha

PORTUGAL

Extremadura

Balearic Islands

Levant

Andalusia

Canary Islands

# Introduction

## The Cuisine of Spain: A Regional Overview

The cuisine of Spain is as varied as its geography. The country is essentially a land of mountains ringed by the sea. The Peninsula has been isolated from Europe for centuries by the imposing Pyrenees mountains. Another high sierra bars the way in the south, having made the crossing into Andalusia difficult before the age of modern transportation. The North is a continuation of rugged mountain ranges that form isolated areas within the country. Communication among the different regions has always been difficult, making the exchange of culinary specialties rare. Today, each region still preserves its cooking secrets and traditions, adhering passionately to its own peculiar manner of cooking. An important base of Spanish cuisine is the *sofrito* which consists of sautéed onions, tomatoes and garlic in olive oil.

## The Cuisine of Andalusia

The cuisine of Andalusia reflects the subtropical climate of the region and the domination by Arab invaders for almost eight hundred years. It is a light, colorful cuisine that uses fresh garden vegetables, olive oil, and garlic as main ingredients. Gazpachos and salads are an important part of the menu, particularly on hot summer days. Fresh fish is deliciously prepared in coastal towns by deep-frying it in olive oil and serving it accompanied by the famous local white wine.

Cured ham is particularly tasty here, especially if it comes from the towns of Jabugo and Trevélez. Serrano ham is similar to Italian prosciutto and cured in the high mountain ranges where winter snow is regularly present. The ham is sweet-salty in taste and crunchy to the bite. Serrano ham must be eaten accompanied by wholesome bread and Manzanilla wine, one of the full-bodied wines of Andalusia.

Many dishes in this region are prepared with sherry, which has been produced in the area of Jerez de la Frontera for centuries. Sherry is a fortified wine containing a small amount of brandy that is aged in oak casks for several years. Andalusians drink sherry while eating tapas before meals or with dessert.

A land of bull breeding, Andalusia offers a series of interesting stews prepared with beef. The desserts have a very strong Arab/Jewish influence. Sweets made with ground almonds, dried figs, honey, and cloves are reminiscent of Middle Eastern lands.

A menu representative of Andalusian cuisine could be:

*Gazpacho andaluz* (Cold Tomato Soup)

*Salmonetes fritos* (Fried Red Mullets)

*Ternera a la sevillana* (Sautéed Veal with Sherry and Green Olives)

*Yemas de San Leandro* (Candied Egg Yolks)

## The Cuisine of the Basque Country

The Basque Country lies in the mountainous regions of northern Spain and southwestern France. Its language, which, so far as is known, bears no relation to any other, may possibly be the survivor of the ancient Iberian languages which was supplanted by Latin, under the Romans. The Basques have preserved their ancient customs, language, and cuisine through the years.

Basque cooking focuses mainly on the preparation of seafood, which is very abundant in the cold waters of the Bay of Biscay. Many dishes are cooked using the dry salt-cod that the Basques have imported from Norway and Newfoundland for generations; hake, tuna, and sea bream are also prepared in several delicious ways. One of the elements that make Basque cuisine different from that of the rest of Spain is its sauces, which are prepared carefully, following old recipes passed from generation to generation.

In the mountains, the temperate humid weather helps pastures stay green and tender. There, calves and sheep grow to become prime veal and tasty lamb. Feathered and furred game, such as quail, duck, woodcock, wild boar, and venison, is cooked in special sauces and garnished with several varieties of local mushrooms. The region is famous for its gastronomical societies with male-only members that gather together to prepare and sample dishes whose recipes are well-kept secrets.

A typical Basque menu could consist of:

*Ollo salda* (Chicken Consommé)

*Angulas a la bilbaina* (Baby Eels Fried in Olive Oil)

*Chuleta alavesa* (Grilled Marinated Veal Chop)

*Leche frita* (Flour/Milk Squares Fried in Oil)

## The Cuisine of Castile

The dry tableland of Castile is politically the most important region of Spain. The wind, the heat, and the drought have forged the strength of the Castilians who have dominated the rest of the country for several centuries. Agriculture and livestock breeding are the essential occupations of Castile, and this is reflected in the cuisine of the region. Far from the ocean, old Castilians did not have available the ever-present seafood of coastal Spain. Their bread, however, has no equal; Castile is know as the land of the best bread, made with the best wheat, and sold with a thick, crunchy crust that is a meal in itself.

Pork is one of the fundamental elements of Castilian cuisine and the base of the famous chorizo of Cantimpalos and Riofrío. Castile has a harsh continental climate that is another important factor in the region's cuisine, causing it to be rich in calories. *Cocido* is its *pièce de resistance.* Sheep are also common in the Castilian steppes, providing excellent cheeses that go very well with the bread and the noble red wines of the area. Segovia is reknown for its roast suckling pig and Avila for the preparation of baby lamb dishes. And then, there is Madrid, where the popular *cocido* could have developed from the *adafina,* a stew which the Spanish Jews used to place on glowing embers on Friday evenings to be eaten on the Sabbath.

A representative Castilian menu could consist of the following dishes:

*Sopa de almendras a la castellana* (Almond Soup)

*Besugo con piñones* (Sea Bream with Pine Nuts)

*Cocido madrileño* (Meat, Sausage, and Chickpea Stew)

*Huesos de santo* (Marzipan Paste Filled with Candied Egg Yolks)

## The Cuisine of Catalonia

Catalonia is a prosperous, industrial region located in the northeastern corner of the Iberian Peninsula. Its people are famous for their pragmatism, their diligence, and their contempt for everything that is not Catalonian. Catalonia could be described as a Mediterranean region that has had strong cultural, commercial, and culinary ties with other peoples living in the coastal areas of this interior sea. Catalonian cuisine resembles that of Provence in Southern France. The gastronomic specialty of its capital city, Barcelona, is seafood. The local restaurants are reknowned for their *zarzuelas*, or fish casseroles reminiscent of the bouillabaisse from Marseilles. Garlic is strongly present in Catalonian dishes, particularly in the garlic-mayonnaise sauce that is similar to Provence's aioli. Inland, the farmers prepare tasty stews consisting of local sausages and dry white beans. Sauces often contain crushed almonds or hazelnuts that grow there profusely.

In spite of its relatively dry climate, Catalonia produces a great variety of fruits. The summer crop consists of peaches, apricots, pears, cherries, melons, and grapes. These fruits are often included in recipes and served as stuffing or garnishes in a variety of dishes.

The wines of Catalonia are of excellent quality and are exported to countries around the world. It is the only region of Spain that produces sparkling wines, called *cava* and comparable in quality to the champagne of France. A Catalonian menu could consist of the following dishes:

**Sopa payesa** (Cabbage and Ham Soup)

**Habas a la catalana** (Sautéed Fava Beans with Chorizo)

**Parrillada de pescado** (Grilled Seafood)

**Crema a la catalana** (Crème Brûlée)

## The Cuisine of Extremadura

The region of Extremadura is largely mountainous, dry, and poor. In the distant past, the people of Extremadura had to leave their native land to find fame and fortune elsewhere. Many *extremeños* took part successfully in the conquest of the New World; Cortés, the conqueror of Mexico, was from the city of Medellín; Pizarro, the conqueror of Perú, was from the town of Trujillo; Balboa, discoverer of the Pacific Ocean, came from Jerez de los Caballeros.

The Guadiana river crosses Extremadura from east to west, providing irrigation along its course for the growing of grain crops. The cuisine of this region is based on dishes cooked with pork, poultry, and game. Chorizo sausage is particularly good in Extremadura, where it is made with meat from hogs that have been fed with acorns, very abundant in the area. Herds of swine are often seen in the fields of Extremadura, foraging for acorns during the day and returning to their pens at sunset.

The cuisine of this austere land is simple and unpretentious. Popular in Extremadura are *migas*, an inexpensive dish prepared with stale bread or flour to which chunks of sausage, ham, and bacon are generously added.

Here is a sample menu from Extremadura:

*Ensalada de judías tiernas* (Green Bean Salad)

*Migas a la serrana* (Sautéed Water-Soaked Bread)

*Faisán a las uvas* (Pot-Roasted Pheasant with Grapes)

*Torta de bellotas* (Acorn Scone)

## The Cuisine of Galicia

Much of the land in Galicia is mountainous and barely arable. Its seacost, however, is incredibly rich in seafood. Galician rivers and the Atlantic Ocean form estuaries where shellfish can be easily collected at low tide. Galicia is the only place in Spain where people play the bagpipes: the Galicians are akin to the ancient Celts who settled Scotland and Ireland in prehistoric times.

The cuisine of this northern region has its roots in pre-Roman Spain; in a kitchen that did not use garlic and olive oil but pork fat, corn bread, and rye flour. The waters of its short but plentiful rivers flowing into the Bay of Biscay are rich in salmon that is prepared following old recipes handed down from generation to generation. Other specialties in the Galician cuisine are boiled octopus and dishes prepared with hard cider, made from the region's abundance of apples.

The wines of Galicia are quite different from those of the south of Spain. The lack of sunshine makes the grapes rich with tannin which causes the wine to be heavy in body and, if red, to develop an almost purplish hue.

A classic Galician menu could be:

*Sopa de centollo* (Spider Crab Soup)

*Empanada de lamprea* (Lamprey Pie)

*Merluza a la gallega* (Hake Galician Style)

*Tarta de Puentedeume* (Almond/Egg Yolk Tart)

# The Cuisine of the Islands

The two Spanish archipelagos have very different characteristics. The Balearic Islands lie in the Mediterranean Sea, off the coast of eastern Spain while the Canary Islands are located just north of the Tropic of Cancer, off the coast of western Africa.

The cuisine of the Balearic Islands is similar to that of Catalonia: typically Mediterranean, although having a strong Jewish flavor. People from ancient Israel are said to have arrived and settled in the islands after the diaspora.

The Canarian cuisine, on the other hand, uses ingredients commonly found in the tropics. Bananas are often used in recipes, together with roasted corn meal, sweet potatoes, and wall rocket. A traditional dish cooked on grand occasions is a stew containing seven kinds of meat: beef, pork, turkey, chicken, rabbit, partridge, and squab.

A menu combining both cuisines could be:

*Sopa mallorquina* (Balearic Cabbage Soup)

*Calamares rellenos* (Balearic Stuffed Squid)

*Cazuela canaria* (Canarian Fish Stew)

*Torta de plátanos* (Canarian Banana Fried Bread)

# The Cuisine of La Mancha

La Mancha is a dry, flat region on the central plateau that extends roughly south from Madrid to the spurs of the Andalusian mountain chains. This is the land of Don Quixote, the mad knight created by Cervantes in the 17th century, who was determined to right any wrong he encountered in his chimerical country. The real La Mancha is a wine, wheat, and olive-growing area teeming with game and sheep.

Cervantes defines the stew prepared in times of Don Quixote as having chunks of beef, lamb, ham, bacon, hen, duck, partridge, calf's brain, giblets, leeks, turnips, carrots, onion, celery, chickpeas, cabbage, rice, lentils, bread, tomato, salt, and cloves. Today, stews are still the main culinary features of this region.

Rabbit, quail, and partridge are also excellently prepared in La Mancha, but the fame goes to a stew called *morteruelo* made with hare, chicken, pork tenderloin, with walnuts, paprika, pepper, cloves, cinnamon, and caraway as condiments.

Cervantes would recommend the following menu when in La Mancha:

*Pisto albacetense* (Ratatouille with Pickled Bonito Fish)

*Bacalao pueblerino* (Salt-cod and Legume Puree)

*Perdices escabechadas* (Pickled Partridges)

*Sopa borracha* (Red Wine-soaked Biscuits)

## The Cuisine of León

The first university on the Iberian Peninsula was established at Salamanca in 1220. Since then, this city in the region of León has been the cultural center of Spain. People believe that the best Castilian is spoken in the country around Salamanca and Valladolid.

León's rivers and reservoirs are famous for their abundance of trout. Chamois, deer, and wild boar are common in the mountains of the region and are an important part of the rich, wholesome cuisine of this area. Trout fishermen here prepare trout by coating them with river mud before baking them on a bed of embers. The region is also famous for its beef and pork roasts.

A typical Leonese menu would offer:

*Sopa leonesa* (Bread and Egg Soup)

*Truchas a la judía* (Sautéed Trout Jewish Style)

*Tostón zamorano* (Roast Suckling Pig)

*Orejas* (Fried Brandy Dumplings)

## The Cuisine of the Levant

The coastal region between Catalonia and Andalusia was the fief of El Cid who wrested it from Arab invaders. The climate is mildly Mediterranean which helps the growth of citrus fruits, vegetables, almonds, dates, figs, mulberries, and rice. Rice is grown in marshlands in the province of Valencia and is the main staple of the area. Home of the world-known paella, the Levant is also famous for many other rice dishes cooked with meat, fish, game, vegetables, snails, or with eels caught in the inland lakes where rice is grown.

The fish is also particularly tasty. Restaurants on the coast prepare a fisherman's rice cooked in the broth left over from boiling several kinds of local fish. The rice is served with *alioli* sauce, a cold, thick, pale yellow sauce with a tangy bite that is the perfect additive to this Mediterranean dish.

In the South, the Arabs built an efficient system of irrigation that is still functional today. A series of canals supplies water to vegetable gardens where peppers, tomatoes, garlic, onions, fava beans, artichokes, and other produce is plentifully grown.

A Levantine menu could offer:

*Ajotomate* (Tomato/Garlic Salad)

*Mújol a la sal* (Mullets Baked in Coarse Salt)

*Paella valenciana* (Meat and Seafood Rice)

*Buñuelos de higo* (Fig Fritters)

## The Cuisine of Portugal

The history of Portugal has been tied to that of Spain for centuries and so has its cuisine. Until the thirteenth century Portugal was one of the medieval kingdoms in the Iberian Peninsula. Spaniards and Portuguese have common ancestors, customs, and methods of cooking. Portuguese cooking, however, is spicier and perhaps richer. While Spanish cooking uses olive oil almost exclusively, in Portugal the use of cream and butter is quite common.

As in Spain, pork and lamb are excellent, while beef is not of the highest quality. Portugal is also a country of plentiful fish that is deliciously grilled on charcoal fires just a few hours after being caught. Like the Basques, Portuguese seamen have been fishing the banks of Newfoundland for generations, bringing to Portugal slabs of salt-cod that is prepared in multiple ways across the country.

Northern Portugal's cooking is very similar to that of Spanish Galicia; its *caldo verde* soup made from dark green cabbage is akin to Galicia's *caldo gallego*. In the South, the cuisine of the Algarve, with strong Arab influence, resembles that of Andalusia.

A menu served in a Portuguese restaurant could offer the following dishes:

*Caldeirada a pescadora* (Fisherman's Style Soup)

*Arroz de caril de camarao* (Spiced Shrimp Rice)

*Frango na pucara* (Chicken in the Pot)

*Bolo de amendoras* (Almond Cake)

## The Cuisine of Rioja/Aragon

Aragon straddles the valley of the largest Spanish river, the Ebro, that runs parallel to the Pyrenees. Cooking here is simple and strong enough to help the people endure the harsh winters when the wind blows from the high mountains in the North. The region is famous for its *chilindrón* sauce a spicy orange-colored combination of tomatoes, peppers, onions, and garlic simmered in olive oil. Chicken and lamb prepared *al chilindrón* are the specialties of Aragon.

Rioja produces the best wines in Spain. The clarets have the reputation of being as good as those of Bordeaux and are exported around the world. Game is abundant in the area and when prepared with red wine sauces are well-appreciated by connoisseurs.

A typical menu served in the area could consist of:

*Sopa oscense* (Veal Liver and Cheese Soup)

*Truchas al Pirineo* (Baked Trout with Cured Ham)

*Chilindrón de cordero* (Lamb in Chilindrón Sauce)

*Peras con vino* (Poached Pears in Red Wine)

# Spanish Cuisine

# *Part I*

## Spanish and Portuguese Dishes, by Course

# TAPAS — SNACKS

Drinks consumed in bars or taverns before lunch or dinner are always accompanied by a variety of snacks served in small portions and eaten informally as appetizers. Tapas are cooked in the establishments where they are served and can range from simple fried almonds or stuffed olives to sophisticated dishes like grilled shrimp, stuffed squid, or pickled quail. The variety of tapas served by any bar depends on its popularity; it is not uncommon to find bars offering thirty or forty varieties of tapas at any given time.

**Aceitunas** Olives.
— *al ajillo* Pickled olives in garlic.
— *aliñadas* Marinated olives.
— *rellenas* Stuffed green olives with anchovy and/or pimiento.
**Al ajillo** Cooked with garlic.
**A la sidra** Cooked with hard cider.
**Albóndigas** Meatballs.
**Albondiguillas** Small pork meatballs.
**Al horno** Baked in the oven.
**Al limón** With lemon.
**Almejas a la diabla** Clams in spicy tomato sauce.
— *al horno* Baked stuffed clams.
**Almendras** almonds.
— *saladas* Fried salted almonds.
**Al pil-pil** Sautéed in oil with garlic and hot peppers.
**Anchoas** Anchovies.
**Angulas** Baby eels.
— *al la bilbaina* Baby eels sautéed in oil with hot pepper.
**Atún en escabeche** Pickled tuna fish.
**Banderillas** Any cold cut, sausage, cheese, olive, or hard-boiled egg on a slice of bread threaded together with a toothpick.
**Barquitas** A stuffed, bite-sized, boat-shaped baked dough tapa.
**Boquerones** Small sardines.
— *en salmuera* Small sardines pickled in salt.
— *en vinagre* Small sardines pickled in vinegar.
**Buñuelos** Fritters.
— *de bacalao* Salt-cod fritters.
— *de chorizo* Chorizo sausage fritters.
— *de jamón* Cured ham fritters.
— *de queso* Fried cheese puffs.
**Caballitos** Deep-fried battered shrimp.
**Calamares a la romana** Deep-fried squid.
— *con cebolla* Fried squid with onions.
— *en su tinta* Squid stewed in its own ink.
— *rellenos* Fried squid stuffed with cured ham.
**Camarones** Prawns.
**Canapé de anchoa y pimiento** Anchovy and pimiento canapé.
— *de atún y tomate* Canned tuna and tomato canapé.
**Caracoles** Snails.
— *picantes* Snails in hot sauce.
**Cebollitas** Small fresh onions.
— *al limón* Chopped fresh onions dressed with olive oil and lemon juice.
— *en vinagre* Chopped vinegar-pickled fresh onions.

*Champiñones al ajillo* Sautéed mushrooms with garlic.
— *rellenos* Meat or seafood-stuffed mushrooms.
*Chanquetes* Deep-fried whitebait.
*Chorizo a la sidra* Chorizo sausage cooked with sliced apples in hard cider.
*Delicias de queso* Fried cheese balls.
*Empanadilla* Small pie.
— *de atún* Tuna fish pie.
— *de carne* Meat pie.
— *de chorizo* Chorizo sausage pie.
— *de jamón* Cured ham pie.
*En escabeche* Pickled.
*Ensaladilla rusa* Potato, vegetable, and mayonnaise salad.
*En salmuera* Cured in brine.
*En su tinta* Cooked in its own ink.
*En vinagre* In vinegar.
*En vinagreta* Dressed with vinaigrette sauce.
*Flamenquines* Deep-fried pork and ham rolls.
*Gambas al ajillo* Sautéed shrimp with garlic.
— *a la plancha* Broiled shrimp.
— *al pil-pil* Chili-hot sautéed shrimp.
— *con gabardina* Batter-fried shrimp.
— *en piperada* Shrimp simmered with tomatoes, peppers and spices.
*Huevas de pescado* Cured fish roe.
*Huevos rellenos* Stuffed hard-boild eggs.
*Mejillones en salsa verde* Mussels in green sauce.
— *en vinagreta* Mussels in vinaigrette.

— *rellenos* Chopped boiled mussels dressed with a wine béchamel and served in their own shell.
*Michirones picantes* Stewed dried fava beans in hot sauce (from Murcia).
*Pasteis de bacalhau* Salt-cod fritters (from Portugal).
*Patatas al all-i-oli* Boiled potatoes with garlic mayonnaise.
— *con ajo* Boiled potatoes with garlic mayonnaise.
*Pelotas en salsa roja* Meatballs in red sherry sauce.
*Pepinillos en vinagre* Pickled gherkins.
*Pepito de ternera* Grilled veal steak sandwich.
*Pinchos morunos* Grilled marinated miniature kabobs.
*Pulpo a la gallega* Boiled octopus dressed with paprika and oil.
— *en vinagreta* Boiled octopus slices with vinaigrette sauce.
*Riñones* Kidneys.
— *al jerez* Veal kidneys in sherry sauce.
*Rissois de camarao* Shrimp *rissolés* (from Portugal).
*Sardinas a la plancha* Grilled fresh sardines.
*Sepia con cebolla* Sautéed cuttlefish with onions.
*Tartaleta* Tartlet.
— *de champiñones* Mushroom-mayonnaise tartlet.
— *de riñones* Tartlets of sautéed kidneys in sherry sauce.
— *de salmón* Salmon tartlet.
*Tortilla de patatas* Potato omelet.
*Tortillitas de camarones* Shrimp fritters.

## ENTREMESES — APPETIZERS

Spanish lunch and dinner normally consist of three courses, often four. Appetizers in Spanish meals might consist of a hot or cold dish according to the time of year or the importance of the meal. A common hors d'oeuvre is a platter of cold cuts, sausages, cheeses, and pickled savories accompanied by a glass of cold dry sherry, preferably manzanilla.

*Aguacate a la valenciana* Avocado-half garnished with grapefruit sections and salad dressing.

*Alcachofas con jamón* Artichoke bottoms filled with chopped cured ham and mayonnaise.

— *en salsa verde* Artichokes in parsley sauce.

*Almejas a la marinera* Clams in white wine sauce.

— *con aceitunas* Clams with olives.

*Ancas de rana* Frog's legs.

— *rebozadas* Sautéed battered frog's legs.

*Aros de cebolla ocultos* Beer-battered, deep-fried onion rings.

*Aspic de langostinos* Shrimp aspic.

*Barquitas de pepino y atún* Mixed cucumber, canned tuna, and mayonnaise barquettes.

*Bolinhos de bacalhau* Deep-fried salt-cod cakes (from Portugal).

*Bolitas de oro* Hard-boiled egg yolks with pâté and gelatine.

— *de queso* Fried battered cheese balls.

— *de zanahoria* Fried battered carrot balls.

*Butifarra catalana* White pork sausage from Catalonia.

*Caracoles a la andaluza* Stewed snails with almonds and paprika.

*Carne fiambre* Cold cuts.

*Cecina* Cured meats.

*Chorizo* Red pork and paprika sausage.

*Ciruelas pasas rellenas* Deep-fried cured-ham-stuffed prunes.

*Cóctel de gambas* Shrimp served in a tomato/mayonnaise sauce.

*Cogollos de Tudela* Hearts of romaine with anchovy vinaigrette.

*Croquetas de gambas* Shrimp croquettes.

— *de jamón* Ham croquettes.

— *de merluza* Hake croquettes.

*Empanada* Pie.

— *asturiana* Chorizo pie (from Asturias).

— *berciana* Pork loin and chorizo pie (from León).

— *de berberechos* Cockle pie (from Galicia).

— *de espinacas* Spinach pie.

— *de lamprea* Lamprey fish pie (from Galicia and northern Portugal).

— *de lomo* Pork loin pie.

— *de sardinas* Sardine pie.

— *gallega* Marinated pork loin pie (from Galicia).

— *mallorquina* Lamb meat pie (from the Balearic Islands).

*Endibias al roquefort* Endive with Roquefort cheese.

*Entremeses variados* Selction of cold appetizers.

*Escabeche de bonito* Pickled striped tuna fish.

*Esgarrat* Sweet red pepper and shredded salt-cod salad (from the Levant).

*Espárragos con mayonesa* Asparagus with mayonnaise.

*Espuma de foie gras* Foie gras mousse.

*Farinatos* Bread-and-pork-fat sausage.

*Fiambre de atún* Tuna fish galantine.

— *de ternera* Veal galantine.

*Fritos de berenjena* Deep-fried battered eggplant and salami slices.

*Gachas* Gruel.

— *gaditanas* Flour gruel with milk and anise seed (from Cádiz).

— *malagueñas* Flour gruel with potatoes and garlic (from Málaga).

*Greixonera de patas de cerdo* Pig's feet baked basserole.

*Hojaldrados de chorizo* Chorizo sausage in puff pastry.

*Hornazo* Pork, partridge, and chorizo pie (from León).

*Huevos a la rusa* Stuffed hard-boiled eggs with shrimp or lobster meat and mayonnaise.

— *en salsa agria* Hard-boiled eggs simmered in a sweet-sour sauce.

*Jamón al jerez* Stewed ham in sherry wine.

— *con tomate* Fried ham with tomatoes and sweet red pepeprs.

— *empanado* Fried breaded ham.

— *en salsa de gitanos* Ham braised in milk and vinegar.

— *serrano* Cured ham.

*Lacón* Cured front leg of pig (from Galicia).

*Langostinos a la rusa* Prawns in aspic mayonnaise.

— *en salsa mahonesa* Prawns in mayonnaise sauce.

— *Villeroy* Fried béchamel-coated prawns.

*Lomo embuchado* Cured smoked pig's loin in a sausage casing.

*Longaniza* thin pork sausage.

*Medallones de langosta* Lobster medallions with mayonnaise.

*Mejillones en salsa picante* Mussels in mustard/mayonnaise.

— *gratinados* Mussels au gratin.

*Melón con jamón* Iced melon with serrano ham slices.

*Merluza a la vinagreta* Poached hake with vinaigrette sauce served cold.

— *bellavista* Cold hake in aspic.

*Migas a la serrana* Sautéed water-soaked bread with crisp pork rinds.

— *canas* Sautéed water-soaked bread (from La Mancha).

— *de la Tierra de Barros* Sautéed water-soaked bread with bacon and dried peppers.

— *de rico* Sautéed water-soaked bread with pork loin.

— *manchegas* Sautéed water-soaked bread with diced cured ham and pork rind.

*Mojama* Cured Mediterranean shark meat.

*Morcilla* Black sausage made with pig's blood.

*Navajas a la plancha* Grilled fresh razor clams.

*Nidos de patata* Deep-fried shredded potato nests filled with sautéed chopped ham, shrimp, green peas, and hard-boiled egg.

*Ostras al limón* Oysters-on-the-half-shell served with lemon.

*Pan relleno* Bread crust stuffed with minced ham, beef tongue, roasted veal, hard-boiled egg, and gherkins.

*Pastel de carne* Puff pastry meat pie (from Murcia).

— *de liebre* Hare pie.

— *de perdices* Partridge pie.

*Paté de gambas* Shrimp paté.

— *del Pirineo* Pork paté with apples and nuts.

*Pechuga de pollo a la suprema* Chicken breast *chaud-froid*.

*Pimientos con huevos de codorniz* Fried quail eggs and sweet peppers.

— *fritos* Fried sweet pappers.

— *rellenos de merluza* Peppers stuffed with hake.

*Pisto de Semana Santa* Sautéed peppers, tomatoes, onions, and canned tuna.

*Pollo a la gelatina* Chicken in aspic.

*Pomelo caliente con crema* Half grapefruit covered with whipped cream and brown sugar lightly broiled.

*Pulpo en vinagreta* Boiled octopus slices in vinaigrette sauce.

*Queso con nueces* Cream cheese with walnuts.

— *frito* Fried cheese.

*Repollo relleno de salchicha* Cabbage leaf stuffed with sausage.

*Riñones a la cántabra* Lamb kidneys, bacon, sausage, and mushrooms on a skewer.

*Rizos de jamón de York* Ham rolls filled with gelatine foie gras.

*Rollitos de lenguado* Sole, bacon, and cheese paupiettes.

*Salchicha* Thin pork sausage.

— *al jerez* Thin pork sausage in sherry wine sauce.

*Salchichón* Thick salami sausage.

*Salmón ahumado* Smoked salmon.

*Salpicón de mariscos* Seafood salmagundi.

*Sobrasada* Chorizo spread from the Balearic Islands.

*Terrina* Terrine.

— *de conejo* Rabbit terrine.

*Timbal de hígado* Liver timbale.

*Tomates rellenos* Stuffed tomatoes.

*Torta de chicharrones* Crisp pork-rind torte.

*Tortitas de arroz* Cold rice, béchamel-battered cakes fried in olive oil.

*Trucha ahumada* Smoked trout.

— *en aceite* Fried trout fillets pickled in olive oil and herbs and served cold.

**DISHES BY COURSE**

# ENSALADAS — SALADS

Seldom is there a lunch served in Spain that does not include a salad. Often salads are served as appetizers; at times it is the main course's side dish. Commonly a big bowl full of crunchy fresh salad vegetables is centered on the table and eaten through the meal. No ready-made dressings are ever used but instead plain oil and vinegar or a garlicky vinaigrette sauce.

When served as first course, salads can be garnished with delicious ingredients, such as pickled bonito fish, canned tuna, marinated olives, capers, or chunks of salt-cod.

**Achicoria** Chicory.

**Ajotomate** Tomato salad dressed with a tomato/garlic vinaigrette.

**Cebolla** Onion.

**Endibia** Belgian endive.

**Ensalada almoraina** Endive lettuce dressed with a pasty blend made with tomato, garlic, cumin, oil and vinegar, and black olives.

— **andaluza** Blanched tomatoes and green peppers dressed with vinaigrette containing chopped hard-boiled egg.

— **bicolor** Chopped romaine, Belgian endive, red cabbage, red onion, and radishes dressed with oil and vinegar.

— **bohemia** Romaine lettuce with string beans, ham, and truffles folded with mayonnaise.

— **catalana** Layered salad containing boiled potatoes, onion, peppers, olives, and canned tuna dressed with vinaigrette and garnished with hard-boiled egg.

— **César** Caesar salad.

— **de abadejo** Poached codfish salad dressed with mustard, capers, parsley, and salt.

— **de achicoria** Chicory salad.

— **de aguacate** Avocado salad.

- **y gambas** Avocado and shrimp salad.

— **de alcachofas** Artichoke heart salad.

— **de apio** Celery salad.

— **de arroz** Rice salad.

- **a la tártara** Cold boiled rice combined with a mixture of cured ham, gherkins, and parsley folded in mayonnaise/mustard sauce.

- **con frutas** Rice salad with fresh fruit.

- **marroquí** Cooked brown rice mixed with banana, orange, and dates dressed with a blend of honey, oil, and pepper.

- **y anchoas** Rice salad with anchovies.

— **de atún** Canned tuna salad.

— **de bayas** Mixed fresh berry salad with pine nuts.

— **de berros** Watercress salad.

— **de brécol** Broccoli salad.

— **de calabacín** Zucchini salad.

— **de champiñones** Mushroom salad.

— **de col** Cabbage salad.

— **de coles de Bruselas** Brussels sprouts salad.

— **de endibias y cítricos** Belgian

endive salad with citrus fruit.
— *de espárragos* Asparagus salad.
— *de espinacas* Spinach salad.
— *de gambas y patatas* Cooked shrimp and potato salad.
— *de garbanzos* Chickpea salad.
— *de granada* Pomegranate salad.
— *de habas tiernas* Fresh fava bean salad.
— *de huevo* Hard-boiled egg salad.
— *de judías blancas* Navy bean salad.
— *de longosta* Lobster salad.
— *de lengua* Cooked veal tongue salad.
— *de lentejas* Lentil salad.
— *de lombarda* Red cabbage salad.
— *de mango* Mango salad.
— *de manzana* Apple salad.
— *de mariscos* Seafood salad.
— *de melocotones* Fresh peach salad.
— *de melón* Melon salad.
— *de naranjas* Orange salad.
— *de ostras* Oyster salad.
— *de peras* Pear salad.
— *de pimiento y tomate* Roasted red pepper and tomato salad.
— *de plátanos* Banana salad.
— *de pollo* Chicken salad.
— *de puerros* Boiled young leeks dressed with vinaigrette sauce.
— *de rape* Poached anglerfish salad.
— *de remolacha* Beet salad.
— *de repollo* Cabbage salad.
— *de requesón* Cottage cheese salad.
— *de San Isidro* Romaine lettuce, onion, tomato, and olives combined with canned tuna and dressed with vinaigrette.
— *de tomate y huevo* Tomato and

hard-boiled egg salad.
— *de tomate y pepino* Tomato and cucumber salad.
— *de verduras* Vegetable salad.
— *koskera* Shredded boiled hake and lobster medallions mixed with pimiento and olives dressed with vinaigrette.
— *Lidia* Diced boiled potatoes, fruits and walnuts dressed with a creamy mustard vinaigrette.
— *lirio del valle* Celery, apple, tomato, and walnuts folded in a light mayonnaise.
— *mallorquina* Tomatoes sprinkled with fresh oregano and marjoram and dressed with a garlicky vinaigrette.
— *manchega* De-salted salt-cod and canned tuna combined with tomatoes, onions, and olives and dressed with vinaigrette.
— *murciana* Escarole lettuce and tomatoes dressed with paprika vinaigrette.
— *piperada* Sweet pepper, cucumber, and tomato salad dressed with vinaigrette.
— *Raquel Meller* Cucumber and tomato salad garnished with smoked herring and dressed with a vinaigrette with mustard.
— *sevillana* Boiled rice, pimientos, tomatoes, scallions, and green olives with vinaigrette.
— *Triana* Escarole lettuce, tomato, onion, and green olives dressed with vinaigrette.
— *tropical* Mixed salad containing tropical fruits.
— *valenciana* Boiled potatoes and sliced oranges with onion and pimiento dressed with vinaigrette.

DISHES BY COURSE

*Escalivada a la catalana* Baked eggplant, fennel, peppers, and onions
dressed with olive oil and garnished with anchovy fillets.

*Escarapuche* Cold sautéed trout
combined with chopped onion
and tomato dressed with vinegar
and lemon juice.

*Escarola* Endive.

*Judías verdes en vinagreta* Green
beans vinaigrette.

*Lechuga* Lettuce.

*Pepinillos en vinagre* Gherkins.

*Pepino* Cucumber.

*Pimiento rojo* Red pepper.

— *verde* Green pepper.

*Pipirrana* Finely chopped green
peppers, onions, tomatoes, and
cucumbers dressed with oil, vinegar, and salt.

*Poti-poti de Mura* Boiled potatoes,
salt-cod, tomato, and onion salad
garnished with red peppers and
black olives.

*Rábano* Radish.

*Remojón* Shredded de-salted salt-
cod and orange slices combined
with black olives and scallions
dressed with a paprika vinaigrette.

*Salada a lisbonense* Cooked Belgian
endive, carrots, and beets combined with fresh tomatoes and
hard-boiled egg with vinaigrette
dressing (from Portugal).

— *de bacalhau* Shredded de-salted
salt-cod combined with green
peppers and tomatoes and dressed
with olive oil, lemon juice, and
fresh chopped parsley (from Portugal).

— *portuguesa* Boston lettuce, watercress, tomato, onion, and anchovy-stuffed olives with vinaigrette dressing (from Portugal).

*Salmorejo* Pasty combination of tomatoes, garlic, soaked bread, vinegar, and olive oil garnished with
diced cured ham and hard-boiled
eggs.

*Tomate* Tomato.

*Trempó mallorquí* Tomato, green
pepper, and onion salad dressed
with a vinaigrette with capers.

*Vinagreta de mejillones* Mussels
vinaigrette.

*Xató de Sitges* De-salted salt-cod
mixed with canned tuna, anchovies, olives, and tomatoes dressed
with a vinaigrette containing almonds and paprika.

## SOPAS — SOUPS

The basis for good soups is the liquids with which they are prepared. A great number of Spanish soups are made with stock to which a bone of cured ham has been added. This special ingredient gives soups a distinct rich taste that makes them particularly hearty and nourishing; often soups are meals in themselves. Fish soups in the South and the Levant are prepared with the broth obtained from simmering fish and shellfish that are particularly tasty as species of the warm waters of the Mediterranean Sea.

In the summer months, a large variety of cold soups called gazpachos are served throughout the country but especially in Andalusia where the heat can be overwhelming for people harvesting crops.

*Ajo blanco con uvas* Cold gazpacho made with crushed almonds and garlic, soaked bread, water, and oil and vinegar garnished with seedless green grapes.

*Caldo* Broth.

— *a la francesa* Clear consommé

— *de perro gaditano* Fish soup with orange juice (from Cádiz).

— *de pescado con pimientos* Fish broth with bell peppers and potatoes seasoned with cumin.

— *de verduras* Vegetable broth.

— *gallego* Hearty beef broth garnished with beef, navy beans, cabbage, and potatoes (from Galicia).

— *navarro* Chicken broth flavored with clove, cinnamon, and saffron

— *verde* Kale and potato soup with chorizo sausage (from Portugal).

*Canja* Chicken soup with mint leaves and lemon (from Portugal).

*Cebollada con almendras* Onion soup with blanched almonds.

*Consomé* Consommé.

— *a la italiana* Consommé with pasta and grated Parmesan cheese.

— *al flan* Consommé *royale.*

— *al jerez* Sherry consommé.

— *de ave* Chicken consommé.

— *doble* Double consommé.

— *madrileño* Beef consommé garnished with diced tomatoes.

— *sencillo* Clear consommé.

*Costrada* Bread, chorizo sausage, and sautéed vegetables soaked in chicken broth and topped with eggs, baked in the oven.

*Crema* Cream.

— *de cangrejos* Cream of crayfish soup.

— *de champiñones* Cream of mushroom soup.

— *de espárragos* Cream of asparagus soup.

— *de espinacas* Cream of spinach soup.

— *de guisantes* Cream of green pea soup.

— *de tomate* Cream of tomato soup.

— *de yemas* Chicken broth with heavy cream and egg yolks.

— *de zanahorias y nabos* Cream of carrot and turnip soup.

— *florentina* Cream of spinach soup.

— **Solferino** Cream of potato and tomato soup.

**Escudella a la catalana** Catalonian thick soup similar to Italian minestrone.

**Gazpacho** Cold soup from Andalusia: blended salad vegetables (no lettuce) with oil, vinegar, and garlic.

— **alentejano** Portuguese gazpacho containing a larger amount of bread than its Spanish counterpart.

— **extremeño** Thick gazpacho with vegetable broth from Extremadura.

— **gaditano** Hot gazpacho from Cádiz.

— **rojo sevillano** Gazpacho made with ripe tomatoes, sherry, and cayenne pepper.

**Gazpachuelo** Hot fish gazpacho made with clam juice, fish, and potatoes, folded with mayonnaise.

**Oliagua amb escarrats** Asparagus, tomato, and garlic soup (from Catalonia).

**Perlas doradas** Chicken stock with tapioca and egg yolks.

**Porrusalda** Salt-cod, potato, and leek soup (from the Basque region).

**Puré** Puree.

— **de patatas y zanahorias** Potato and carrot puree.

— **dorado** Navy bean and pumpkin puree.

— **leontino** Thick vegetable soup with milk.

**Sopa** Soup.

— **a alentejana** Coriander and garlic soup with poached eggs (from Portugal).

— **a la malagueña** Clam broth with a sofrito and seasoned with paprika.

— **a la marinera** Fisherman-style soup made with shellfish.

— **a la reina andaluza** Beef broth enhanced by a *sofrito* thickened with flour and garnished with diced roasted green pepper.

— **al cuarto de hora** Seafood broth with rice and green peas. The name means "quarter of an hour soup" because it takes about fifteen minutes to prepare.

— **asturiana** Made with sorrel, leeks, and corn meal to which a *sofrito* is added.

— **aterciopelada** Beef broth with tapioca, whipped cream, and egg yolks.

— **balear** Made with minced beef, ham, *sofrito*, and bread soaked in red wine.

— **burgalesa** Chicken broth enhanced with sautéed lamb meat and crayfish.

— **catalana** Stock enhanced with a *sofrito* made with vegetables, ham, and egg yolks (from Catalonia).

— **de ajo** Garlic Soup.

- **a la castellana** Garlic soup with bread croutons.

- **con huevos** Garlic soup with added egg yolks.

— **de albondigas** Meatball soup.

— **de almejas** Clam soup.

— **de almendras** Almond soup.

— **de apio** Celery soup.

— **de Béjar** Chicken broth enhanced with a *sofrito* made with paprika and garnished with bread slices (from León).

— *de berros a la castellana* Watercress soup with potatoes and whipped cream.

— *de boda* Chicken broth with chicken giblets and slices of bread (from León).

— *de Cádiz* Chicken broth garnished with cured ham, sherry, and hard-boiled eggs.

— *de calabacín* Zucchini soup.

— *de cebolla* Onion soup.

— *de centollo a la gallega* Spider crab soup containing bacon and grated cheese (from Galicia).

— *de cerezas* Cherry soup made with wine and milk.

— *de cerveza* Beer soup made with eggs, ham, milk, and bread slices.

— *de col* Cabbage soup.

— *de coliflor* Cauliflower soup.

— *de congrio* Conger eel soup.

— *de gallina* Chicken broth.

— *de gambas* Shrimp soup.

— *de garbanzos* Chickpea soup.

— *de habas tiernas* Fresh fava bean soup.

— *de jamón* Ham soup.

— *de lentejas* Lentil soup.

— *de mariscos* Shellfish soup.

— *de mejillones* Mussel soup.

— *de menudillos* Chicken giblet soup.

— *de mero con arroz* Sea bass soup with rice.

— *de ostras pontevedrense* Chopped oyster soup (from Galicia).

— *de pedra* Red kidney bean soup with vegetables and chorizo sausage (from Portugal).

— *de perdiz* Partridge soup with sherry wine.

— *de pescado* Fish soup.

- *con fideos* Fish soup with thin spaghetti.

— *de picadillo* Chicken broth with diced cured ham, hard-boiled egg, and mint.

— *de pimientos* Bell pepper soup flavored with paprika.

— *de queso* Cheese soup.

— *de rabo de buey* Oxtail soup.

— *de rape* Anglerfish soup.

— *de remolacha* Beet soup.

— *de setas* Wild mushroom soup.

— *de tomate* Tomato soup.

— *de tomillo* Thyme soup.

— *de vigilia* Fish stock with a *sofrito* of shredded boiled fish and cauliflower florets.

— *de yogur* Yogurt soup.

— *Donosty* Crab soup enhanced with shallots, truffles, red wine, and brandy (from the Basque Country).

— *granadina* Bread soup with a *sofrito* flavored with saffron.

— *juliana* Vegetable soup with garlic.

— *leonesa* Made with sautéed onions, bread slices, and eggs and flavored with paprika.

— *mahonesa* Chicken broth enhanced with sautéed bread soaked in milk and beaten eggs (from the island of Menorca).

— *mallorquina* Dry soup made with vegetables and unsalted bread slices.

— *manchega* Chicken broth with a *sofrito* made with garlic, asparagus tips, and saffron.

— *montañesa* Vegetable broth enhanced with a thick *sofrito* and macaroni.

— *oscense* Beef broth containing

**Sopa oscense** (cont.)
minced veal liver and grated cheese (from Aragón).

— **payesa** Navy bean and rice soup containing cabbage, onion, cured ham, and paprika (farmer's soup from Catalonia).

— **real** Seasoned stock garnished with cured ham, chicken, hard-boiled egg, and sherry.

— **tinerfeña** Rice soup with a *sofrito* and lemon juice (from the Canary Islands).

— **torrada** Chicken broth garnished with meat balls and fried bread slices.

**Sopas gatas** Garlic soup with beaten egg and bread.

## PESCADOS Y MARISCOS — SEAFOOD

Spain has hundreds of miles of coast on two oceans and a great abundance of seafood. The Atlantic Ocean provides cold-water fish like turbot, hake, and haddock of firm, silvery meat, while the Mediterranean offers a great variety of specially tasty fish, like *salmonetes* (red mullets), *mero* (grouper), and *rape* (angler). There is also a great diversity of shellfish in the river estuaries of Galicia where *centollos* (spider crab), *navajas* (razor clams), and *berberechos* (cockles) thrive and are prepared in delectable ways by local cooks.

Very popular throughout the country is *bacalao* (salt-cod), a specialty of the Basques who prepare it in multiple ways using earthenware casseroles. Squid is also popular and is found in almost any bar *a la romana* (deep-fried dusted in flour) or *en su tinta* (cooked in its own ink).

*Albóndigas de bacalao* Fish balls made with salt-cod.

*Almejas* Clams.

— *a la sanluqueña* Steamed clams in white wine sprinkled with paprika.

*Anguila* Eel.

— *a la morisca* Eel medallions, larded with anchovy fillets, and baked in the oven with lemon juice, oil, and white wine.

— *a la valenciana* Eel simmered in paprika sauce.

*Angulas* Baby eels.

— *a la ovetense* Fried baby eels with garlic and hot chili peppers.

*Arenques* Herring

— *a la nórdica* Herring simmered in a champagne sauce with fresh mint.

*Atascaburras* Blend of boiled potatoes and shredded salt-cod folded with egg yolk and walnuts.

*Atún* Tuna fish.

— *a la barquera* Tuna baked in a thick *sofrito* containing almonds.

— *con alcaparras* Fried fresh tuna steaks with capers.

— *con tomate* Fried tuna steaks in tomato sauce.

— *mechado* Larded tuna in casserole.

— *pamplonica* Poached tuna garnished with minced onion, parsley, and hard-boiled egg.

— *provenzal* Tuna fish baked in an anchovy sauce with black olives.

*Bacalao* Codfish.

— *ajoarriero* Salt-cod simmered in a tomato sauce with vinegar and paprika.

— *a la manchega* Flaked salt-cod baked in a *sofrito* containing roasted peppers and topped with eggs.

— *a la navarra* Boiled salt-cod dressed with a *sofrito* containing red peppers.

— *a la riojana* Salt-cod stew with white beans and red peppers.

— *a la valenciana* Baked salt-cod with a *sofrito* containing rice, green peas, and pimiento.

— *a la vizcaina* Baked salt-cod in a hot dried pepper and olive oil sauce garnished with sweet red peppers.

— *al pil-pil* Fried salt-cod with garlic and hot peppers.

— *con manzanas* Simmered salt-cod with sautéed apples.

— *de Alcántara* Pot-roasted salt-cod with spinach.

— *en sanfaina* Sautéed shredded salt-cod with ratatouille.

**Bacalhau a Gomes de Sa** Salt-cod baked in a sauce containing milk and boiled potatoes (from Portugal).

**Besugo** Red porgy.

— *a la madrileña* Baked porgy with white wine and bread crumbs.

— *al horno* Baked red porgy.

— *con almendras* Sautéed red porgy in a wine sauce containing almonds.

— *donostiarra* Baked red porgy with lemon juice, garlic, and hot red pepper.

**Boga** Sea bream.

**Bogas a las finas hierbas** Fried sea bream in a parsley *sofrito.*

**Bonito** Bonito (striped tuna).

— *a la oriotarra* Fried bonito steak dressed with tomato and green pepper puree.

**Caballa** Mackerel.

**Caballas a la parrilla** Grilled mackerel, usually served with fried chopped tomato in olive oil.

— *a la vizcaina* Baked mackerel with bread crumbs, garlic, parsley, paprika, and hard cider.

— *trianera* Baked mackerel with ratatouille.

**Cachelada gallega** Octopus stew with new potatoes.

**Calamares** Squid.

— *a la bilbaina* Squid simmered in a sofrito containing the squid's own ink.

— *al jerez* Squid simmered in sherry sauce.

— *encebollados* Squid braised with onions.

— *rellenos menorquina* Braised squid stuffed with pine nuts, raisins, and fresh mint (from the island of Menorca).

**Caldereta asturiana** Seafood stew with white wine, paprika, and peppercorns (from Asturias).

— *de pescado* Fish stew.

**Camarones** Prawns.

— *a la andaluza* Fried prawns garnished with fried tomato and garlic.

**Cangrejo** Crab.

— *de mar al jerez* Sautéed sea crab in sherry sauce.

— *de río al vino blanco* Sautéed crawfish in white wine.

**Centollo** Spider crab.

— *al vino blanco* Spider crab braised in white wine.

**Ceviche al coco** Raw fish strips marinated in lemon juice dressed with shredded coconut and whipping cream.

**Chanquetes** Whitebait.

— *fritos* Deep-fried whitebait dusted with flour.

**Congrio** Conger eel.

— *a la bilbilitana* Cured conger eel simmered with pine nuts, tomato sauce, and eggs.

— *en cazuela* Conger eel casserole.

**Coquinas** Cockles.

— *a la andaluza* Cockles simmered in a spicy *sofrito.*

— *con tomate* Boiled cockles sautéed with tomatoes and onions.

*Corvina* Corbina.
— *a la andaluza* Baked corbina dressed with a *sofrito* containing pimientos and sherry wine.
— *al vino blanco* Baked corbina in white wine sauce.
*Croquetas de pescado* Fish croquettes.
*Dorada* Dorado.
— *al hinojo* Baked dorado with fresh fennel.
— *de Alcántara* Dorado stuffed with minced pike and baked in a red wine sauce.
— *gaditana* Fried dorado in a spicy sherry sauce (from Cádiz).
— *a la sal* Baked dorado covered with coarse salt.
— *al all-i-pebre* Baked dorado in a garlic sauce with saffron, almonds, and parsley.
*Espetones de sardinas* Sardines grilled on a skewer.
*Flan de mariscos* Seafood timbale.
*Fritura de pescado* Assorted fried fish.
— *malagueña* Deep-fried battered mixed fried fish.
*Gambas* Shrimp.
— *con gabardina* Battered-fried shrimp.
— *Villeroy* Béchamel-battered deep-fried shrimp.
*Gastaika* Poached ray dressed with a sauce made of oil, vinegar, and hot chili peppers.
*Lamprea* Lamprey.
— *a la gallega* Lamprey casserole with wine and paprika.
*Langosta* Lobster.
— *a la americana* Lobster sautéed in brandy sauce.
— *a la catalana* Braised lobster

with almonds, garlic, hazelnuts, saffron, and chocolate.
— *a la marinera* Lobster braised in a *sofrito*, with wine and paprika.
— *al archiduque* Lobster sautéed in béchamel sauce with whiskey.
— *con pollo* Lobster with chicken.
— *Costa Brava* Lobster shell stuffed with the lobster meat sautéed in a *sofrito* mixed with white sauce.
*Langostinos* Prawns.
— *con clavo* Prawns in a clove-flavored marinade.
*Lenguado* Sole.
— *a la gaditana* Milk-marinated sole fillets dusted in flour and deep-fried.
— *a la riojana* Sole fillets sautéed with red peppers, garlic, and cayenne pepper.
— *al plato* Sole fillets baked in meat broth, white wine, olive oil, and bread crumbs.
— *al vino tinto* Sole fillets simmered in red wine with onions and mushrooms.
— *al whiskey* Grilled sole fillets egg-washed in whiskey batter.
— *Bombay* Poached sole fillets served with curried rice.
— *con champiñones* Sautéed sole fillets dressed with a creamy mushroom sauce.
— *con salsa de nueces* Sole in walnut sauce.
— *Capri* Fried sole fillet served with fried bananas on a bed of rice.
— *grenoblesa* Sautéed sole fillets with capers.
*Lisa* Striped mullet.
— *en amarillo* Striped mullet simmered in a *sofrito* containing

**Lisa en amarillo** (cont.)
crushed fried bread, lemon juice,
and saffron.
**Lubina** Striped bass.
— *a la greca* Poached striped bass
garnished with boiled vegetables
in white wine.
— *al ajillo* Baked striped bass
dressed with fried garlic in olive
oil.
— *a las hierbas* Grilled striped bass
with fresh fennel and sage.
— *a las uvas* Baked striped bass
with green grapes and white wine
sauce.
— **Albufera** Baked striped bass in
a garlic and almond sauce.
— *al hinojo* Striped bass in fennel
sauce.
**Marmitako** Basque fish stew made
with white wine and potatoes.
**Mejillones** Mussels.
— *al gratén* Mussels au gratin with
spinach and garlic mayonnaise.
**Merluza** Hake.
— *a la Alhambra* Marinated hake
fillets baked in a mixture of bread
crumbs, parsley, and lemon juice.
— *a la asturiana* Baked hake in a
hard cider sauce.
— *a la chiclanera* Hake baked in a
liquid made of oil, garlic, water-
soaked bread, and vinegar.
— *a la española* Fried hake garnished with sautéed onions and
sweet red peppers.
— *a la gallega* Hake casserole with
fish fumet and paprika.
— *a la koskera* Hake sautéed in
white wine with clams garnished
with hard-boiled egg and parsley.
— *a la serrana* Baked hake with
cured ham and mushroom sauce.

— *a la sevillana* Hake simmered
in a *sofrito* of fried bread crumbs,
sherry, pine nuts, almonds, and
walnuts.
— *a la vasca* Hake steak casserole
prepared with white wine and
green peas.
— *al jerez* Baked hake with
shrimp puree and sherry wine.
— *al rojo y blanco* Poached stuffed
hake served with béchamel sauce
and decorated with tomato sauce.
— *con ajo* Poached hake with garlic sauce.
— *en blanco* Poached hake served
with mayonnaise diluted in the
poaching fumet.
— *en salsa lucentina* Poached
hake dressed with a blend of water-soaked bread, oil, and vinegar
and garnished with hard-boiled
eggs.
— *en salsa verde* Poached hake in
parsley sauce with almonds,
green peas, and hard-boiled egg.
— *gratinada a la andaluza* Hake
au gratin dressed with bread
crumbs, garlic, parsley, and oil.
**Mero** Grouper.
— *a la tarraconense* Grilled grouper dressed with a sauce made
with olive oil, almonds, hazelnuts, and hot red peppers.
— *a la valenciana* Sautéed grouper served with a thickened garlic sauce containing saffron.
— *en salsa de ostras* Baked grouper in a *sofrito* containing chopped
oysters.
**Mousse de pescado** Fish mousse.
**Mújol** Mullet.
— *a la sal* Baked mullet covered
with coarse salt.

**Navajas** Razor clams.
— *a la plancha* Grilled razor clams.
**Pagel** Sea bream.
— *a la jerezana* Baked sea bream with sherry and fennel.
— *a la playera* Sea bream simmered with vegetables and saffron.
— *al vino blanco* Baked sea bream with a thickened *sofrito* containing flour and white wine.
— *en salsa de pepinillos* Baked sea bream with a *sofrito* containing saffron and garnished with gherkins.
**Palometa** Yellow jack.
— *a la gaditana* Baked yellow jack with a *sofrito* of fish broth thickened with flour and garnished with sliced hard-boiled eggs.
— *con anchoas* Grilled yellow jack garnished with anchovy mayonnaise.
**Papandúas** Simmered shredded salt-cod with flour, yeast, and saffron worked to a dough and deep-fried in small portions.
**Paté de mariscos** Seafood pâté.
**Pescadilla** Whiting.
— *a la alcarreña* Baked stuffed whiting with béchamel sauce.
— *a la malagueña* Poached whiting dressed with mayonnaise diluted in the poaching fumet.
— *a la mayordoma* Fried whiting served with maître d'hôtel butter.
— *a la monegasca* Fried whiting served with ratatouille.
— *en escabeche* Fried whiting marinated in vinegar flavored with saffron, cumin, ginger, and bay leaf.

**Pez espada** Swordfish.
— *a la plancha* Grilled swordfish.
— *en adobo* Marinated swordfish.
**Pimientos rellenos de merluza** Red peppers stuffed with flaked poached hake in béchamel sauce.
**Pixin a la asturiana** Monkfish in hard cider sauce with apples.
**Pulpo** Octopus.
— *a la feria* Sliced boiled octopus in a paprika marinade.
**Rape** Angler or monkfish.
— *a la Costa Brava* Baked angler in wine sauce flavored with saffron.
— *a la malagueña* Braised angler with a *sofrito* containing fried bread and saffron.
— *con pimentón* Simmered angler in a liquid containing oil, garlic, paprika, and bay leaf.
— *comodoro* Fried angler with mushrooms and artichokes.
— *con piñones* Sautéed angler with pine nuts.
— *Pompadour* Poached angler medallions with hollandaise sauce, garnished with tomato sauce and mushrooms.
— *marinera* Angler casserole with clam juice, green peas, pimiento, and paprika.
— *hawayana* Fried angler with onion rings and grilled pineapple.
**Rodaballo** Turbot.
— *a la andaluza* Baked turbot in a fumet containing sautéed vegetables.
— *California* Poached turbot with brandy sauce.
— *con grelos y almejas* Cooked turbot with vegetable greens and clams (from Galicia).

— *miramar* Grilled turbot seasoned with lemon juice, salt, and pepper.

**Rubio** Red gurnard.

— *a la casera* Red gurnard simmered with a *sofrito* containing lemon juice, saffron, and fish fumet.

**Salmón** Salmon.

— *a la alicantina* Grilled salmon steak previously marinated in olive oil, lemon juice, red peppers, and seasonings.

— *a la andaluza* Salmon simmered in a liquid containing oil, vinegar, green olives, and parsley and served garnished with hard-boiled eggs.

— *a la sidra* Baked salmon with ham and hard cider.

**Salmonetes** Red mullets.

— *a la nizarda* Fried red mullets garnished with a *sofrito* containing anchovies and gherkins.

— *en escabeche* Pickled red mullets.

**Sancocho canario** Salt fish stew with potatoes, sweet potatoes, and roasted corn meal.

**Santola recheada fría** Cold stuffed crab (from Portugal).

**Sardinas** Sardines.

— *a la navarra* Baked sardines with a blend of bread crumbs, paprika, and spices.

— *a la vinagreta* Sardines simmered in a vinaigrette sauce containing saffron and hard-boiled egg.

— *al Sacromonte* Sardines simmered in a liquid containing oil, onion, tomato, and paprika.

— *siciliana* Baked sardines stuffed with pine nuts, almonds, raisins,

and bread crumbs.

**Sepia** Cuttlefish.

— *guisada* Cuttlefish stew with potatoes.

**Shangurro** Stuffed spider crab Basque-style.

**Soufflé de atún** Tuna soufflé.

**Suquet de pescadores** Seafood casserole with a saffron *sofrito*.

**Terrina de ahumados** Smoked fish terrine.

**Trucha** Trout.

— *a la catalana* Sautéed trout simmered in a spicy stock containing cumin.

— *a la cazuela* Trout casserole.

— *a la judía* Trout baked with onion, olive oil, and flour.

— *a la montañesa* Trout simmered in fish stock with white wine.

— *a la navarra* Trout stuffed with cured ham slices and sautéed in oil.

— *al champán* Poached trout in a champagne sauce.

— *al horno* Baked trout.

— *con almendras* Fried boned trout with a béchamel containing almonds.

— *rellena jironesa* Trout stuffed with chopped olives, pimiento, almonds, and mushrooms and cooked *en papillote*.

**Txangurro** Stuffed spider crab (from the Basque Country).

**Vieiras** Sea scallops, in Galicia.

— *de Santiago* *Coquilles St. Jacques* made with a spicy tomato and wine sauce.

— *gratinadas* Scallops au gratin.

**Zancho canario** Boiled grouper and potatoes served with a sauce called *mojo colorado*, made with chili peppers, garlic, oil, cumin, and paprika.

**Zarzuela a la vasca** Seafood casserole in a garlicky white sauce.

— *de pescado* Seafood casserole made with shellfish fumet spiced with brandy and paprika.

**Zurrucutuna** Salt-cod casserole with paprika and toasted bread slices.

# HUEVOS — EGGS

When in Spain, do not expect to have eggs for breakfast; instead, they will be part of your evening meal. Eggs are also an important ingredient in many dishes and are often incorporated into soups, fish, and stews. The best-known of egg dishes in the Peninsula is undoubtedly *tortilla de patatas,* the potato omelet always present in family picnics and in tapas menus.

Often, eggs are served as a main dish when they are prepared fried in plentiful olive oil accompanied by a generous serving of cured ham, chorizo or *morcilla* sausage, fried potatoes, and, on the side, a glass of hearty red wine. The Spanish word for omelet is *tortilla,* which has nothing to do with the thin, round, unleavened cake used in the preparation of Mexican tacos.

*Huevos* Eggs.

— *a la alicantina* Potato barquettes filled with tomato puree and chopped prawns, topped with poached eggs and napped with white sauce.

— *a la andaluza* Fried eggs garnished with fried chorizo sausage and potatoes.

— *a la castellana* Eggs *en cocotte* cooked with sautéed onion and minced meat and covered with béchamel sauce.

— *a la cordobesa* fried eggs garnished with sliced fried potatoes, pimiento, and sautéed chorizo.

— *a la cubana* Fried eggs garnished with boiled rice, fried tomato puree, and bananas.

— *a la flamenca* Shirred eggs with ham, chorizo, asparagus tips, and green peas.

— *a la madrileña* Shirred eggs with sautéed tomato and breakfast sausage.

— *a la navarra* Shirred eggs with tomato sauce, chorizo, and grated cheese.

— *a la romana* Shirred eggs over a bed of sautéed spinach, grated cheese, and anchovies dressed with Mornay sauce.

— *a la roncalesa* Baked eggs with Italian-style sausage and crumbled fried bread (from Navarra).

— *a la rusa* Poached eggs on a bed of lettuce, cured ham, tomato, and diced cheese dressed with mustard sauce.

— *a la sevillana* Fried eggs garnished with fried cured ham, potatoes, and artichokes.

— *a la turca* Shirred eggs with chicken livers sautéed in sherry wine.

— *al estilo de Sóller* Fried eggs on ham with a sauce made with vegetables, milk, and white wine (from the island of Majorca).

— *al plato* Shirred eggs.

- *al curry* Shirred eggs with lamb in a curried béchamel.

- *chiclanera* Shirred eggs over a bed of fried garlic, almonds, and bread flavored with saffron, cumin, and cinnamon.

— *al queso azul* Hard-boiled eggs dressed with blue cheese sauce.

— *Aurora* Hard-boiled eggs with a béchamel sauce containing tomato puree.

— *Bella Otero* Potato barquettes filled with béchamel sauce topped with soft-cooked eggs napped with the same béchamel.

— *chiclanera* Poached eggs over a layer of a *sofrito* containing chopped ham and chorizo, napped with béchamel sauce and browned in the oven.

— *con champiñones* Shirred eggs with sautéed minced mushrooms.

— *cuajados* Soft-cooked eggs.

- *con espinacas* Soft-cooked eggs over a bed of fried spinach with garlic, vinegar, and paprika.

- *con jamón* Soft-cooked eggs over a slice of cured ham.

- *con tomate* Soft-cooked eggs over tomato sauce.

- *Giralda* soft-cooked eggs over a bed of rice mixed with chicken livers and ham and flavored with saffron (from Seville).

- *sevillana* Soft-cooked eggs over a bed of minced prawns, pimiento, and green peas.

— *duros* Hard-boiled eggs.

— *empanados* Poached eggs covered with bread crumbs, dipped into egg wash and bread crumbs again and fried until golden.

— *en cama* Baked eggs on a bed of mashed potatoes with tomato sauce

— *en camisa* Baked egg yolks covered with their beaten whites and sprinkled with grated cheese.

— *en cocotera* Eggs *en cocotte.*

- *con higadillos* Eggs *en cocotte*

with chicken livers.

— *en sorpresa* Shirred eggs with chicken livers, mushrooms, and bread crumbs.

— *escalfados* Poached eggs.

- *a la española* Poached eggs garnished with *sofrito.*

- *americana* Poached eggs over a bed of rice combined with a shellfish fumet containing wine and brandy.

- *Aranjuez* Au gratin poached eggs napped with Mornay sauce and garnished with asparagus.

- *Bohemia* Foie gras-stuffed tartlettes topped with a poached egg dressed with wine sauce and baked in the oven.

- *Clamart* Poached egg on a crouton garnished with green peas and dressed with a cream sauce containing truffles.

- *con almejas* Poached eggs with clam sauce.

- *con besamel* Poached eggs dressed with béchamel sauce.

- *con gelatina* Jellied poached eggs.

- *portuguesa* Poached eggs on a crouton garnished with a tomato sauce containing mushrooms and truffles.

- *Rossini* Poached eggs on a tartlette stuffed with foie gras and dressed with a sauce made with Madeira wine.

— *escondidos* Scrambled eggs wrapped in ham slices and rolled in crepes.

— *florentina* Poached eggs on boiled spinach puree.

— *fritos* Fried eggs.

- *a la española* Eggs fried in abundant olive oil.
- *al ajillo* Fried eggs with garlic, vinegar, and paprika.
- *con migas* Fried eggs garnished with fried diced bread.
- *con patatas* Fried eggs garnished with fried potatoes.
- *con pimientos* Fried eggs garnished with fried green peppers.
- *en sorpresa* Deep-fried dough nest containing tomato sauce and one egg inside.
— *Herminia* Hard-boiled eggs and boiled potatoes dressed with mayonnaise sauce and garnished with sautéed green peas.
— *moscovita* Hard-boiled eggs on artichoke bottoms topped with anchovy fillets and napped with mayonnaise containing caviar.
— *napolitana* Fried eggs over spaghetti with tomato sauce.
— *nizarda* Potato barquettes filled with sautéed green peas and tomato, topped with a soft-cooked egg, and napped with white sauce.
— *pasados por agua* Soft-boiled eggs.
— *presidencia* Hard-boiled eggs stuffed with a mixture of the yolks and liver pâté, placed on a bed of boiled spinach, covered with béchamel sauce, and baked briefly.
— *rellenos* Deviled eggs.
- *con anchoas* Deviled eggs with anchovies.
- *de gambas* Stuffed hard-boiled eggs with a mixture of shrimp and egg yolk.
— *revueltos* Scrambled eggs.

- *al pisto* Scrambled eggs garnished with *pisto* (ratatouille).
- *con setas* Scrambled eggs with mushrooms.
- *portuguesa* Scrambled eggs garnished with reduced tomato sauce.
- *princesa* Scrambled eggs with asparagus.
— *turbigo* Soft-cooked eggs garnished with grilled lamb kidneys and grilled tomatoes.
— *Villeroy* Soft-cooked eggs in cold béchamel sauce dipped in egg wash and breadcrumbs and fried in oil.
*Omeleta de atun* Canned tuna omelet (from Portugal)
*Ovos Quinta das Torres* Fried eggs covered with cold cheese béchamel sauce dipped in egg wash and bread crumbs and deep-fried (from Portugal).
*Pastel de tortillas* Four omelets placed over each other: one mushroom, one shrimp, one potato, one mixed vegetables, cut like a cake, and served with tomato puree.
*Piperrada* Flat omelet with sweet peppers, onions, garlic, cured ham, and tomato (from the Basque Country).
*Tarta de huevos* Eggs baked over a meat or fish pie.
*Tortilla a la andaluza* Omelet stuffed with *sofrito*.
— *a la gallega* Potato omelet with chorizo sausage, diced pimiento, and touch of paprika.
— *alicantina* Omelet containing onion, tomato, shrimp, ham, asparagus tips, and canned tuna.

— *al Sacromonte* Omelet made with lamb's brains, cured ham, potatoes, pimiento, and green peas.

— *asturiana* Omelet containing onion, tomato, and canned tuna.

— *bretona* Omelet with fried onions and mushrooms.

— *canaria* Omelet with chopped onion, tomato, tarragon, mint, and parsley.

— *catalana* Omelet made with canned white beans, onion, tomato, and chorizo sausage.

— *chilena* Folded omelet stuffed with a mixture of lamb's brains, ham, and spices.

— *coruñesa* Potato omelet with bacon and paprika.

— *de angulas* Baby eel omelet.

— *de bacalao* Salt-cod omelet.

— *de berenjena* Eggplant omelet.

— *de cebolla a la andaluza* Omelet made with onion simmered until very soft and browned.

— *de champiñones* Mushroom omelet.

— *de chanquetes* Omelet with fried whitebait (from Málaga).

— *de gambas* Shrimp omelet.

— *de garbanzos* Canned chickpea omelet with onion and pimiento.

— *de habas* Fresh fava bean omelet.

— *de hierbas* Omelet with watercress, celery, and parsley.

— *de riñones* Kidney omelet.

— *española* Flat, thick potato omelet, with chopped onion.

— *francesa* Plain folded omelet.

— *granadina* Omelet with ground veal, green peas, and pimientos.

— *madrileña* Omelet containing sweetbreads, ham, onion, tomato, and sherry wine.

— *murciana* Omelet with mixed vegetables.

— *paisana* Flat omelet containing diced cured ham and a medley of vegetables.

— *rellena* Stuffed folded omelet.

— *de San Juan* Egg dumplings made with bread, garlic, parsley, and saffron (from Andalusia).

— *sevillana* Omelet with onion and red peppers garnished wth sautéed mushrooms and tomatoes.

DISHES BY COURSE

# ARROZ — RICE

Rice is to Spain what pasta is to Italy: an ever-present staple on the nation's menus. Rice cooked in Spain has very little resemblance to the rice dishes prepared elsewhere in the world. Most of the time, unlike in other cuisines, rice is served as the main course of meals for it can be, in itself, a hearty, nutritious, delicious meal.

There are several "secrets" that must be known before preparing rice the Spanish way: the rice is briefly sautéed in a *sofrito* (basically onion, tomato, and sweet peppers sautéed in olive oil) before the cooking liquid is added; a *majado* (garlic, parsley, saffron, spices, and seasonings crushed in a mortar) is added with the cooking liquid; short grain is used instead of long grain; the rice is cooked in shallow containers with flame applied to the entire base at any given time.

A great variety of ingredients can be cooked in rice to create many variations of this succulent dish, of which paella is the most famous and one of the national dishes. Although cooked throughout the country, rice is best prepared in the Levant where, tradition says, it was originally used.

*Arroz* rice.

— *a banda* Fishermen's rice made with fish broth and served with garlic mayonnaise.

— *a la alicantina* Rice with a *sofrito* containing crushed sweet dry peppers, meat, and shellfish.

— *a la americana* Rice with chopped ham but no saffron.

— *a la andaluza* Rice with *sofrito*, chicken, cured ham, bacon, and chorizo.

— *a la catalana* Rice with *sofrito*, rabbit, cured ham, sausage, and diced pork.

— *a la criolla* Plain boiled rice garnished with bacon strips, fried eggs, fried bananas, and tomato sauce.

— *a la cubana* Plain boiled rice garnished with fried eggs and bananas.

— *a la griega* Rice containing onion, green pepper, prunes, walnuts, and black olives. Served cold.

— *a la italiana* RIce with fresh sausage, chicken livers, white wine, grated cheese but no saffron.

— *a la malagueña* Rice with *sofrito*, clams, shrimp, asparagus, green peas, saffron, and paprika.

— *a la mallorquina* Rice with *sofrito*, seafood, and paprika-spread sausage (*sobrasada*).

— *a la milanesa* Rice with ham, green peas, and grated Parmesan.

— *a la primavera* Rice with assorted vegetables.

— *a la sevillana* Rice with *sofrito*, fish broth, squid, angler, cured ham, and green peas and garnished with crayfish, roasted peppers, hard-boiled egg, and fried chorizo slices.

— *al curry* Curried rice.

— *al horno* Rice cooked in the oven.

— *blanco* Plain boiled rice.
— *canario* Rice garnished with fried eggs and fried bananas dredged in flour and beaten egg.
— *con alcachofas* Rice with artichokes.
— *con almejas* Rice with clams.
— *con azafrán* Saffron rice.
— *con bacalao* Rice with salt-cod.
— *con calamares* Rice with squid.
— *con caracoles* Rice with snails (escargots).
— *con cerdo* Rice with diced pork.
— *con chipirones* Rice with squid.
— *con conejo* Rice with rabbit.
— *con cordero* Rice with lamb.
— *con costra* Rice with meatballs, chicken, sausage, and chickpeas, topped with beaten eggs.
— *con jerez* Rice with sherry wine.
— *con jibia* Rice with cuttlefish.
— *con langostinos* Rice with prawns.
— *con magra* Rice with fresh pork.
— *con mariscos* Rice with shellfish.
— *con mejillones* Rice with mussels.
— *con menudillos* Rice with chicken giblets.
— *con pavo* Rice with turkey.
— *con perdiz* Rice with partridge.
— *con pescado* Rice with fish.
— *con picadillo* Rice with a *sofrito* containing diced pork, cured ham, and chicken livers.
— *con pichones* Rice with squab.
— *con pollo* Rice with chicken.
— *con rape* Rice with anglerfish.
— *con riñones* Rice with veal kidneys.
— *con verduras* Rice with mixed vegetables.
— *con vino* Rice with chicken and

a *sofrito* containing white wine.
— *de Cádiz* Rice with *sofrito* and fish broth, seasoned with lemon juice.
— *en caldero* Rice cooked with fish broth, dried red peppers and abundant garlic (from Murcia).
— *frío en ensaladilla* Plain boiled rice mixed with canned tuna, pimiento, hard-boiled egg, capers, and gherkins.
— *frito* Fried rice.
— *integral* Brown rice.
— *jerezano* Rice with a *sofrito* containing sherry wine.
— *murciano* Rice with pork and garden vegetables.
— *navarro* Rice with lamb (from Navarra).
— *negro* Rice with squid and its ink.
— *pamplonica* Rice with salt-cod and sweet peppers (from Navarra).
— *verde con almejas* Soupy rice with clams, green peppers, and parsley.
— *viudo* Rice with artichokes, red peppers, snow peas, onions, and tomatoes.
**Frango com arroz** Chicken with rice (from Portugal).
**Paella** Meat, seafood, and vegetable rice with *sofrito*, and saffron.
— *barcelonesa* Paella variation containing sausages.
— *huertana* Paella made with assorted vegetables.
— *marinera* Seafood paella.
— *valenciana* Traditional paella made with chicken and seafood.
**Pastel de arroz** Diced cooked seafood folded in mayonnaise placed

**Pastel de arroz** (cont.)
between two layers of rice and boiled in the seafood fumet.

**Rosca de arroz con salmón** Béchamel sauce with shredded salmon sur-rounded by a circle of white rice.

**Tartaletas de arroz** Tartlets filled with plain boiled rice mixed with mayonnaise and napped with to-mato sauce.

## PASTAS — PASTA

Pasta dishes are not common on Spanish menus since rice is much more popular. *Canelones*, however, is a type of pasta that is prepared deliciously throughout the country. *Canelones* are thin wafers of pasta dough, about two inches in diameter,that once boiled are filled with a variety of stuffings and served with several types of sauces.

*Canelones* Cannelloni.

— *con espinacas* Baked cannelloni stuffed with spinach, anchovies, and béchamel sauce.

— *con jamón* Baked cannelloni stuffed with minced cured ham and tomato puree.

— *con langostinos* Baked cannelloni stuffed with prawns in white sauce.

— *de pescado* Baked cannelloni stuffed with flaked boiled fish, mushrooms, and hard-boiled egg.

— *de pollo* Baked cannelloni stuffed with minced chicken in tomato sauce.

— *de vigilia* Baked cannelloni stuffed with a paste made with fish, truffles, tomato puree, white wine, and Parmesan cheese.

— *Rossini* Baked cannelloni stuffed with a paste of chicken livers, calf's brain, and spices.

*Espaguetis* Spaghetti.

— *con almejas* Spaghetti with a *sofrito* containing clams.

*Fideos* Thin spaghetti.

— *a la cazuela* Thin spaghetti casserole garnished with pork ribs and sausages.

— *al ajo* Thin spaghetti with fried garlic and hot red peppers in olive oil topped with Parmesan.

— *al ajoaceite* Thin spaghetti with a blend of olive oil, garlic,

and egg yolk.

— *campesinos* Thin spaghetti with a *sofrito* containing tomato, zucchini, garlic, black olives, and parsley.

— *con almejas* Thin spaghetti in a soupy stew made with fish stock and clams.

— *con moluscos* Thin spaghetti in a white souce with clams and mussels.

*Fideua de mariscos* Thin spaghetti cooked in a *sofrito* containing seafood and saffron (from Catalonia).

*Lasaña* Lasagna.

— *de mariscos* Shellfish lasagna.

*Macarrones* Macaroni.

— *a la capuchina* Baked macaroni mixed with fried garlic, anchovies, chopped cucumbers, black olives, and capers.

— *a la española* Au gratin macaroni with onion, cured ham, and tomato puree.

— *a la italiana* Baked macaroni in a rich tomato sauce containing beef stock and Parmesan.

— *a la maltesa* Baked macaroni with a mix of ground pork, ground beef, chicken livers, mushrooms, tomato sauce, and Parmesan cheese.

— *al gratén* Au gratin macaroni in a tomato and cheese sauce made with butter.

— *con chorizo* Macaroni in a thick tomato sauce containing chorizo and cured ham.

— *con espinacas* Macaroni in a creamy spinach sauce.

— *con frutos secos* Macaroni with a blend of crushed walnuts, hazelnuts, pine nuts, olive oil, milk, and Parmesan.

— *con huevos* Baked macaroni with egg yolks, butter, and grated cheese.

— *con mayonesa y atún* Macaroni mixed with shredded canned tuna and mayonnaise.

— *con riñones* Macaroni with lamb kidneys sautéed in white wine.

— *con salsa americana* Macaroni with a blend of egg, olive oil, lemon juice, ketchup, and brandy.

— *con tomate* Baked macaroni in tomato sauce with minced sautéed onions.

— *escondidos* Macaroni folded into a sauce consisting of sautéed onion and tomato, chorizo, and grated cheese, covered with a thin layer of pie dough, and baked.

— *saboyarda* Baked macaroni in a white sauce with chopped cooked ham.

*Ñoquis al gratén* Au gratin gnocchi.

— *de patatas y jamón* Gnocchi made with mashed potatoes and cooked ham.

— *de sémola* Gnocchi made with semolina flour.

*Pasta a la bechamel* Pasta with béchamel sauce.

— *al curry* Pasta in curry sauce.

— *con albondiguillas* Pasta with meat balls.

— *con pisto* Pasta served combined with ratatouille.

*Pastel de macarrones* Baked macaroni with a mixture of ground beef, tomato, onion, and white wine sautéed in olive oil.

*Ravioles* Ravioli.

— *con tomate* Ravioli in tomato sauce.

— *regios* Ravioli in a sauce containing foie gras, whipping cream, brandy, and Parmesan cheese.

*Tallarines* Noodles.

— *a la alsaciana* Baked noodles in a thick white sauce containing ham, chicken livers, truffles, and grated cheese.

— *a la boloñesa* Noodles with a minced meat tomato sauce.

— *a la carbonara* Noodles with egg, bacon, garlic, and butter.

— *con anchoas* Buttered noodles with a paste of crushed anchovies, garlic, parsley, and egg yolk.

# LEGUMBRES Y VERDURAS — VEGETABLES

Anyone visiting Spain for the first time will be impressed by the freshness, quality, and great variety of vegetables displayed by farmers at open markets. Back in the eighth and ninth centuries, the Arabs introduced several plants and trees from the Middle East. After the discovery of America, Spain was the first European country to receive new vegetables, of which tomatoes, potatoes, peppers, corn, and beans are just a small sample.

Vegetables are seldom used as garnishes in dishes; instead, they are used as ingredients in stews or served as dishes themselves. Often, they are prepared sautéed in *sofritos*, taking different names depending on the regions where they are prepared. The name in Catalonia is *samfraina*, in La Mancha it is *pisto*, and in Aragon *chilindrón*. Another peculiarity with vegetable cooking is the use of dry legumes in stews throughout the country, especially garbanzos (chickpeas), *judías* (white beans), and *lentejas* (lentiles).

**DISHES BY COURSE**

*Acelgas* Swiss chard.
— *al la malagueña* Boiled Swiss chard sautéed in olive oil with garlic and sultana raisins.
— *a la napolitana* Boiled Swiss chard simmered in a *sofrito* containing thyme and white wine.
— *con pasas y piñones* Swiss chard sautéed with raisins and pine nuts.
— *en adobillo* Boiled Swiss chard sautéed in olive oil, vinegar, paprika, and bread soaked in water.
— *rehogadas* Sautéed Swiss chard.
*Alcachofas* Artichokes.
— *a la cordobesa* Artichokes simmered in meat broth containing garlic, flour, and saffron.
— *a la española* Artichokes simmered with onion, white wine, vinegar, and chicken stock thickened with flour and sprinkled with fresh parsley.
— *a la sevillana* Sautéed artichoke hearts, potatoes, and garlic simmered in chicken stock with saffron and thickened with flour.

— *con dos salsas* Boiled artichokes separated into hearts and outer leaves: the hearts are served with garlic mayonnaise and vinaigrette is served in individual bowls for the leaves to be dipped.
— *con jamón* Sautéed artichokes with cured ham.
— *con tomate* Sautéed artichokes with tomato.
— *en aceite* Boiled artichokes: artichokes are set in a pan pressed against each other; olive oil is poured into the center of each artichoke; water is added to the pan to just cover the base of the artichokes and the artichokes are boiled until tender.
— *en cazuela* Artichoke casserole.
— *mojadas* Artichokes simmered in chicken broth with wine, bacon, and garlic.
*Apio* Celery.
— *a la iruñesa* Boiled celery stewed in olive oil, white wine, tomato, garlic, and parsley (from the Basque Country).

– *con salsa holandesa* Boiled celery with hollandaise sauce.

***Batatas*** Potatoes, in Portuguese.

— *a portuguesa* Sliced sautéed potatoes (from Portugal).

***Berenjena*** Eggplant.

***Berenjenas a la crema*** Fried eggplant slices dredged in flour napped with cream sauce and browned in the oven.

— *a la eibarresa* Baked eggplant stuffed with anchovies, bread soaked in milk, and fried tomato.

— *a la mallorquina* Baked stuffed eggplant with chorizo spread napped with white sauce.

— *a la parrilla* Grilled eggplant dressed with a sauce made with meat broth, olive oil, parsley, bread crumbs, and lemon juice.

— *con queso* Baked eggplant topped with cheese slices.

— *fritas* Eggplant slices dredged in flour and fried in olive oil.

— *duquesa* Eggplant stuffed with diced ham, tomato, mushrooms, and white wine.

— *rellenas* Eggplant stuffed with bread soaked in milk, garlic sausage, and egg.

— *rebozadas* Slices of eggplant, cooked ham, and cheese dipped in beaten egg, dredged in flour, and deep-fried.

— *salteadas* Sautéed eggplant simmered in a touch of stock with tomato.

***Berza*** Cabbage.

— *a la campesina* Boiled cabbage leaves stuffed with minced pork and ham.

— *con patatas* Boiled cabbage and potatoes sautéed with chorizo

sausage and bread slices (from the Basque Country).

***Cachelos*** New potatoes (in Galicia).

— *a la castellana* Diced boiled new potatoes dressed with fried garlic, paprika, and vinegar and garnished with chopped hard-boiled egg.

***Calabacín*** Zucchini.

***Calabacines a la marinera*** Baked zucchini stuffed with a mixture of poached fish, mushrooms, onion, egg, and bread crumb.

— *a la turca* Boiled zucchini, stuffed with sautéed chicken livers, onion, tomato, and rice, sprinkled with Parmesan and baked.

— *al horno* Baked zucchini.

— *empanados* Deep-fried zucchini.

— *rellenos andaluza* Deep-fried zucchini stuffed with sautéed onion, minced pork, hard-boiled egg, and bread crumbs.

— *salteados* Boiled zucchini fried with onion and garlic.

***Cebollas rellenas*** Baked boiled onions stuffed with minced pork, egg yolk, and seasonings.

***Champiñones*** Mushrooms.

— *a la murciana* Simmered button mushrooms with garlic, onion, diced cured ham, chorizo slices, and paprika.

— *a la polonesa* Baked mushrooms napped with white sauce garnished with chopped hard-boiled egg.

— *al jerez* Mushrooms sautéed in sherry wine.

— *con salsa holandesa* Boiled mushrooms with hollandaise sauce.

— *salteados* Sautéed mushrooms.
**Coles de Bruselas** Brussels sprouts.
— *a la crema* Boiled Brussels sprouts napped with cream sauce.
— *salteadas* Sautéed Brussels sprouts.
**Coliflor** Cauliflower.
— *a la granadina* Boiled cauliflower florets sautéed with bacon and onion and dressed with chicken broth containing vinegar and saffron.
— *al ajoarriero* Boiled cauliflower dressed with a thin oil-garlic-vinegar sauce.
— *al estilo de Badajoz* Boiled cauliflower marinated in garlic and vinegar, dusted in flour, dipped in beaten egg, and deep-fried.
— *al gratén* Cauliflower au gratin.
— *al horno* Baked cauliflower.
— *con salsa holandesa* Boiled cauliflower with hollandaise sauce.
— *duquesa* Au gratin cauliflower florets garnished with potato puree containing egg yolk and butter and dressed with béchamel sauce.
**Dolmas** Simmered vine leaves stuffed with raisins, pine nuts, rice, mint, lemon, and parsley.
**Endibias** Belgian endive.
— *a la sartén* Belgian endive simmered in milk with cured ham, onion, and parsley.
**Espárragos** Asparagus.
— *a la andaluza* Simmered asparagus dressed with a blend of garlic, fried bread, paprika, and vinegar garnished with fried croutons.
— *a la manchega* Boiled asparagus with a sauce made with egg yolk, cumin, and seasonings.

— *a la navarra* Boiled asparagus and sautéed ham garnished with whole eggs and simmered until the eggs are set.
— *a la sevillana* Boiled asparagus dressed with crushed sautéed garlic and bread, garnished with hard-boild egg.
— *bella Elena* Boiled asparagrus combined with thin slices of pancake and napped with béchamel sauce.
— *mimosa* Cooked asparagus dressed with vinaigrette, garnished with a julienne of hard-boiled egg whites and sprinkled with the chopped yolks.
— *salteados* Sautéed asparagus.
**Espinacas** Spinach.
— *a la cordobesa* Boiled spinach sautéed with onion, garlic, vinegar, paprika, and cinnamon.
— *a la española* Boiled spinach sautéed in olive oil and garlic.
— *al Sacromonte* Boiled spinach sautéed in olive oil with almonds, garlic, vinegar, bread, and saffron (from Granada).
— *con garbanzos* Spinach and chickpea casserole.
— *con pasas y piñones* Boiled spinach sautéed with raisins and pine nuts.
**Faves** Fava beans in Portuguese.
— *a portuguesa* Fava beans with bacon, onion, and garlic cooked in a small amount of meat broth until tender.
**Fondos de alcachofa a la gitana** Boiled artichoke bottoms sautéed with garlic and green pepper and dressed with a vinaigrette sauce containing tarragon.

*Fritada de tomates y pimientos* Simmered tomatoes, sweet pepers and onions in olive oil.

*Frito huertano* Sautéed onion, eggplant, sweet peppers, tomato, and paprika, thickened with a touch of flour (from Murcia).

*Fritos de patata* Potato fritters.

*Garbanzos* Chickpeas.

— *a la catalana* Chickpeas cooked with a *sofrito* containing breakfast sausage and diced cured ham.

— *refritos* Chickpeas leftover from a previous stew sautéed with chorizo and pimiento.

*Grelos* Spring greens (in Galicia).

— *salteados* Spring greens sautéed in olive oil with garlic.

*Guiberludiños* Sautéed wild mushrooms dressed with bread crumbs, garlic, and parsley.

*Guisantes* Green peas.

— *a la escocesa* Green peas boiled with diced ham and chopped lettuce thickened with beurre manié.

— *a la española* Green peas braised with onions and cured ham, garnished with fresh mint.

— *a la maña* Green peas fried in bacon fat with diced cured ham (from Aragón).

— *a la murciana* Sweet peas simmered in a *sofrito* containing cured ham, chorizo slices, paprika, and a touch of flour garnished with quartered hard-boiled eggs.

— *con lechuga* Boiled green peas and lettuce sautéed with diced cured ham, garlic, and nutmeg.

— *con salchichas* Green peas with Italian-style sausages sautéed in a tomato and onion sauce.

— *levantina* Green peas simmered in a liquid containing water, wine, sauteed onion, and garlic garnished with pimiento strips.

*Habas* Fava beans.

— *a la andaluza* Fava beans and artichokes sautéed with tomato, onion, and cumin.

— *a la asturiana* Fava beans simmered in meat broth and white wine with potatoes, ham, onions, and carrots.

— *a la catalana* Fava beans, onion, garlic, and tomato simmered in wine and brandy with chopped chorizo and herbs.

— *a la rondeña* Fava beans sautéed with cured ham, hard-boiled egg, and parsley.

— *con jamón* Fava beans sautéed with cured ham.

— *con mejillones* Fava beans sautéed with mussels.

— *huertanas* Fava beans sautéed with diced cured ham and *morcilla* sausage (from Murcia).

*Habichuelas verdes* Green beans.

— *a la sevillana* Boiled green beans dressed with melted lard and vinegar.

*Hervido* Potatoes and assorted vegetables boiled in water with lemon juice, olive oil, and touch of paprika.

*Judías verdes* Green beans.

— *a la castellana* Boiled green beans fried with pimiento, garlic, and parsley.

— *a la gallega* Sautéed green beans with onion, garlic and potatoes.

— *a la lionesa* Boiled green beans sautéed with bacon and onions.

— *a la mayordoma* Boiled green beans sautéed in butter and lemon juice.

— *a la riojana* Stewed green beans with fried pork chops, onion, garlic, and sausage.

— *con jamón* Boiled green beans sautéed with cured ham.

— *salteadas* Sautéed green beans.

**Lechuga** Lettuce.

— *al jugo* Braised lettuce au jus.

— *al queso* Boiled lettuce in chicken broth baked and dressed with melted butter and parmesan cheese.

**Liadillos sevillanos** Boiled stuffed cabbage leaves.

**Lombarda** Red cabbage.

— *a la San Quintín* Red cabbage simmered with bacon, onion, apple slices, new potatoes, and vinegar.

— *con manzanas* Boiled shredded red cabbage simmered with sliced apples, vinegar, and caraway.

— *con tocino* Boiled red cabbage simmered in broth with bacon.

— *de Navidad* Braised boiled red cabbage with apple slices.

**Michirones** Boiled dried fava beans with hot chilis (from Murcia).

**Nabos** Turnips.

— *a la Badajoz* Sautéed turnips with cured ham simmered in water thickened with flour and flavored with nutmeg.

**Pastel de alcachofas** Pie shell filled with boiled artichokes, butter, beaten egg, and milk set in a double boiler and baked until the egg is done.

**Patatas** Potatoes.

— *a la extremeña* Simmered potatoes, green beans, onion, tomato, and green peppers.

— *a la brava* Potatoes browned in oil dressed with a sautéed onion and garlic sauce containing tomato sauce, wine, hot pepper, and Tabasco.

— *a la castellana* Sautéed potatoes sprinkled with flour and paprika cooked in a small amount of chicken broth until almost dry.

— *a la flamenca* Boiled potatoes sautéed in oil and dressed with vinegar and mustard.

— *al ajo cabañil* Sautéed sliced potatoes dressed with a blend of water, garlic, vinegar, and parsley.

— *a la judía* Boiled diced potatoes cooked in wine and dressed with egg yolk, olive oil, vinegar, and mustard.

— *a la leonesa* Potatoes sautéed with onions.

— *a la malagueña* Potatoes simmered in a *sofrito* containing paprika and green olives.

— *a la mallorquina* Baked stuffed potatoes with chorizo spread napped with white sauce.

— *a la riojana* Fried sliced potatoes simmered in a touch of water containing vinegar, garlic, and pepper.

— *aliñadas* Sliced boiled potatoes dressed with a blend of garlic, parsley, hard-boiled egg, oil, and vinegar.

— *a lo pobre* Sliced potatoes simmered in olive oil sprinkled with minced garlic and parsley.

— *al vapor* Steamed potatoes.

— *Ana* Baked buttered sliced potatoes.

— *con bacalao* Potatoes cooked in a liquid containing a *sofrito* with paprika and shredded salt-cod.

— *con chorizo* Sliced potatoes sautéed with chorizo and bacon.

— *con huevos duros* Sliced potatoes cooked in a *sofrito* and garnished with hard-boiled eggs.

— *doradas* Steamed potatoes brushed with melted butter and baked until golden.

— *duquesa* Duchess potatoes.

— *en ajopollo* Potatoes cooked in broth containing sautéed garlic, bread, almonds, and parsley.

— *en salsa verde* Potatoes in green sauce.

— *estofadas* Stewed potatoes.

— *goncourt* Potatoes browned in oil cooked in a touch of broth containing chopped tomatoes, thyme, and bay leaf.

— *paja* Straw potatoes.

— *picantes* Sautéed boiled potatoes seasoned with paprika, chili pepper, and garlic.

— *rellenas* Baked stuffed potatoes.

— *salteadas* Sautéed potatoes.

— *San Florentino* Potatoes pureed with egg yolk, butter, and diced ham shaped like a pear and deep-fried in olive oil.

— *Susana* Baked potatoes stuffed with béchamel sauce mixed with diced ham, chicken breast, and truffles.

**Pimientos** Peppers.

— *con nata* Grilled sweet peppers napped with whipped cream.

— *fritos* Fried peppers in olive oil.

— *morrones* Pimientos.

— *rellenos* Stuffed peppers.

— *rojos* Red peppers.

— *verdes* Green peppers.

**Pisto** Ratatouille.

— *castellano* Vegetables sautéed in bacon grease, simmered in chicken stock with a beaten egg.

— *manchego* Zucchini, tomato, green pepper, onion, and bacon ratatouille.

**Puerros** Leeks.

— *con bechamel* Baked leeks with béchamel sauce.

**Remolacha** Beet.

— *aliñada* Boiled beets dressed with oil and vinegar and garnished with quartered hard-boiled egg.

— *con atún* Diced boiled beets, mixed with canned tuna in oil and dressed with minced garlic, fresh parsley, oil, and vinegar.

**Repollo con salsa holandesa** Boiled shredded cabbage with hollandaise sauce.

**Respigos** Sautéed turnip greens with bacon, anchovies, and green peppers.

**Salsifis** Salsify.

— *al gratén* Au gratin salsify.

**Setas** Wild mushrooms.

— *a la casera* Wild mushrooms simmered with onion and sherry wine and garnished with chopped hard-boiled egg.

— *a la navarra* Wild mushrooms sautéed with white wine, crushed almonds, garlic, and paprika.

— *con salsa de almendras* Wild mushrooms sautéed in butter, thickened with flour, and simmered in meat broth with crushed almonds and paprika.

— *salteadas* Sautéed wild mushrooms.

*Tarta de cebolla* Pie shell filled with sautéed onion in bacon fat, eggs, milk, and seasonings.

— *de legumbres* Pie shell filled with a layer of spinach puree, another of chopped cooked leeks, and one of cooked potatoes, then sprinkled with grated cheese and baked.

*Tirabeques* Snow peas.

— *rellenos* Fried snow peas stuffed with a fine paste made with ground meat and cured ham.

*Tomatada a la navarra* Tomatoes simmered in olive oil with cured ham, chorizo, strips of veal, and sweet peppers.

*Tomate* Tomato.

*Tomates a la florentina* Stuffed tomatoes with creamed spinach.

— *al horno* Baked tomatoes.

*Tomates rellenos alicantina* Baked halved tomatoes stuffed with sautéed spinach, grated orange peel, and crushed sautéed almonds.

*Zanahorias* Carrots.

— *a la crema* Creamed carrots.

— *con jamón* Sautéed carrots with diced cured ham.

— *salteadas con apio* Boiled carrots and celery sautéed with garlic and cured ham.

*Zarangollo* Fried zucchini and onions combined with beaten egg and simmered until the egg sets (from Murcia).

## GUISOS, OLLAS, POTAJES, Y PUCHEROS — STEWS

No cuisine is more prolific in meals-in-a-pot than Spanish cooking. In some regions, different types of meats, together with a chunk of cured ham bone, are simmered for hours to produce a delicious, nourishing broth that is sometimes served as a soup or used as the liquid to cook legumes. Spanish stews may contain meat, furred and feathered game, fish, offal, snails, vegetables, and legumes.

As in many other dishes in Spanish cuisine, there are two basic components to stews: the *sofrito* (sautéed onions, garlic, tomatoes, and peppers in olive oil) and the *majado* (a blend of crushed-in-the mortar paste containing spices, herbs, and often, nuts). The most famous is the *cocido madrileño*, an adaptation of the *adafina*, a stew which the Spanish Jews used to place in glowing embers on Friday evening to eat on the Sabbath.

**Acelgas guisadas** Swiss chard stewed with a *sofrito* containing pine nuts and raisins.

**Ajo colorado** Mashed potatoes and sweet red peppers with a *majado* made with oil, cumin, and garlic (from Almeria).

**Ajoharina** Stew made with diced pork, chorizo, milk mushrooms, and fried garlic, thickened with flour.

**Alubias** Dry beans.

— **castellanas** Dry bean casserole with a *sofrito* with cured ham, wine, and paprika, thickened with flour.

— **con patatas** Dry bean casserole with sliced potatoes and a *sofrito* containing bacon.

— **en potaje** Dry bean stew with a *sofrito* containing fresh sausage and garnished with quartered hard-boiled eggs.

— **a la Urgel** Dry bean stew with braised pork loin, chicken, fresh sausage, fried tomato, and herbs.

**Atascaburras** Mashed boiled potatoes and shredded salt-cod blended with olive oil and hard-boiled egg yolks and dressed with a *majado* made with garlic, parsley, and walnuts.

**Cachelada gallega** Sliced boiled octopus and new potato (*cachelos*) stew with a *sofrito* and the liquid from boiling the octopus (from Galicia).

**Caldeirada** Stew of assorted fish with tomato, peppers, onion, potatoes, and paprika (from Galicia).

**Caldereta a la menorquina** Lobster casserole with fish fumet and a *majado* of onion, tomato, garlic, and parsley.

— **asturiana** Seafood stew with fish fumet, brandy, green peppers, lemon juice, and cayenne pepper.

— **de cordero** Lamb stew with *sofrito*, cured ham, white wine, and thyme.

— **de lomo** Casserole of pork medallions and artichokes stewed in meat broth and white wine.

— **de rape** Anglerfish casserole with sliced potatoes, *sofrito* and a *majado* with saffron, garlic, clove,

almonds, hazelnuts, and parsley.
— *extremeña* Cubed-lamb stew with lamb's liver, red wine, and a *majado* with garlic, black peppercorns, paprika, and vinegar.
— *de Tarazona* Rabbit, lamb, and potato casserole with a *majado* of walnuts and the rabbit's liver.
— *manchega* Lamb shoulder casserole containing a *majado* made with sautéed lamb's brain, liver, and bread.
*Caldero de pastor* Lamb and potato casserole with onion and tomato *sofrito*.
*Caldo de jaramago* Boiled navy beans, potatoes, salt pork, and wall rocket leaves (*jaramago*) mixed with corn meal and dressed with vinegar (from the Canary Islands).
*Callos* Beef tripe.
— *a la asturiana* Tripe casserole with chickpeas and white wine.
— *a la madrileña* Tripe casserole with cured ham, ox feet, chorizo, *morcilla* sausage, paprika, and chili peppers.
— *murcianos* Tripe stew with calf's feet, chorizo, cured ham, and chickpeas and flavored with saffron and fresh mint.
*Caracoles* Snails (escargots).
— *a la andaluza* Snails stewed with *sofrito* and a *majado* made with garlic, fried almonds, and fried bread.
— *picantes* Snails stewed with chili peppers.
*Carne a la montañesa* Cubed leg of veal stew with sautéed onion, white wine, and meat broth.
*Casolet* Dry white bean stew with lamb, pork loin, and fresh sausage.
*Cazuela canaria* Sautéed assorted fish casserole with a *sofrito* with paprika and garnished with potatoes, corn, banana, pumpkin, and pineapple.
— *de espárragos* Asparagus casserole with a *majado* made with fried garlic, bread, vinegar, and paprika and garnished with beaten egg and browned in the oven.
— *de ternera con berenjenas* Veal casserole with eggplant.
*Chanfaina de ave* Chicken casserole with hard-boiled eggs, and a *majado* containing pig's liver, fried almonds, and roasted garlic.
*Chilindrón de cordero* Lamb stewed in *chilindrón* sauce.
*Cochifrito* Lamb casserole with meat broth, lemon juice, and sherry.
*Cocido con pelotas* Chickpea stew with beef, turkey, chorizo, potatoes, and green beans, garnished with meat balls made with bread, bacon, chicken livers, garlic, pine nuts, and parsley.
— *gaditano* Veal-and-pork-meat stew with chickpeas, bacon, onion, green beans, potatoes, pumpkin, chorizo, and paprika flavored with a *majado* made of garlic, cumin, tomato, and vinegar.
— *gallego* Veal, salt pork, pig's head, and chickpea stew with cabbage and chorizo sausage (from Galicia).
— *madrileño* Chickpea stew with beef brisket, salt pork, ham hock, beef bone, chicken, chorizo, *morcilla* sausage, boiled potatoes, cabbage, and spices.

— *valenciano* Veal and chickpea stew with bacon, cured ham, chorizo, potatoes, and assorted vegetables and garnished with dumplings made with poultry blood, bacon, egg, corn meal, and bread crumb.

— *zamorano* Chickpea and bacon stew with rice, sliced potatoes, chorizo, and *sofrito* containing paprika.

*Conejo guisado* Rabbit stuffed with bread soaked in milk, bacon, veal marrow, and parsley, simmered in white wine, and dressed with boiled onion puree (from the Canary Islands).

*Cordero a la pastora* Marinated lamb stewed with rosemary, thyme, and meat stock and thickened with flour.

*Ensopado de borrego* Lamb stew with potatoes (from Portugal).

*Escudella catalana* Cabbage, potato, and rice casserole with bacon and pasta (from Catalonia).

*Estofado a la catalana* Beef stew with red wine, bouquet garni, new potatoes and garlic sausage.

— *de cordero a la andaluza* Lamb stew in a flour-thickened broth with a *majado* of garlic and fresh mint.

— *de ternera* Veal stew.

— *de toro* Beef stew.

— *de vaca aragonesa* Diced beef stewed in white wine with a *sofrito* containing thyme.

— *a la montañesa* Cubed beef stew flavored with cocoa.

*Fabada asturiana* Dry bean stew with pig's feet, brisket of beef, chorizo, *morcilla*, and paprika sausage.

*Gachas gaditanas* Wheat flour gruel with aniseed.

— *malagueñas* Wheat flour gruel with minced sautéed potatoes and garlic.

— *manchegas* Wheat flour gruel garnished with sautéed pork liver, bacon, potato, and chorizo (from La Mancha).

*Garbanzos a la catalana* Chickpea stew with *sofrito* and *butifarra* sausage garnished with chopped hard-boiled egg.

— *a la andaluza* Chickpea casserole with beef tripe, chorizo sausage, and a *sofrito* with crushed almonds.

— *con huevos duros* Chickpea stew with a *sofrito* containing cured ham and chorizo and *majado* with hazelnuts and cloves and garnished with hard-boiled eggs.

— *con tomate* Chickpea casserole with a *sofrito*, additional fried tomato and paprika and garnished with fried croutons.

*Guisado de ternera* Veal ragout with white wine, bouquet garni and nutmeg.

— *de vaca al estilo de Vigo* Beef stew with white wine, nutmeg, and cloves.

*Guiso de albondigas de bacalao* Artichoke and green pea stew with salt-cod dumplings.

— *de calamares y patatas* Stewed potatoes with squid.

— *de cordero* Lamb stew with *sofrito* and a *majado* with garlic, parsley, and sherry wine.

— *de gurullos con hierbabuena* Chickpea stew with *sofrito*, small pieces of flour dough, and fresh mint (from Murcia).

— *de menudos de cerdo* Pork tripe casserole.

— *de patatas* Fried sliced potatoes and boiled green peas with a *sofrito* containing fresh sausage stewed in meat broth and garnished with hard-boiled eggs.

— *de pulpo con patatas* Octopus stew with potatoes, *sofrito*, and paprika (from Galicia).

— *de sangre de cerdo* Pig's blood stew with a *sofrito* with paprika.

— *de trigo* Stewed wheat with pig's feet, chickpeas, turnips, and a *sofrito* with paprika.

— *de vaca al coñac* Beef stew with brandy, cream, and paprika.

*Habas secas con rabo* Stew of dried fava beans with oxtail.

*Jarrete cacerola* Beef shank casserole with white wine, herbs and assorted vegetables.

*Judías* Dry beans.

— *a la bilbaina* Navy bean casserole with *sofrito*, cured ham, and green peppers.

— *a la bretona* Navy bean casserole with sautéed onions and tomatoe puree.

— *a la maconesa* Kidney bean casserole with bacon and *sofrito* containing red wine.

— *a la madrileña* Navy bean stew with a *sofrito* containing chorizo and paprika.

— *al caserío* Navy bean casserole with *sofrito*, bacon, and red peppers.

— *a lo tío Lucas* Navy bean stew with a *sofrito* containing paprika, vinegar, cumin, clove, and parsley.

— *con chorizo* Navy bean stew with chorizo.

— *con mano de cerdo* Navy bean stew with pig's feet.

— *con perdiz* Navy bean and potato stew with partridge.

— *estofadas* Stewed dry beans.

— *pintas con cerdo* Pinto bean stew with fresh pork.

*Lacón con grelos* Salted shoulder of pork (*lacón*) with vegetable greens (*grelos*) and dry white beans (from Galicia).

*Lentejas* Lentils

— *a la burgalesa* Lentil stew with bacon and a *sofrito* containing nutmeg.

— *a la cubana* Lentil stew with a *sofrito* containing nutmeg.

— *a lo pobre* Lentil stew with a sofrito with paprika, garnished with quartered hard-boiled eggs.

— *con almejas* Stewed lentils with clams and *sofrito*.

— *con arroz* Stewed lentils with rice and *sofrito*.

— *con chorizo y tocino* Lentil stew with chorizo, salt pork, and sautéed onion.

— *con oreja de cerdo* Lentil stew with pig's ear.

— *finas hierbas* Lentil casserole with a *sofrito* with cured ham, silver onions, and bouquet garni.

— *Villalar* Boiled lentils sautéed in lard with nutmeg and garnished with minced hard-boiled egg and croutons.

*Marmitako* Fresh tuna stew with white wine and potatoes (from Basque Country).

*Menestra* Vegetable and/or meat casserole.

— *a la bilbaina* Mixed-vegetable casserole with *sofrito* containing diced cured ham, white wine, and chicken stock and garnished with chopped hard-boiled egg.

— *a la catalana* Vegetable casserole with fresh sausage, cubed pork tenderloin, and white wine.

— *a la extremeña* Swiss chard and potato casserole dressed with beaten egg.

— *a la murciana* Assorted vegetable casserole.

— *a la riojana* Sautéed vegetables mixed with a *sofrito* with cured ham, baked, and garnished with quartered hard-boiled eggs and pimiento strips.

— *a la rondeña* Artichoke, fava bean, and green pea casserole with morcilla sausage and *sofrito*.

— *a la tudelana* Artichoke and fava bean casserole with *majado* of garlic, parsley, almonds, fried bread, and saffron garnished with sliced hard-boiled egg.

— *con jamón* Ham and vegetables casserole.

— *de ternera* Diced veal stewed with spring vegetables.

— *de verduras* Assorted vegetable casserole.

— *gallega* Casserole of assorted vegetables sautéed with diced cured ham and garnished with poached eggs.

— *ribereña* Stew of assorted vegetables with cured ham and *sofrito*.

**Mojo de cerdo** Pig's lung and heart casserole with a *sofrito* with white wine and a *majado* made with oregano, thyme, cumin, vinegar,

and paprika (from the Canary Islands).

**Morteruelo manchego** Minced boiled hare, hen, and pork loin with bread crumb summered in the liquid and flavored with cloves, paprika, and caraway.

**Olla de cerdo** Boiled dry beans, rice, and turnips with bacon slab, *morcilla*, pig's ear, garlic, and tomato.

— *gitana con peras* Chickpea stew with potatoes, green beans, pumpkin, fresh pears, and *sofrito*.

— *podrida* Veal, pork, mutton, poultry, duck, partridge, veal's brain, and chicken liver stew with assorted vegetables and *sofrito* (from La Mancha).

**Orejas de cerdo a la leonesa** Pig's ear casserole with sautéed onion, bacon, and meat broth.

**Patatas con bacalao** Potatoes and salt-cod stew.

— *con rape* Potatoes and anglerfish casserole.

— *con raya* Potatoes and skate casserole.

**Patorra extremeña** Sautéed diced mutton liver, lungs, and blood simmered in meat broth with sautéed onion, paprika, and flour, and garnished with beaten egg (from Extremadura).

**Pebre murciano** Boiled shoulder of lamb with a *majado* made with boiled tomatoes and cumin (from Murcia).

**Potaje blanco** Navy bean, chickpea, and rice stew with a *sofrito* made with lard.

— *de garbanzos con acelgas* Chickpea and Swiss chard stew

with a *sofrito* containing almonds and vinegar.

— *de viernes* Chickpea and spinach stew with salt-cod, *sofrito*, and paprika.

***Pote asturiano*** Salt pork, pig's ear, *morcilla* sausage, navy beans, potatoes, and cabbage stew flavored with smoked lard.

— *del Cantábrico* Cabbage, potatoes, and dry bean stew with salted pork shoulder meat (*lacón*), chorizo, and *morcilla* sausage.

***Puchero canario*** Beef brisket, chorizo, *morcilla* sausage, and chickpea stew with potatoes, sweet potatoes, pumpkin, corn, cabbage, and pears and a *majado* containing clove, saffron, and garlic.

— *casero* Cabbage and potato stew with chorizo and *morcilla* sausage.

— *de gallina* Broth-simmered hen stuffed with bacon, cured ham, the hen's liver, garlic, parsley, tarragon, bread crumb, egg, and white wine.

— *de las Hurdes* Rabbit stewed with potatoes, vinegar, olive oil, and minced onion (from Extremadura).

***Rabo de toro a la andaluza*** Oxtail stew with a *sofrito* containing cured ham and paprika.

— *a la jerezana* Oxtail stew with bouquet garni, meat broth, white wine, and a *sofrito* containing paprika.

***Ragout de cordero*** Lamb ragout.

— *de ternera* Veal ragout.

***Rancho*** Stew in Portuguese.

— *a Porta Nova* Chickpea stew with pork shank, beef brisket, macaroni, and *sofrito* with cumin (from Portugal).

***Ropa vieja*** Chopped leftover stewed beef sautéed with diced potatoes, onion, tomato, eggplant, and thyme.

***Sancocho canario*** Stew made with salt fish, yams, potatoes, and corn meal and a *majado* containing garlic, cumin, cayenne, bread, and vinegar (from the Canary Islands).

***Sepia guisada*** Cuttlefish stew with potatoes, *sofrito*, and chicken stock.

***Suquet de pescadores*** Assorted seafood stewed with *sofrito*, white wine, and a *majado* made with saffron, garlic, almonds, and parsley (from Cataluña).

***Ternera a la sevillana*** Beef tenderloin simmered with green olives, toasted almonds, sherry wine, and *sofrito*.

— *a la sidra* Veal casserole with green peas, hard cider, and *sofrito*.

— *con guisantes* Veal stew with green peas.

***Vaca guisada a la flamenca*** Beef stew with bouquet garni and bock beer.

***Zarzuela de pescado*** Assorted seafood stewed in fish fumet with a *sofrito* containing brandy and a *majado* made of saffron, garlic, pine nuts, and parsley.

**DISHES BY COURSE**

## AVES — POULTRY

Mass-production chicken farms were practically unknown in Spain until recently. Instead of buying poultry frozen, Spaniards purchase chickens and turkeys alive, often in open farmers' markets. As a result, the quality of the meat is extremely good and its taste of superior quality. These birds have been raised pecking around small farms where they can find nutritious feed by themselves.

Although poultry meat often appears cooked in conjunction with other meats, seafood, and legumes, there are many imaginative recipes for cooking birds. As with other dishes, *sofritos* and *majados* are almost always added to provide the very special flavors of Spanish foods.

*Alas de pollo* Chicken wings.

— *al vino* Sautéed chicken wings with garlic, tomato, white wine, and oregano.

*Capón* Capon.

— *a la andaluza* Roast capon stuffed with raisins, pine nuts, bacon, milk-soaked bread, egg, sherry, and cinnamon.

— *al estilo de Lazcano* Baked chicken stuffed with a mixture of apples, chestnuts, bacon, milk, and hard cider (from the Basque Country).

— *asado* Roast capon.

— *borracho* Capon sautéed in olive oil and simmered in white wine.

— *picante* Capon sautéed in oil with *sofrito* containing paprika and hot chili peppers.

*Frango* Chicken in Portuguese.

— *a portuguesa* Chicken simmered in wine garnished with fried eggs and boiled rice.

*Gallina* Hen.

— *a la cubana* Hen poached in broth simmered in chicken stock with roux, egg yolk, and whipping cream.

— *a la gallega* Fried chicken simmered in wine with bouquet garni, noodles, and a *sofrito* with saffron and nutmeg.

— *a la granadina* Hen simmered in white wine, sautéed onion, and parsley and garnished with sautéed yams and bananas.

— *a la italiana* Boiled hen simmered in a sauce of onion, garlic, mushrooms, and wine.

— *al estragón* Hen in tarragon sauce.

— *dorada* Baked hen basted with a mixture of meat broth and sherry wine.

— *en aceite* Hen sautéed with garlic and parsley simmered in white wine, broth, and thyme with a *majado* made of olive oil, almonds, and the yolk of a hard-boiled egg.

— *en pepitoria* Hen braised in chicken stock with dry sherry and a sauce made with crushed toasted almonds, fried bread, garlic, nutmeg, and cloves.

— *en salsa* Hen simmered in a liquid made of broth, wine, vinegar, crushed tomato, and cinnamon.

*Muslos de gallina rellenos* Stuffed hen thighs.

*Pavo* Turkey.

— *adobado* Turkey marinated in wine, cloves, peppercorns, onion, and bay leaf, sautéed, and then simmered in the liquid of the marinade with tomato, cinnamon, and clove.

— *a la madrileña* Roast turkey basted with wine and dressed with its own pan gravy.

— *a la menorquina* Roast turkey stuffed with bread crumbs, butter, honey, raisins, lemon rind, egg, and cinnamon.

— *con verduras* Turkey casserole with assorted vegetables.

— *en salsa de almendras* Sautéed turkey simmered in meat broth with a *sofrito* containing crushed almonds with a gravy flavored with lemon juice and thickened with flour.

— *trufado* Roast turkey stuffed with ground veal, ground pork loin, truffles, milk-soaked bread crumb, egg, sherry, and nutmeg.

*Pechuga de pollo* Chicken breast.

*Pechugas de pollo a la naranja* Chicken breasts in orange sauce.

— *con piñones* Sautéed chicken breasts simmered with onion, garlic, parsley, pine nuts, and white wine.

— *rellenas* Stuffed chicken breasts.

— *Villeroy* Deep-fried chicken breasts coated with a sauce made with roux, chicken stock, milk, and nutmeg.

*Pollo* Chicken.

— *a la andaluza* Floured chicken fried in olive oil simmered in broth, sherry, and *sofrito* with a *majado* made from fried garlic, almonds, saffron, parsley, and hard-boiled egg yolk.

— *a la bilbaina* Sautéed chicken simmered in a *sofrito* containing sweet red peppers and white wine.

— *a la bordelesa* Truffle-stuffed chicken *en cocotte* with onion, brandy, wine, tomato, and chicken stock dressed with a sauce made with shallots, mushrooms, and chervil.

— *a la buena mujer* Roast chicken *en cocotte* with sherry, potatoes, silver onions, bacon, and brandy.

— *a la castellana* Sautéed chicken simmered in wine, chicken broth, pureed onion, and spices.

— *a la catalana* Sautéed chicken simmered in a *sofrito* with white wine, zucchini, and eggplant.

— *a la cerveza* Chicken simmered in beer with sautéed potatoes and onions.

— *a la chilena* Pulled chicken meat cooked in a mixture of milk and cream, garnished with spaghetti.

— *a la española* Chicken sautéed in casserole with sautéed onions, white wine, chicken stock, basil, garlic, parsley, and pine nuts.

— *a la extremeña* Sautéed chicken simmered in a sauce made of lemon rind, honey, rosemary, and white wine.

— *a la flamenca* Chicken sautéed in lard with minced onion, parsley, and garlic simmered in chicken broth and white wine thickened with flour.

DISHES BY COURSE

— *al ajillo* Fried chicken with garlic.

— *a la manchega* Sautéed chicken simmered in a *sofrito* with cured ham and fried garlic and flavored with thyme, bay leaf, and cinnamon.

— *a la molinera* Chicken stuffed with sautéed mushrooms, chicken liver, onion, brandy, and sherry and simmered in white wine.

— *a la murciana* Chicken simmered in a *sofrito* with tomatoes, red peppers, and a touch of sugar.

— *a la navarra* Chicken simmered with wild mushrooms and a *majado* with the chicken's liver, garlic, and white wine.

— *a la pimienta* Pepper-seasoned fried chicken simmered in stock with chili peppers, saffron, and nutmeg and a *majado* of garlic, parsley, toasted almonds, and pine nuts.

— *a la piña* Roast chicken with pineapple sauce.

— *a la praviana* Sautéed chicken simmered in hard cider with sautéed cured ham, onion, garlic, paprika, and blanched shrimp garnished with fried bread (from Asturias).

— *a la sal* Chicken covered with a paste made with coarse salt and water and roasted in the oven.

— *a la santanderina* Sautéed chicken simmered in a *sofrito* with white wine and brandy.

— *a las finas hierbas* Chicken casserole with bacon, parsley, potatoes, and green onions.

— *al ast* Spit-roasted chicken.

— *al café* Sautéed chicken with sherry and walnuts simmered in coffee and thickened with cornstarch.

— *al champán* Chicken in champagne sauce.

— *al chilindrón* Chicken braised in olive oil with sweet red peppers, tomatoes, onions, and diced cured ham.

— *al horno* Roast chicken.

— *al pimentón* Chicken in paprika sauce.

— *al vino tinto* Chicken in red wine sauce.

— *campurriano* Chicken sautéed in bacon fat stewed in chicken stock and white wine with a *sofrito* with paprika.

— *con caracoles* Chicken casserole with *sofrito*, snails, and a paste made with the chicken's liver and olive oil.

— *con col* Chicken boiled in liquid containing olive oil, vinegar, and cloves and a *sofrito* with shredded boiled cabbage and white wine.

— *con gambas* Sautéed chicken and shrimp simmered in wine, chicken broth, and brandy.

— *con higos* Chicken simmered in a sauce made with fresh figs, white wine, olive oil, and cinnamon.

— *con jamón serrano* Chicken pieces larded with cured serrano ham sautéed with onions, tomatoes, and brandy and simmered until tender.

— *con langosta* Chicken and lobster sautéed in casserole with a sauce of almonds, hazelnuts, saffron, and bitter dark chocolate.

— *con manzanas* Roast chicken with apples.

— *con naranjas* Chicken à l'orange.

— *con piñones* Chicken stewed with onions, olive oil, and pine nuts.

— *con pisto* Sautéed chicken with ratatouille.

— *con salsa de ajo* Sautéed chicken simmered in wine and saffron with a *majado* of garlic and fried bread.

— *con tomate* Fried chicken in tomato sauce.

— *empanado* Deep-fried breaded chicken.

— *en chanfaina* Sautéed chicken with onion, garlic, eggplant, peppers, tomato, white wine, and thyme.

— *hervido con bechamel* Poached chicken napped with béchamel sauce.

— *jerezano* Bacon-larded chicken baked until brown with carrots, onion, garlic, and parsley; then meat broth and sherry wine are added and the whole simmered until the chicken is done.

— *morisco* Sautéed chicken simmered in water with crushed almonds, onion, and raisins.

— *relleno* Stuffed chicken.

— *riojano* Sautéed chicken simmered in a *sofrito* containing sweet red peppers, hot chilis, and white wine.

— *salteado* Sautéed chicken.

— *vienesa* Boiled chicken pieces breaded and fried in oil.

DISHES BY COURSE

## CARNES — MEATS

In the far north of the Peninsula, where mountain valleys are covered with abundant green grass, beef is of very good quality. On the central plateau and in the coastal regions cattle is not especially tender and is best prepared in pots and casseroles, simmered in stewed tomato and herbs or pre-tenderized in tasty marinades.

Pork and lamb, on the other hand, are often prepared when very young, and their meat is particularly delicious. Eating roast suckling pig or baby lamb is an experience to remember.

### CERDO — PORK

**Chuleta** Chop.

**Chuletas de cerdo a la asturiana** Sautéed pork chops and apple slices simmered in meat broth and hard cider.

— *a la madrileña* Marinated pork chops sautéed in olive oil.

— *a la mostaza* Grilled pork chops dressed with mustard and chopped gherkins.

— *a la naranja* Pork chops in orange sauce.

— *a la portuguesa* Sautéed pork chops simmered in wine, sautéed onion, and bouquet garni and garnished with shredded boiled cabbage.

— *al jerez* Sautéed pork chops simmered in sherry and crushed almonds.

— *con ciruelas pasas* Browned pork chops simmered in a sauce made with prunes, red wine, sugar, and cinnamon.

— *con espinacas* Sautéed pork chops simmered in sherry garnished with sautéed spinach.

— *con pimientos y jamón* Browned pork chops simmered in a *sofrito* containing pimiento and diced cured ham.

— *con tomate* Sautéed pork chops with tomato.

— *empanadas* Fried breaded pork chops.

— *riojana* Seared pork chops simmered with sautéed onion, garlic, tomato, and sweet red peppers.

**Cochinillo** Suckling pig.

— *asado* Roast suckling pig.

**Costillas de cerdo** Pork ribs.

— *a la bejarana* Potato, green pepper, and pork rib stew.

— *con setas* Fried pork ribs simmered in wine, sautéed mushrooms, and onions.

**Filetes de cerdo con queso** Fried breaded pork fillets stuffed with cheese.

**Jamón** Ham.

— *a la plancha* Broiled ham.

— *asado con pasas* Roast fresh leg of pork dressed with red wine and raisin sauce.

— *de York al oporto* Baked canned ham dressed with port wine sauce.

**Lechón** Suckling pig.

— *asado* Roast suckling pig.

**Lomo** Loin.

**Lomo de cerdo adobado** Sautéed marinated pork loin.

— *a la andaluza* Roast pork loin garnished with fried green peppers in olive oil.

— *a la aragonesa* Marinated pork loin simmered in meat broth with sautéed onion, wine, and vinegar.

— *a la baturra* Sautéed pork loin medallions simmered in wine, tomato puree, sautéed onion, cured ham, and green olives (from Aragón).

— *a la miel* Roast pork loin dressed with a sauce made with red wine, vinegar, meat broth, and honey.

— *a la vasca* Sautéed pork loin with garlic and onion simmered in milk until tender.

— *con almejas* Marinated pork loin sautéed with onions simmered in the marinade's liquid with clams (from Portugal).

— *con castañas* Roast pork loin basted with brandy and garnished with chestnut puree.

— *con escalibada* Roast pork loin garnished with sautéed sweet red peppers and eggplant (from Catalonia).

— *con lombarda* Roast pork loin garnished with boiled red cabbage.

— *relleno* Stuffed pork loin.

— *trufado* Stuffed pork loin with truffles.

*Magra con tomate* Sautéed diced fresh ham with tomato.

*Manos de cerdo* Pig's trotters.

— *a la catalana* Boiled pig's trotters simmered in wine with a *sofrito* containing pine nuts.

— *al limón* Boiled pig's trotters in lemon sauce.

— *con salsa roja* Boiled pig's trotters with red pepper sauce.

— *gratinadas* Boiled pig's trotters au gratin.

*Pierna* Leg.

*Pierna de cerdo encebollada* Simmered leg of pork with onion, green peppers, tomato, paprika, cloves, and oil and a *majado* of garlic, paprika, and saffron.

— *estofada* Braised leg of pork.

*Prueba de cerdo* Fried cubed pork meat with onion, garlic, hot chilis, cayenne, thyme, and paprika (served to "test" the meat of the pig that has just been butchered).

*Solomillo* Tenderloin.

*Solomillo de cerdo a la malagueña* Roast pork tenderloin dressed with a sauce made of sautéed onion, meat broth, lemon juice, nutmeg, and flour and garnished with sliced hard-boiled egg, green peas, and cubed cured ham.

— *al jerez* Roast bacon-larded pork loin basted with meat broth and sherry wine.

— *con aceitunas* Roast pork tenderloin with green olive sauce.

## CORDERO — LAMB and CABRITO — YOUNG GOAT

*Brochetas* Brochettes.

— *de cordero* Lamb borchettes.

*Cabeza de cordero al horno* Roast lamb's head.

*Cabrito* Young goat.

— *a la castellana* Sautéed diced young goat baked dressed with a *majado* made with garlic, parsley, and vinegar.

— *a la extremeña* Young goat casserole with a *majado* made with its liver, garlic, pimiento, and paprika.

— *al ron* Broiled young goat marinated in rum sauce.

*Carnero* Mutton.

— *a la española* Roast leg of mutton with garlic and rosemary
dressed with its own gravy and
garnished with green peas.

— *en adobo* Sautéed marianted
mutton.

*Chuletas* Cutlets.

*Chuletas de cordero a la aragonesa*
Fried breaded lamb chops simmered in fried tomato.

— *a la bechamel* Grilled lamb cutlets wrapped in béchamel sauce.

— *al ajo cabañil* Fried lamb cutlets dressed with a *majado* made
with garlic and vinegar.

— *a la navarra* Sautéed lamb cutlets simmered in a *sofrito* with
diced cured ham and chorizo sausage.

— *a la parmesana* Fried lamb cutlets baked covered with potato
puree blended with egg yolk, butter, and nutmeg.

— *a la parrilla* Grilled lamb cutlets.

— *asadas* Grilled lamb cutlets.

— *Villarreal* Baked lamb cutlets
with sautéed onions in bacon fat
and bouquet garni.

— *Villeroy* Lamb cutlets dipped in
béchamel sauce, breaded and
deep-fried in olive oil.

*Cordeiro a transmontana* Rolled leg
of lamb roasted with fresh mint
(from Portugal).

*Cordero a la almendra* Baked lamb
medallions in almond sauce.

— *a la menta* Roast saddle of lamb
with mint sauce.

— *a la murciana* Baked leg of

lamb with new potatoes, garlic,
parsley, and pine nuts.

— *a la riojana* Roast leg of lamb
basted with wine and dressed
with its own gravy combined with
garlic, meat stock, and vinegar.

— *a la sal* Baked leg of lamb covered with a casing of coarse salt.

— *al chilindrón* Diced lamb simmered in a *sofrito* with white wine,
saffron, and dry red peppers.

— *asado a la manchega* Roast
lamb basted with white wine and
dressed with its own gravy spiced
with peppercorns and garlic.

— *a la segoviana* Baked leg of
lamb dressed with thyme, garlic,
and sherry.

— *a la vallisoletana* Baked half
baby lamb dressed with lard, parsley, and vinegar.

— *en salsa picante* Baked leg of
lamb dressed with piquant sauce.

— *en su jugo* Roast lamb au jus.

*Espalda* Shoulder.

*Espalda de cordero con nabos* Lamb
shoulder casserole with turnips.

— *rellena* Roasted stuffed shoulder of lamb.

*Lengua* Tongue.

— *de cordero a la murciana* Boiled
lamb tongue simmered in meat
stock with crushed almonds, raisins, and lemon juice and thickened with flour.

*Manos de cordero a la catalana*
Boiled lamb's trotters cut into
pieces, breaded and deep-fried.

— *a la madrileña* Boned boiled
lamb's trotters dressed with a
sauce made with sautéed onion,
garlic, diced cured ham, paprika,
and thickened with flour.

*Medallones de cordero Marengo* Lamb leg medallions simmered in sherry with sautéed onions, garnished with sautéed bacon, carrots, and zucchini.

*Pierna* Leg.

*Pierna de cordero a la cordobesa* Roast leg of lamb with wine, bouquet garni, meat broth, and tomato sauce.

— *a la orensana* Leg of lamb roasted in meat broth and garnished with cooked navy beans (from Galicia).

— *asada* Roast leg of lamb.

— *con alioli de membrillo* Roast leg of lamb garnished with quince *alioli*.

— *mechada* Roast larded leg of lamb.

*Sesos* Brains.

*Sesos de cordero rebozados* Breaded fried lamb's brains.

*Ternasco* Baby lamb.

— *asado* Roast baby lamb.

*TERNERA — VEAL* and *VACCA — BEEF*

*Aguja de ternera* Shoulder of veal.

— *a la jardinera* Shoulder of veal stewed with assorted vegetables.

*Bifes de cebollada* Beefsteak with onions (from Portugal).

*Bistec a la andaluza* Grilled beefsteak garnished with baked eggplant stuffed with ham and fried tomatoes with onions.

— *con pimientos* Grilled beefsteak garnished with roasted sweet peppers.

*Blanqueta de ternera* Veal blanquette.

*Cachopo* Fried veal cutlet with cheese and ham.

*Chuleta de lomo a la bilbaina* Marinated beef loin chop breaded, grilled, and garnished with minced garlic and parsley.

*Chuleta de ternera* Veal chop.

— *a la alavesa* Grilled marinated veal chop garnished with fried sweet red peppers.

— *a la castellana* Fried veal chop simmered in white wine with onions and noisette potatoes.

— *a la guipuzcoana* Fried veal chop baked in meat broth, hard cider, sliced potatoes, and bouquet garni.

— *al ajo cabañil* Fried veal chop simmered in meat broth, garlic, paprika, and vinegar.

— *a la hortelana* Fried veal chop garnished with sautéed onion, garlic, chopped cured ham, mushrooms, pimiento, and thyme.

— *con habas* Fried veal chop garnished with a *sofrito* containing fresh fava beans.

— *Villagodio* Grilled veal chop basted with olive oil.

— *zíngara* Fried veal chop simmered in brown sauce and garnished with thin slices of ham.

*Churrasco de ternera* Veal meat baked with wine, meat broth, garlic, onion, and carrots.

*Entrecote a la bordelesa* Grilled beefsteak dressed with red wine sauce containing shallots and veal marrow.

— *a la mayordoma* Grilled beef steak with maître d'hôtel butter.

*Escalope* Escalope.

*Escalope de ternera a la catalana* Fried veal escalope dressed with a sauce containing white wine and hazelnuts.

— *a la madrileña* Fried breaded veal escalope garnished with sautéed onion and tomato sauce.

*Escalopines al limón* Veal escallopinni with lemon sauce.

*Filete* Fillet - cutlet.

— *a caballo* Fried veal cutlet garnished with one fried egg on a slice of French bread.

— *de vaca con crema de anchoas* Grilled beef fillet garnished with anchovy butter.

— *mechado con jamón* Roast beef fillet larded with prosciutto ham.

— *de ternera empanado* Breaded veal cutlet.

*Granadinas de ternera a la vasca* Veal grenadins simmered in the oven with a *sofrito* containing white wine, veal tongue julienne, and bouquet garni.

*Hígado* Liver.

— *de ternera con lechuga* Fried veal liver garnished with shredded romaine lettuce and dressed with oil and vinegar.

— *encebollado* Sautéed veal liver and onions.

*Lengua* Tongue.

— *de ternera con ensalada* Cold boiled veal tongue garnished with salad.

*Lomo* Loin.

— *mechado Enrique IV* Roast larded beef loin garnished with artichoke bottoms and green peas.

*Medallón* Medallion.

*Medallones de ternera Montpensier* Fried veal medallions garnished

with artichoke bottoms filled with sautéed asparagus tips.

*Popietas a la romana* Beef paupiettes stuffed with minced pork, hard-boiled egg, and minced gherkins.

*Redondo de ternera* Veal round.

— *al horno* Roast veal round.

*Solomillo* Tenderloin.

— *a la andaluza* Roast larded beef tenderloin garnished with stewed mushrooms and onions.

— *a la granadina* Roast beef tenderloin garnished with turnips, carrots, onions, and tomatoes.

— *a la naranja* Beef tenderloin with orange sauce.

— *a la pimienta* Grilled beef tenderloin dressed with a sauce containing peppercorns, brandy, and whipping cream.

— *con salsa de berros* Beef tenderloin with watercress sauce.

— *de vaca al vino* Baked beef tenderloin with wine sauce.

*Ternera a la provenzal* Veal ragout with onions and thyme.

— *al jugo* Roast veal au jus.

— *asada* Roast veal.

*Tournedos a la alsaciana* Fried beef tournedos on toast garnished with a creamy sauce containing green peas and onions.

— *Rossini* Fried beef tournedos on toast garnished with foie gras and truffles.

— *royale* Fried beef tournedos on toast garnished with green beans and dressed with a creamy tomato sauce.

# CAZA — GAME

Spain has some of the best hunting in Europe. *Caza mayor*, big game, refers to the hunting of deer, ibex, and wild boar which are numerous in the mountainous region of the Peninsula. *Caza menor*, small game, comprises a large variety of wild birds which cross Spain on their migration journeys to and from Africa. The number of partridges, quail, wood pigeons, hare, and rabbit hunted every year across the country is substantial.

It is quite common to find game dishes offered in Spanish restaurants, particularly in small towns far from areas of heavy traffic. Famous throughout the country are the red-legged partridges which fly in large flocks on their way to Africa. High up in the Pyrenees, the Basques catch large numbers of thrushes by setting gossamer nets in the mountain passes. Restaurants in the Basque Country often feature thrush dishes that are much appreciated by the local patrons.

**Becada** Woodcock.
— *a la bilbaina* Woodcock braised in broth, sherry, turnips, and a *majado* of fried bread and potato puree.
— *a la guadalupe* Woodcock braised with a *sofrito* containing wine and the woodcock's giblets.
— *al jerez* Roast woodcock basted with sherry wine.
**Codorniz** Quail.
**Codornices a la aragonesa** Quail braised in wine with assorted vegetables.
— *a la bilbaina* Roast quail in grapevine leaves, flamed with brandy, and served on toast.
— *a la burgalesa* Quail braised in a broth made with the quail's giblets and white wine.
— *a la gallega* Quail stewed with white beans.
— *a la riojana* Quail simmered in a *sofrito* with wine, cured ham, and sweet green peppers.
— *a las uvas* Roast quail dressed with a white sauce containing

grapes flamed in port wine and brandy.
— *asadas* Roast quail.
— *con jamón* Quail stuffed with cured ham braised in broth with a *majado* of roasted almonds, garlic, and parsley.
— *con pochas* Quail simmered in a *sofrito* with cured ham and chorizo sausage, garnished with cooked white beans.
**Conejo** Rabbit.
— *agridulce* Sweet and sour rabbit
— *a la alicantina* Rabbit marinated in garlic and orange juice, fried in olive oil, and garnished with sautéed fava beans.
— *a la asturiana* Sautéed rabbit braised in a *sofrito* with turnips, carrots, and potatoes and a *majado* with the rabbit's liver and pine nuts.
— *a la bilbaina* Rabbit braised in stock, wine, garlic, hazelnuts, the rabbit's liver, and chocolate.
— *a la burgalesa* Rabbit stewed in

**Conejo a la burgalesa** (cont.) wine, meat stock, the rabbit's pureed liver, thyme, and nutmeg.

— **a la campesina** Rabbit marinated in wine simmered in a *sofrito* with the liquid of the marinade and brandy.

— **a la castellana** Rabbit braised in a *sofrito* containing vinegar and paprika.

— **a la cazadora** Rabbit simmered in a *sofrito* containing cured ham, brandy, wine, and thyme.

— **al alioli** Grilled rabbit served with garlic mayonnaise.

— **a la montañesa** Sautéed rabbit braised in wine, mushrooms, bouquet garni, and cinnamon with a *majado* of garlic, pinenuts, and toasted almonds (from Santander).

— **a la navarra** Rabbit braised in wine, garlic, tomato, and rosemary.

— **a las hierbas** Rabbit braised in white wine and a *sofrito* containing thyme, oregano, and toasted almonds.

— **almogávar** Rabbit simmered in *sofrito* with stock, wine, and a *majado* of garlic, roasted almonds, parsley, chocolate, unsweetened cake bread, and the rabbit's liver.

— **al romero** Rabbit marinated in wine, braised in the liquid of the marinade with a *majado* of garlic, fried bread, and rosemary.

— **con castañas** Braised rabbit with a *sofrito* containing sherry, brandy, and broth and garnished with boiled chestnuts.

— **con caracoles** Sautéed rabbit and snails simmered in wine, anise liquor, and meat stock with a *majado* containing saffron, garlic, pine nuts, almonds, and the rabbit's liver.

— **con chocolate** Marinated rabbit braised in the liquid of the marinade with a *majado* made of garlic, toasted almonds, pine nuts, and chocolate.

— **con tomate** Rabbit simmered in tomato sauce.

— **en ajillo pastor** Rabbit sautéed with onions, simmered in wine, brandy, saffron, thyme, and peppercorns.

— **en salmorejo** Marinated rabbit braised in a sauce made of hot peppers, garlic, and paprika.

**Faisán** Pheasant.

— **con salsa de pan** Roast pheasant dressed with a sauce made with bread, milk, whipping cream, minced onion, and cayenne pepper.

— **de Alcántara** Roast pheasant in port wine with truffles.

— **en cocotte** Stuffed pheasant with marrons glacés and truffles en cocotte with wine, brandy, and mushrooms.

**Faisao com Madeira** Roast pheasant with Madeira sauce (from Portugal).

**Jabalí** Wild boar.

— **a la cazadora** Marinated wild boar medallions sautéed in olive oil and dressed with a sauce made of red wine, pinenuts, and raisins.

**Liebre** Hare.

— **a la cacereña** Hare marinated in red wine and braised in the liquid of the marinade with a *majado* made of garlic, clove, and nutmeg.

— *con lentejas* Hare stewed with lentils.

— *en civet* Hare braised in its own blood, red wine, bouquet garni, and herbs.

*Oca* Goose.

— *con peras* Goose casserole with pears (from Cataluña).

*Paloma torcaz* Ringdove.

— *al vino tinto* Ringdove braised in red wine.

*Pato* Duck.

— *a la andaluza* Duck stew with chickpeas.

— *a la gallega* Braised duck with wine, anise liquor, turnips, carrots, onions, bouquet garni, and garlic.

— *a la maltesa* Roast duck dressed with a sauce of wine and orange juice.

— *a la montañesa* Duck braised in a *sofrito* with sherry, stock, and paprika.

— *a la naranja* Duck *à l'orange*.

— *a la sevillana* Braised duck with green olives and sherry sauce.

— *a la vasca* Duck braised in wine, stock, tarragon, thyme, and cloves.

— *asado con manzanas* Roast duck with apples.

— *con nabos* Baked duck dressed with a *majado* made of sautéed turnips, onion, carrots, parsnips, and wine.

— *con aceitunas* Duck braised in green olive sauce.

— *con salsa de alcaparras* Duck casserole with a *sofrito* containing capers, almonds, green olives, and raisins.

— *con higos* Roast duck in a dried fig sauce.

— *en salsa de almendras* Duck braised in almond sauce.

*Perdiz* Partridge.

— *a la andaluza* Simmered partridge stuffed with its giblets, bacon, and anchovies and simmered in wine, tomato, and green peppers.

— *a la Briand* Stuffed partridge with fresh sausage meat, egg yolk, and truffles simmered in sherry with minced onion and carrots.

— *a la catalana* Partridge stew garnished with shredded boiled cabbage.

— *a la cortijera* Partridge braised in stock with boiled shredded cabbage, bacon, chopped salami, and bouquet garni.

— *a la manchega* Partridge braised in a *sofrito* with thyme, cured ham, and touch of cinnamon.

— *a lo tío Lucas* Partridge braised with a *majado* made of truffles, pine nuts, onion, parsley, bread, and sherry, garnished with a mixture of ground veal and bacon.

— *al vino tinto* Partridge braised in red wine.

— *con almendras* Partridge braised with a *majado* made of garlic, toasted almonds, parsley, and sherry wine.

— *con coles* Partridge braised with cured ham and fresh sausage, garnished with boiled Brussels sprouts.

— *en escabeche* Braised marinated partridge.

— *estofada* Partridge stewed in wine and vinegar with vegetables and garlic.

*Pichón* Squab.

**Pichones a la andaluza** Squab larded with anchovy fillets braised in white wine with garlic and parsley.

— *a la dogaresa* Squab stuffed with ground veal, egg, truffles, and nutmeg and simmered in a *sofrito* containing sherry and mushrooms.

— *en chocolate* Braised squab with chocolate sauce.

— *en compota* Squab browned in bacon fat, braised in wine and broth, and garnished with fried bread triangles.

**Pintada** Guinea fowl.

— *al vino tinto* Guinea fowl braised in red wine.

**Tordo** Thrush.

**Tordos a la tudelana** Thrush stuffed with diced cured ham and braised in wine, onion, garlic, and cloves.

— *al vino blanco* Thrush braised in white wine.

— *fritos* Thrush fried in olive oil dressed with sautéed bread crumb and parsley.

**Venado** Venison.

— *con salsa de Cabrales* Roast venison with blue cheese sauce.

## POSTRES, FRUTAS, Y NUECES —
## DESSERTS, FRUITS, AND NUTS

Spain claims the best selection of fruits in Europe. Many of them were introduced by the Moors when they settled in the Peninsula in the eighth century. After the discovery of America, sugar became plentiful, and chocolate was a Spanish monopoly for several decades. Sweets of Arab and Jewish ancestry are common today, particularly those made for special occasions, such as at the Christmastime when sweets are made with honey, toasted almonds, dates, dried figs, sweet wines, cinnamon, and cloves. Many of these ancient recipes have been preserved in convents where nuns have the reputation of preparing the best sweets of all.

A very common breakfast food is *churros*, which are made by deep-frying batter in a cauldron of boiling olive oil. Dipped in powdered sugar, churros are delicious when eaten hot accompanied by a cup of thick *café con leche* or hot chocolate. Regular meals are commonly ended with a bowl of fruit or, less often, with a selection of cheeses. Most restaurant menus offer *flan*, a rich, sweet, egg custard dessert or *tocino de cielo* which is still richer and sweeter than flan.

*Albaricoque* Apricot.

*Alfajores* Sweetmeats made of ground almonds, honey, aniseed, cinnamon, and raisins.

*Almendra* Almond.

*Almendrados de Castellón* Baked blanched almonds mixed with egg white, sugar, cinnamon, and grated lemon rind.

*Almendras garrapiñadas* Candied almonds.

*Almojábanas* Baked mixture of flour, egg, sugar, and olive oil.

*Arándanos* Blueberries.

*Arrope cántabro* Assorted candied fruit flavored with rum.

*Arroz con leche* Rice pudding.

— *a la asturiana* Rice pudding flavored with anise liquor.

*Arroz emperatriz* Rice pudding with candied fruit macerated in brandy.

*Avellanas* Hazelnuts.

*Baba al ron* Rum-soaked savarin-dough cake.

*Babarúa arlequín* Chilled vanilla and chocolate custard garnished with mandarin sections.

*Babarúa de café* Chilled custard with coffee flavor.

*Bartolillos* Fried pastries filled with custard.

*Bayas* Berries.

*Bienmesabes* Baked ground hazelnuts with butter, sugar, egg yolks, and cinnamon.

*Bilbaos* Ground toasted almonds mixed with flour, sugar, grated orange, and lemon.

*Bizcocho* Cake.

— *borracho* Liqueur-soaked cake.

— *de almendra* Almond cake.

— *de avellana* Hazelnut cake.

— *de San Lorenzo* Chestnut-puree cake.

— *de reina* Layer cake filled with strawberry jam.

**Blanco y negro** Iced coffee with vanilla ice cream.

**Bocaditos de dama** Apricot jam-filled cake with lemon icing.

**Bolas de Berlín** Deep-fried pâte-à-choux balls filled with quince jelly.

— **de castaña** Fried balls made with pureed chestnuts boiled in milk.

**Borrachuelos** Fried pâte-à-choux pastries flavored with anise liquor.

**Brazo gitano** Rolled cream-filled sponge cake.

**Budín** Pudding.

— **a la cántabra** Baked mixture of pound cake, grated toasted almonds, pineapple chunks, eggs, and brandy.

— **puertorriqueño** Milk and wine-soaked pound cake mixed with raisins, toasted almonds, and cinnamon.

**Buñuelos** Fritters.

— **del Ampurdán** Fritters with aniseed, coriander, and cinnamon.

— **de manzana** Apple fritters.

— **de San Isidro** Fritters filled with custard.

— **de San José** Rice fritters flavored with sweet sherry wine.

**Cabello de ángel** Candied squash meat.

**Cacahuetes** Peanuts.

**Canutillos** Custard-filled puff pastry cylinders.

**Caqui** Persimmon.

**Casadielles** Turnovers filled with ground walnuts and cinnamon and flavored with anise liquor (from Asturias).

**Castañas** Chestnuts.

— **en almíbar** Chestnuts in vanilla syrup.

**Cerezas** Cherries.

— **infernales** Cherries boiled in syrup and flamed with kirsch.

**Churros** Deep-fried batter.

**Ciruela** Plum.

**Coco** Coconut.

**Compota** Stewed fruit.

**Confitura** Jam.

— **de higos** Fig jam.

— **de naranja** Orange marmalade.

**Coquillos** Coconut cookies.

**Cordiales** Baked ground almonds mixed with egg, sugar, and grated lemon rind.

**Crema catalana** Crème brûlée with added cinnamon and lemon zest.

— **de chocolate** Chocolate cream.

— **de Málaga** Cream made with Malaga wine.

— **de naranja** Orange cream.

— **de San José** Egg custard with cinnamon and lemon peel.

— **quemada** Crème brûlée.

**Cuajada con miel** Curdled milk with honey.

**Dátil** Date.

**Dulce de membrillo** Quince jelly.

**Ensalada de fruta** Fruit salad.

— **a la madrileña** Fruit salad flavored with sweet sherry and rum.

**Fariñes** Cornmeal mush with honey (from Galicia).

**Filloas** Egg pancakes (from Galicia).

**Flan** Caramel custard.

— **de naranja** Caramel custard with orange juice.

**Flao** Fresh cheese torte.

**Frambuesas** Raspberries.

**Fresas** strawberries.

— **al vino tinto** Macerated strawberries in red wine, cinnamon,

sugar, cloves, and lemon rind.
— *con anís* Strawberries with anise liquor.
*Fresón* Large strawberry.
— *con nata* Large strawberries with whipped cream.
*Granada* Pomegranate.
*Granadinas* Ground almonds, lard, and sugar cookies.
*Granizado* Iced drink.
— *de café* Iced coffee drink.
— *de limón* Iced lemon drink.
*Grosellas* red currants.
— *silvestres* Gooseberries.
*Guindas* Cherries.
*Helado* Ice cream.
— *de fresa* Strawberry ice cream.
*Higos* Figs.
*Huesos de santo* Marzipan rolls filled with candied egg yolk.
*Leche frita* Fried custard squares.
— *merengada* Mixture of iced milk and whipping cream, flavored with cinnamon.
*Lenguas de gato* Butter, flour, and egg-white cookies, flavored with vanilla extract.
*Limón* Lemon.
*Macedonia de frutas* Fruit salad.
*Manjar de monjas* Pudding made with rice flour, milk, sugar, and cinnamon.
*Mantecados* Lard (or butter), sugar, and flour cookies.
*Manzanas* Apples.
— *asadas* Roasted apples, usually filled with powdered almonds and raisins.
— *rellenas* Baked apples stuffed with custard.
— *salteadas con ajonjolí* Butter-sautéed rings of tart apple sprinkled with sesame seeds.

*Marañuelas* Cookies flavored with white wine.
*Marquesa de chocolate* Chocolate mousse with added semi-sweet chocolate.
*Melocotón* Peach.
*Melocotones a la maña* Peaches marinated in red wine, sugar, and cinnamon (from Aragon).
— *al vino* Peaches simmered in red wine, cinnamon, and orange peel.
— *asados al vino* Peaches baked in red wine.
*Melón* Melon.
*Merengue* Meringue.
*Merengues de fresa* Strawberry-flavored meringue.
*Miel* Honey.
*Moras* Mulberries.
*Naranja* Orange.
*Natillas* Cream custard.
*Nueces* Walnuts.
*Pan de higo* Ground dried figs mixed with ground almonds, hazelnuts, chocolate, cinnamon, grated lemon rind, and anise liquor.
*Pastel* Cake, pie.
— *cordobés* Candied squash torte.
— *vasco* Black cherry tart (from the Basque Country).
*Pera* Pear.
*Peras con vino* Pears simmered in red wine and cinnamon.
— *de Lérida* Pears simmered in milk, folded with a mixture of the simmering liquid and beaten egg whites.
*Perrunillas* Cookies made with lard, eggs, anise liquor and cinnamon.
*Pestiños de anís* Deep-fried pâte-à-choux pastries flavored with anise liquor.

*Piña* Pineapple.

*Piñones* Pine nuts.

*Piononos* Cream rolls.

*Plátano* Banana.

— *a la catalana* Baked banana puree combined with sugar, ground hazelnuts, and brandy.

— *a la puertorriqueña* Bananas fried with wine, sugar and cinnamon.

— *con miel y piñones* Bananas sautéed in butter mixed with honey and garnished with pine nuts.

*Polvorones* Shortbread.

— *de Écija* Shortbread flavored with cinnamon and brandy.

*Roscos* Baked dough rings made of flour, lard, egg, sugar, and grated lemon rind.

*Rosquillas* Deep-fried rings made with a dough containing white wine and olive oil.

*Sabayón de naranja* Orange sabayon.

*Sandía* Watermelon.

*Sorbete* Sorbet.

— *de champán* Champagne sorbet.

*Suspiros de Murcia* Baked ground toasted almonds folded with egg white.

*Tarta al whiskey* Frozen whiskey layer cake with vanilla ice cream.

— *de manzana* Apple custard tart.

— *de Portomarín* Torte made with

ground almonds, eggs, and syrup.

— *de Sacromonte* Tart made with toasted bread crumbs, milk, egg, lard, and cinnamon.

— *de Santiago* Almond cake with coffee cream frosting.

— *quemada helada* Frozen orange custard with brittle caramel.

*Tocino de cielo* Egg yolk-rich caramel custard.

*Torrijas* Fried milk-soaked bread flavored with cinnamon and dusted with powdered sugar.

*Torta* Torte, scone.

— *A la navarra* Torte made with bread, milk, raisins, and cinnamon.

*Tortada* Sponge cake soaked in syrup and covered with meringue (from Murcia).

*Torta de almendras* Almond torte.

— *de miel y nueces* Honey and walnut torte.

— *de queso* Cheese torte.

— *de chanchigorri* Sweet bread studded with fried pork rind.

*Turrón* Almond and honey nougat.

*Uvas* Grapes.

*Yemas de coco* Candied egg yolks with grated coconut.

— *de Santa Teresa* Candied egg yolks flavored with lemon.

*Zurracapote* Simmered dried apricots and prunes in red wine, cinnamon, and lemon peel.

# QUESO — CHEESE

Ewe's- and goat's-milk cheeses are very common throughout Spain and Portugal; many are of very good quality. Cow's-milk cheese is made mainly in the north of the Peninsula, where pastures are green and tender most of the year. Every area has its own specialty cheese but the most famous is *queso manchego*, which is made in the central region of La Mancha. There are specialized shops called *mantequerías* where cheeses are sold; here, aged, fresh,cured, smoked, soft, and hard cheeses are displayed and sold wholesale or by the gram.

**Alicante** Fresh goat's-milk cheese from Alicante provine.

**Armada** Semi-hard ewe's-milk cheese from León. It is bitter in taste and very flavorful.

**Burgos** Fresh ewe's-milk cheese from Castile.

**Cabrales** Blue-streaked cow's-milk cheese from Asturias.

**Cádiz** Goat's-milk cheese, hard and mellow in taste, from the province of Cádiz.

**Camerano** Very soft goat's-milk cheese from the Rioja.

**Cebrero** Galician cow's-milk cheese, creamy and sharp in taste.

**Cervera** Fresh white ewe's-milk cheese from Valencia.

**Da serra** Ewe's-milk cheese from northern Portugal. It is creamy and of exquisite flavor.

**Gamonedo** Blue-veined cheese from Asturias. It is semi-hard and milder in taste than Cabrales.

**Gorbea** Semi-hard cheese from the Basque Country. It is made of ewe's milk and is creamy and yellowish in color.

**Grazalema** Ewe's-milk cheese, from Andalusia molded in esparto grass bands. It is often cured in olive oil.

**Huelva** Semi-hard goat's-milk cheese with a very strong flavor from the province of Huelva.

**Idiazábal** Smoked ewe's-milk cheese from the Basque Country.

**León** Cow's-milk cheese heavy in fat.

**Mahón** Soft cow's-milk cheese with a tangy taste, from the Balearic Islands.

**Málaga** Creamy, semi-soft cheese made with goat's milk, from Andalusia.

**Manchego** Ewe's-milk cheese from La Mancha, sold throughout the country.

**Mato** Soft fresh goat's-milk cheese from Catalonia. It is often eaten with honey.

**Morón** Soft, creamy cheese made from ewe's milk, from the province of Seville.

**Orduña** Hard ewe's-milk cheese from the Basque Country.

**Pasiego** Fresh, soft cow's-milk cheese from the province of Santander.

**Pedroches** Piquant, semi-hard ewe's-milk cheese from La Mancha.

**Plasencia** Semi-hard goat's-milk cheese from Extremadura.

**Puzol** Fresh cheese from Valencia.

**Queso de bola** Gouda-style cheese.

— *de cabra* Goat's-milk cheese.

— *de oveja* Ewe's-milk cheese.

— *de vaca* Cow's-milk cheese.

**Roncal** Ewe's-milk cheese with a smoky flavor, from Navarra.

**San Simón** Smoked cow's-milk cheese from Galicia.

**Serena** Hard ewe's-milk cheese from Extremadura. It is creamy but bitter in flavor, although very tasty.

**Soria** Fresh goat's-milk cheese from Castile.

**Tetilla** Creamy, pear-shaped cow's-milk cheese from Galicia.

**Tronchón** Ewe's-milk cheese from Aragon. It is semi-hard and mild in taste.

**Ulloa** Soft cheese from Galicia made with cow's milk.

**Villalón** Ewe's-milk cheese from the region of León. It is sold fresh and is quite mild in flavor.

## PAN Y PASTELERIA — BREADS AND PASTRY

Bread in Spain is of very good quality and a meal in itself. The crumb in Spanish bread is solid, compact and tasty; the crust crunchy. No table is quite set in Spanish homes without having a fresh loaf of bread placed in the center. Bread is always eaten fresh, even if that implies a daily trip to the nearest baker. Castile, where the best wheat in Spain is grown, is famous for making the best bread, although the quality in other regions is also excellent.

Sweet breads and pastries are also very good in the Peninsula where they are consumed in large amounts at breakfast and tea time (*merienda*). Although nowadays pastries are commercially distributed in wholesale plastic bags, the best baked goods are found in specialized shops called *pastelerías*.

**Bollos de aceite** Sweet rolls made with olive oil.

**Boronitas** Sweet cornmeal squares.

**Broa** Cornbread (from Portugal).

**Coca de San Juan** Sweet bread containing marzipan, candied fruits, and pine nuts.

**Ensaimadas** Fluffy sweet rolls (from Majorca).

— **de Tudela** Sweet rolls flavored with aniseed.

**Españoletas** Small brioches.

**Galletas** Biscuits.

**Hojaldre** Puff pastry.

**Hornazo** Castilian bread studded with chorizo and *morcilla* sausages and hard-boiled eggs.

**Lacitos** Puff pastry bow rolls.

**Magdalenas** Madeleines, small sponge cakes.

**Mantecados** Shortbread.

— **de almendra** Almond shortbread.

— **de Antequera** Almond shortbread with cinnamon.

— **manchegos** Shortbread with orange juice and white wine (from La Mancha).

**Mazapán** Marzipan.

**Mediasnoches** Small brioches.

**Mojicones** Flour snaps.

**Mostachones** Brioches topped with chopped almonds.

**Pajas al queso** Cheese straws.

**Palmeras** Puff pastry biscuits.

**Pan blanco** White bread.

— **candeal** Bread made with white flour.

— **de caridad** Bread made with olive oil and cumin.

— **de cebada** Barley bread.

— **de centeno** Rye bread common in Galicia.

— **de pasas** Raisin bread.

— **de pueblo** Regular wheat bread.

— **de Santa Teresa** French toast.

— **dulce** Sweet bread.

— **integral** Whole wheat bread.

— **quemado** Baked sweet bread topped with egg white and sugar (from Valencia).

**Panecillo** Roll.

— **de Viena** Rolls made with milk.

**Rollos de anís** Single knot sweet rools made with *aguardiente* liquor.

— *de manteca* Single knot sweet rolls made with lard.

**Roscos de candelilla** Single knot sweet rolls made with honey and lemon juice.

— *de Reinosa* Single knot sweet rolls made with dry sherry.

**Roscón de Reyes** Large ring-shaped brioche containing minced candied fruit.

**Roscos de vino** Single knot sweet rolls made with wine and flavored with aniseed.

**Rosquillas de La Mancha** Single knot sweet rolls made with lemon juice and aniseed.

**Sequillos** Club rolls made with *aguardiente* liquor.

**Suizos** Sweet rolls.

**Tortas de aceite** Sweet rolls made with olive oil.

— *de manteca* Sweet rolls made with lard and sherry wine.

— *de Pascua* Sweet rolls made with lard (from Murcia).

**Tortells de Mallorca** Sweet bread containing marzipan.

# SALSAS — SAUCES

Most dishes in Spanish cuisine are prepared with sauce as an integral part rather than adding it afterwards. The basic characteristic of sauce in Spanish cooking is *sofrito* which is used in a great number of dishes, particularly in stews.

*Salsa* Sauce.

— *a la mostaza* Mustard sauce made from butter, flour, egg yolk, stock, dry mustard, salt, and pepper.

— *a la naranja* Sauce made with orange juice, onion, butter, flour, sugar, and salt.

— *al jerez* Sherry sauce made with butter, shallots, flour, stock, parsley, salt, and pepper.

— *al limón* Cold lemon sauce made with lemon juice, onion, parsley, gherkins, capers, hard-boiled egg, olive oil, and salt.

— *al vino blanco* White wine sauce with butter, egg yolks, shallots, and lemon juice.

— *alioli* Garlic mayonnaise sauce.

— *amarilla* Cold sauce made from egg, olive oil, French mustard, vinegar, salt, and pepper.

— *aranjuez* Sauce made with asparagus, leeks, carrot, rice, butter, whipping cream, egg yolk, salt, and pepper.

— *bechamel* White sauce made from flour, butter, milk, nutmeg, salt, and pepper.

— *campesina* Sauce made with tomato, red wine, mushrooms, onion, paprika, vegetable broth, bread crumb, herbs, olive oil, and salt.

— *castellana* Sauce made from crushed fried bread, garlic, egg,

minced cured ham, paprika, olive oil, and salt.

— *catalana* Sauce made from minced beef, egg, garlic, onion, pureed celery and turnip, tomato puree, parsley, fresh mint, bay leaf, olive oil, salt, and pepper.

— *chateaubriand* White wine sauce with butter, shallots, mushrooms, meat juice, tarragon, lemon juice, parsley, salt, and pepper.

— *chilindrón* Tomato sauce made from sweet peppers, onions, garlic, and olive oil.

— *de aceitunas* Green olive sauce with butter, onion, flour, broth, parsley, dry white wine, and salt to taste.

— *de aguacate* Cold avocado sauce with onion, lemon juice, mayonnaise, Tabasco, salt, and pepper.

— *de ajo* Cold sauce with garlic, vinegar, bread crumb, meat broth, paprika, and salt.

— *de albahaca* Fresh mint sauce with onion, dry vermouth, lemon juice, corn starch, whipping cream, oil, salt, and pepper.

— *de alcachofas* Pureed artichoke bottoms with butter, milk, whipping cream, flour, salt, and pepper.

— *de alcaparras* White sauce made with capers, butter, flour, nutmeg, milk, whipped cream, lemon juice, and salt.

— *de almejas* Clam sauce made with fish broth, onion, whipping cream, flour, parsley, garlic, tomato puree, saffron, olive oil, and salt.

— *de almendras* Sauce made with puree of blanched almonds, tomatoes, olive oil, salt, and pepper.

— *de anchoas* Sauce made with canned anchovies, butter, and cream cheese.

— *de apio* Béchamel sauce with pureed celery, onion, garlic, egg yolk, parsley, brandy, bay leaf, olive oil, salt, and pepper.

— *de arroz* Sauce made with boiled rice, meat broth, butter, parsley, hard-boiled egg, and salt.

— *de atún* Cold sauce made with canned tuna fish, egg yolk, garlic, olive oil, vinegar, and salt.

— *de azafrán* Sauce made with fish broth, egg yolk, whipping cream, corn starch, saffron, and salt.

— *de castañas* Chestnut sauce made from chestnut puree, raisins, meat broth, butter, and salt.

— *de ciruelas* Sauce made from pureed plums, butter, sugar, corn starch, pine nuts, and salt.

— *de espinacas* Spinach sauce made with butter, milk, raisins, pine nuts, whipping cream, flour, salt, and pepper.

— *de gambas* Sauce made with pureed shrimp, butter, garlic, onion, tomato puree, white wine, flour, brandy, thyme, parsley, salt, and pepper.

— *de majillones* Sauce made with pureed mussels, butter, egg yolks, milk, corn starch, ketchup, nutmeg, and salt.

— *de mariscos* Seafood sauce made from pureed seafood, butter, flour, tomato puree, whipping cream, white wine, brandy, salt, and pepper.

— *de olivas* Cold sauce made from black olives, minced onion, and cream cheese.

— *de ostras* Oyster sauce made from béchamel, oyster fumet, parsley, salt, and pepper.

— *de pan* Bread sauce made with milk, onion, whipping cream, butter, cayenne, and salt to taste.

— *de pimiento* Cold sauce consisting of a blend of canned pimientos, shallots, garlic, parsley, and salt.

— *de pimientos rojos* Sauce made from sweet red peppers with onion, garlic, olive oil, and salt.

— *de rábanos* Béchamel sauce with pureed boiled radishes, and dry mustard.

— *de remolacha* Sauce made with pureed beets, meat broth, whipping cream, salt, and pepper.

— *de tomate* Tomato sauce made with sautéed fresh tomatoes, onions, garlic, paprika, and salt.

— *española* Brown sauce made from a reduced sherry deglazed rich stock.

— *frito* Fried bread sauce made with fried bread crumbs, butter, stock, diced ham, onion, parsley, and lemon juice.

— *madera* Madeira wine sauce made with butter, shallots, flour, stock, parsley, salt, and pepper.

— *mahonesa* Mayonnaise sauce made from eggs, olive oil, dry

mustard, lemon juice, and salt.
— *mornay* Béchamel sauce with beer, grated cheese, and cayenne.
— *moruna* Cold sauce made with lemon juice, oilive oil, paprika, Tabasco, salt, and pepper.
— *murciana* Sauce made from tomato, toasted almonds, garlic, vinegar, paprika, parsley, mayonnaise, salt, and pepper.
— *muselina* White wine sauce with egg yolks, butter, and lemon juice.
— *oscura* Sauce for furred game made from butter, chopped carrot, onion, flour, garlic, marjoram, meat stock, and red wine.
— *picada* Blend of toasted almonds, hazelnuts, saffron, herbs, and spices added to fish dishes or meat stews.
— *primavera* Butter sauce with flour, broth, egg yolk, salt, and pepper.
— *riojana* Salsa española with sautéed onion and dry red wine.
— *romesco* Sauce from Catalonia consisting of a blend of toasted almonds, hot chili peppers, garlic, fried bread, tomatoes, olive oil, vinegar, white pepper, and salt.

— *salmorejo* Cold sauce made from water, vinegar, olive oil, salt, and pepper.
— *sofrito* Basic sauce in Spanish cuisine widely used throughout the country. It consists of minced onion, garlic, tomatoes (and often sweet peppers), sautéed in olive oil with seasonings, herbs, and spices, especially saffron and paprika.
— *tártara* Mayonnaise sauce with chopped capers, parsley, gherkins, tarragon, dry mustard, and cayenne pepper.
— *vasca* Sauce made from fish broth, garlic, flour, asparagus puree, white wine, parsley, olive oil, and salt.
— *verde* Sauce made with parsley, olive oil, garlic, flour, ginger, milk, white wine, salt, and pepper.
— *victoria* Sauce for game dishes made from black currant jelly, stock, orange juice, sherry, cloves, cayenne, salt, pepper, and a dash of cinnamon.
— *vinagreta* Vinaigrette sauce made from olive oil, vinegar, garlic, chopped parsley, salt, and pepper.

## CONDIMENTOS, HIERBAS, Y ESPECIAS — CONDIMENTS, HERBS, AND SPICES

A common way of incorporating flavor in dishes in Spanish cooking is using a *majado*. *Majados* are blends of condiments, herbs, and spices crushed in a mortar or mixed in a blender and added to dishes. A basic *majado* consists of crushed garlic, parsley, spices, and seasonings. Often, other ingredients are included, such as olive oil, broth, nuts, stock, wine, liquor, or herbs.

*Ajo* Garlic.
*Ajonjolí* Sesame seed.
*Albahaca* Basil.
*Alcaravea* Caraway.
*Anís* Aniseed.
*Azafrán* Saffron.
*Canela* Cinnamon.
*Cardamomo* Cardamon.
*Cayena* Cayenne.
*Cebolla* Onion.
*Cebollino* Chives.
*Chalotas* Shallots.
*Cilantro* Coriander.
*Clavo* Clove.
*Cominos* Cummin seed.
*Coñac* Brandy.
*Enebrina* Juniper berry.
*Eneldo* Dill.
*Estragón* Tarragon.
*Guindilla* Hot chili pepper.
*Hinojo* Fennel.
*Jengibre* Ginger.
*Laurel* Bay leaf.
*Majado* Blend of condiments, herbs, spices, seasonings, and other ingredients used to flavor dishes in Spanish cooking. The blend is usually prepared using a mortar and pestle.
*Mejorana* Marjoram.
*Menta* Mint.
*Mostaza* Mustard.
*Nuez moscada* Nutmeg.
*Orégano* Oregano.
*Perejil* Parsley.
*Perifollo* Chervil.
*Pimentón* Paprika.
*Pimienta* Pepper.
— *blanca* White pepper.
— *inglesa* Allspice.
— *negra* Black pepper.
— *roja* Red pepper.
*Raspadura de limón* Grated lemon rind.
— *de naranja* Grated orange rind.
*Romero* Rosemary.
*Sal* Salt.
*Salvia* Sage.
*Tomillo* Thyme.
*Vainilla* Vanilla.
*Vino* Wine.
*Zumo de limón* Lemon juice.

# VINOS — WINES

Wine is ever present on Spanish dinner tables; as a matter of fact, it is also present on tables for lunch. Wine has always been part of the Spanish culture; introduced to the Peninsula by the Phoenecians, vines, together with olive trees, have been part of the landscape since ancient times. Most wines in the southern part of Spain are very dry, due to the fierce sun that shines on the land most of the year, while in the North, the wines are fresh and fruity.

Sherry, a fortified wine, is without doubt the best known of Spanish wines. This dry, golden, high-in-alcohol drink has been exported worldwide since the British discovered it some centuries ago. The best reds are produced on the banks of the River Duero and in the Rioja and Penedés regions. Some of the barrel-aged reds bottled in these areas are comparable in quality to France's Bordeaux and Burgundy.

Champagne-method sparkling wines are produced in Penedés where over 125 million bottles are filled yearly. The name given to sparkling wines is *cava* which Spaniards drink at Christmastime and on special occasions.

**Albariño** Fresh, crisp wine from Galicia.

**Amontillado** Amber-colored aged sherry with a distinct nutty flavor.

**Barril** Barrel.

**Bodega** Cellars where wines are matured; also, tavern.

**Cariñena** Wine-producing area of Aragón.

**Cava** Spanish sparkling wine.

**Chacolí** White, delicate, fruity wine from the Basque Country.

**Champán** Common name given to sparkling wine.

**Clarete** Light red wine.

**Codorniú** Largest *cava* producer in the Penedés region.

**Coñac** Generic name for Spanish brandy.

**Domecq** Bottler of brandy and sherry wines.

**Espumoso** Sparkling.

**Federico Paternina** Vintage wine from Rioja.

**Fino** Very dry sherry drunk chilled as an aperitif.

**Garnacha** Type of wine grape.

**Gran reserva** Aged wine of guaranteed quality.

**Jerez** Fortified wine matured in casks that have a distinct nutty flavor and are high in alcohol content.

**— de la Frontera** Area in Andalusia where the world-famous sherry is produced.

**— dulce** Sweet sherry.

**— seco** Dry sherry.

**Jumilla** Area in Murcia producing quite robust red wines high in alcohol content.

**Madera** Sweet wines from the island of Madeira.

**Málaga** Sweet dessert wine from the Mediterranean coastal area of Malaga.

DISHES BY COURSE

*Manzanilla* Aged amber-colored sherry with a nutty flavor.

*Marqués de Murrieta* Vintage wine from Rioja.

— *de Riscal* Vintage wine from Rioja.

*Moscatel* Sweet dessert wine.

*Oloroso* Dry dark-amber sherry.

*Oporto* Port, dessert wine from Portugal.

*Palomino* Type of grape used to make sherry wine.

*Penedés* Catalonian region where excellent table wines and *cava* sparklers are made.

*René Barbier* Vintage wine from Penedés.

*Reserva* Aged wine of special quality.

*Ribeiro* Area in Galicia producing fruity wines of low alcohol content.

*Ribera del Duero* Region where the famous *Vega Sicilia* wines are made.

*Rioja* Region south of the Basque Country where some of the best-known table wines are made.

— *Bordón* Vintage wine from Rioja.

*Sangre de Toro* Vintage wine from Penedés.

*Sidra* Hard cider produced in the region of Asturias.

*Solera* Aged wine used to strengthen new vintage.

*Uva* Grape.

*Valdepeñas* Area of La Mancha producing a large quantity of common table wine.

*Vega Sicilia* One of the best Spanish red wines, from the Ribera del Duero area.

*Vinhos verdes* Fruity, fresh wines from northwestern Portugal.

*Vino blanco* White wine.

— *corriente* Unlabeled wine.

— *de la casa* House wine.

— *peleón* Unsophisticated wine.

— *rosado* Rosé wine.

— *tinto* Red wine.

*Viña* Vine

— *Sol* Vintage wine from Penedés.

*Viñedo* Vineyard.

# BEBIDAS Y REFRESCOS —
# BEVERAGES AND REFRESHMENTS

Many beverages in Spain are made by mixing wine with fruit and by combining fruit juices with stronger drinks. The popular refreshing sangria wine cup has been prepared in Andalusia since the Romans drank it during the hot summer months.

*Agua* Water.
— *mineral* Bottled water.
- *mineral con gas* Carbonated bottled water.
- *mineral sin gas* Still bottled water.
*Aguardiente* Grape spirit.
*Anís* Anise liquor
*Café* Coffee.
— *con leche* Coffee and Milk.
— *solo* Black coffee.
*Carajillo* Black coffee with dash of brandy.
*Chocolate* Hot chocolate.
*Coñac* Common name for brandy.
*Cortado* Coffee with a touch of milk.
*Cremat* Flamed hot black coffee spiked with brandy, rum, anisette, sugar, cinnamon stick, and lemon peel (from Catalonia).
*Expreso* Espresso coffee.
*Gaseosa* Sweetened carbonated water.
*Horchata de almendras* Iced drink made with crushed almonds, water, sugar, and shaved ice.
— *de chufa* Iced drink made with crushed sedge roots, sugar, cinnamon, and shaved ice.
*Leche merengada* Iced milk with sugar, egg white, cinnamon, and grated lemon rind.
*Licor de hierbas* Macerated leaves of mint, thyme, rosemary, savory, lemon verbena, and salvia in a mixture of anise liquor and anis-

ette, flavored with orange peel (from the island of Ibiza).
*Limonada* Water, lemon juice, sugar, lemon quarters, red wine, sugar, and cubed peaches.
*Manzanilla* Camomile tea.
*Mazagrán* Black coffee, soda water, lemon juice, sugar, and crushed ice.
*Naranjada* Orangeade.
*Pacharán* Sloeberry liqueur from Navarra.
*Ponche* Hot punch made from milk, chopped almonds, egg yolks, sugar, brandy, and vanilla extract.
— *de leche* Milk with beaten egg, sugar, and a dash of brandy.
— *romano* Iced tea with sugar, rum, lemon and orange juice, and triple sec liqueur.
*Queimada* Hot toddy made by flaming marc liquor (from Galicia).
*Sangría* Refreshing drink generally made with red wine, brandy, fresh fruits, and soda water.
— *menorquí* Red wine, water, sugar, cinnamon stick, strips of lemon and orange peel, and nutmeg (from the Island of Menorca).
*Sidra* Hard cider.
*Té* Tea.
*Tila* Linden tea.
*Vino caliente* Hot wine with sugar, lemon peel, cinnamon stick, and water.

DISHES BY COURSE

# Part II

## Spanish Food and Beverage Vocabulary

# SPANISH PRONUNCIATION KEY

a ...... **(ah)** like the *a* in *cat*: nada, casa

b ...... **(beh)** like *b* in *boy*: bar, botón

c....... **(seh)** like *c* in *car*, before *a, o, u*: cama, caja;
like *s* in *cent*, before *e, i*: cena, cien

ch .... **(cheh)** like *ch* in *child*: chile, chocolate

d ...... **(deh)** like *d* in *done*: dedo, duro

e ...... **(eh)** like *e* in *bet*: enero, escoba

f ....... **(eh-feh)** like *f* in *far*: favor, fuego

g ...... **(heh)** like *g* in *gate*, before *a, o, u*: gana, gota;
like *h* in *ham*, before *e, i*: gente, ginebra
When followed by *ue* or *ui*, the *u* is silent and the *g* sounds like
the *g* in *gate*: guinda

h ...... **(ah-cheh)** always silent, like the *h* in *hour*: huevo, higo

i ....... **(ee)** like *ee* in *feet*: vino, fino

j ....... **(hoh-tah)** like *h* in *ham*: jamón, jerez

k ...... **(kah)** like *k* in *kilo*: kilo, kiwi

l ....... **(eh-leh)** like *l* in *let*: libro, litro

ll ...... **(eh-yeh)** like *y* in *yet*: lluvia, llave

m ..... **(eh-meh)** like *m* in *man*: mano, menú

n ...... **(en-neh)** like *n* in *no*: niño, nieve

ñ ...... **(en-nyeh)** like *ny* in *canyon*: baño, piña

o ...... **(oh)** like *o* in *organ*: ocho, once

p ...... **(peh)** like *p* in *put*: pan, pera

q ...... **(koo)** like *k* in *kilo* (always followed by *ue* or *ui*, but the *u* is silent):
queso, quince

r ....... **(eh-reh)** like *r* in *rat*: caro, toro

rr ..... **(eh-rreh)** like *r* in *rat* but strongly rolled: carro, perro

s ....... **(eh-seh)** like *s* in *see*: siete, seta

t ....... **(teh)** like *t* in *top*: teléfono, tenedor

u ...... **(oo)** like *oo* in *boot*: jugo, cubo

v ...... **(oo-beh)** like b in boy: vino, vaso

x ...... **(eh-kees)** like *s* in *sit*, before a consonant: expreso, excusa like *x* in
*examine*, before a vowel: éxito, exacto

y ...... **(ee)** like *ee* in *feet*, when alone or at the end of a word: y, doy like *y*
in *yet*, as a consonant: yema, yarda

z....... **(seh-tah)** like *s* in *see*: zapato, zumo

## STRESS IN SPANISH WORDS

Words with an accent mark *(é)* always receive the stress on the syllable that carries the accent mark: jabón (hah-*bohn*), difícil (dee-*fee*-seel). Words without an accent mark are governed by the following two rules:

1) In words that end in a vowel, *n* or *s*, the stress falls on the next-to-the-last syllable: mesero (meh-*seh*-roh), lavan (*lah*-bahn), carros (*cah*-rrohs).

2) In words that end in a consonant except *n* or *s*, the stress falls on the last syllable: hotel (oh-*tehl*), usted (oos-*tehd*), favor (fah-*vohr*).

# A

**Abadejo** (ah-bah-déh-hoh) Cod fish.

**Aceitunas** (ah-seh-ee-tóo-nahs) Olives.

— **al ajillo** (ahl ah-hée-yoh) Pickled olives in garlic.

— **aliñadas** (ah-lee-nyáh-dahs) Marinated olives.

— **rellenas** (reh-yéh-nahs) Stuffed olives with anchovy and/or pimiento.

**Acelgas** (ah-séhl-gahs) Swiss chard.

— **a la malagueña** (ah lah mah-lah-guéh-nyah) Boiled Swiss chard sautéed in olive oil with garlic and sultana raisins.

— **a la napolitana** (ah lah nah-poh-lee-táh-nah) Boiled Swiss chard simmered in a *sofrito* containing thyme and white wine.

— **en adobillo** (ehn adoh-bée-yoh) Boiled Swiss chard sautéed in olive oil, vinegar, paprika, and bread soaked in water.

— **guisadas** (guee-sáh-dahs) Stewed Swiss chard with a *sofrito* containing pine nuts and raisins.

— **rehogadas** (reh-oh-gáh-dahs) Sautéed Swiss chard.

**Achicoria** (ah-chee-kóh-ree-ah) Chicory.

**Adafina** (ad-dah-fée-nah) Stew made by Spanish Jews on Friday evenings to be eaten on the Sabbath.

**Agua** (áh-goo-ah) Water.

— **mineral** (mee-neh-ráhl) Bottled mineral water.

— **mineral con gas** (mee-neh-ráhl kohn gahs) Bottle carbonated mineral water.

— **mineral sin gas** (mee-neh-ráhl seen gahs) Bottled still mineral water.

**Aguacate** (ah-goo-ah-káh-teh) Avocado.

— **a la valenciana** (ah lah bah-lehn-see-áh-nah) Avocado-half garnished with grapefruit sections and salad dressing.

**Aguardiente** (ah-goo-ahr-dee-éhn-teh) Grape spirit.

**Aguja de ternera** (ah-góo-hah deh tehr-néh-rah) Shoulder of veal.

— **a la jardinera** (ah lah hahr-dee-néh-rah) Stewed shoulder of veal with assorted vegetables.

**Ajo** (áh-hoh) Garlic.

— **blanco con uvas** (bláhn-koh kohn óo-bahs) Cold gazpacho made with crushed almonds and garlic, soaked bread, water and oil, and vinegar and garnished with seedless green grapes.

— **colorado** (koh-loh-ráh-doh) Mashed potatoes and sweet red peppers with a *majado* made with oil, cumin, and garlic (from Almeria).

**Ajoharina** (ah-hoh-ah-rée-nah) Stew made with diced pork, chorizo, milk mushrooms, and fried garlic, thickened with flour.

**Ajonjolí** (ah-hohn-hoh-lée) Sesame seed.

**Ajotomate** (ah-hoh-toh-máh-teh) Chopped tomatoes dressed with a garlic, vinegar, oil, and cumin blend.

**Al ajillo** (ahl ah-hée-yoh) Cooked with garlic.

**A la romana** (ah lah roh-máh-nah) Dusted in flour and deep-fried.

**Alas de pollo** (áh-lahs deh póh-yoh) Chicken wings.

— **al vino** (ahl bée-noh) Chicken wings sautéed with garlic, tomato, white wine, and oregano.

**A la sidra** (ah lah sée-drah) Cooked with hard cider.

**Albahaca** (ahl-bah-áh-kah) Basil.

**Albaricoque** (ahl-bah-ree-kóh-keh) Apricot.

**Albariño** (ahl-bah-rée-nyoh) Fresh, crisp wine from Galicia.

**Albóndigas** (ahl-bóhn-dee-gahs) Meat balls.

— **de bacalao** (deh bah-kah-láh-oh) Fish balls made with salt-cod.

**Albondiguillas** (ahl-bohn-dee-guée-yahs) Small pork meat balls.

**Alcachofas** (ahl-kah-chóh-fahs) Artichokes.

— **a la cordobesa** (ah lah kohr-doh-béh-sah) Artichokes simmered in meat broth containing garlic, flour, and saffron.

— **a la española** (ah lah ehs-pah-nyón-lah) Artichokes simmered with onion, white wine, vinegar, and chicken stock, thickened with flour, and sprinkled with fresh parsley.

— **a la sevillana** (ah lah seh-bee-yáh-nah) Sautéed artichoke hearts, potatoes, and garlic simmered in chicken stock with saffron and thickened with flour.

— **con dos salsas** (kohn dohs sáhl-sahs) Boiled artichokes are separated into hearts and outer leaves: hearts are served with garlic mayonnaise. A vinaigrette is served in individual bowls for dipping the leaves.

— **con jamón** (kohn hah-móhn) Atrichoke bottoms filled with chopped prosciutto ham and mayonnaise.

— **con tomate** (kohn to-máh-teh) Artichokes sautéed with tomato.

— **en aceite** (ehn ah-séh-ee-teh) Boiled artichokes are set standing in a pan pressed against each other; olive oil is poured in the center of each artichoke; water is added to the pan just to cover the base of the artichokes; and artichokes are boiled until tender.

— **en cazuela** (ehn kah-soo-éh-lah) Artichoke casserole.

— **en salsa verde** (ehn sáhl-sah béhr-deh) Artichokes in parsley sauce.

— **mojadas** (moh-háh-dahs) Artichokes simmered in chicken broth with wine, bacon, and garlic.

**Alcaravea** (ahl-kah-rah-béh-ah) Caraway.

**Alfajores** (ahl-fah-hóh-rehs) Sweetmeats made of ground almonds, honey, aniseed, cinnamon, and raisins.

**Al horno** (ahl óhr-noh) Baked in the oven.

**Alicante** (ah-lee-káhn-teh) Fresh goat's-milk cheese from Alicante province.

**al limón** (ahl lee-móhn) With lemon.

**Almejas** (ahl-méh-hahs) Clams.

— **a la diabla** (ah lah dee-áh-blah) Clams in spicy tomato sauce.

— **a la marinera** (ah lah mah-ree-néh-rah) Clams in white wine sauce.

— **a la sanluqueña** (ah lah sahnloo-kéh-nyah) Steamed clams in white wine, sprinkled with paprika.

— *al horno* (ahl óhr-noh) Baked stuffed clams.

— *con aceitunas* (kohn ah-seh-eetóo-nahs) Clams with olives.

*Almendra* (ahl-méhn-drah) Almond.

*Almendrados de* **Castellón** *(*ahl-mehn-dráh-dohs deh kahs-tehyóhn) Baked blanched almonds mixed with egg-white, sugar, cinnamon, and grated lemon rind.

*Almendras garrapiñadas (*ahl-méhn-drahs gah-rrah-pee-nyáh-dahs) Candied almonds.

— *saladas* (sah-láh-dahs) Salted fried almonds.

*Almojábanas* (ahl-moh-háh-bah-nahs) Baked mixture of flour, egg, sugar, and olive oil.

*Al pil-pil* (ahl peel-péel) Sautéed in olive oil with garlic and hot peppers.

*Alubias* (ah-lóo-bee-ahs) Dry beans.

— *castellanas* (kahs-teh-yáh-nahs) Dry bean casserole with a *sofrito* with cured ham, wine, and paprika, thickened with flour.

— *con patatas* (kohn pah-táh-tahs) Dry bean casserole with sliced potatoes and a *sofrito* containing bacon.

— *en potaje* (ehn poh-táh-heh) Dry bean stew with a *sofrito* containing fresh sausage and garnished with quartered hard-boiled eggs.

— *a la Urgel* (ah lah oor-héhl) Dry bean stew with braised pork loin, chicken, fresh sausage, fried tomato, and herbs.

*Amendora* (ah-méhn-doh-rah) Almond, in Portuguese.

*Amontillado* (ah-mohn-tee-yáhdoh) Amber-colored aged sherry with a distinct nutty flavor.

*Ancas de rana* (áhn-kahs deh ráhnah) Frog's legs.

— *rebozadas* (reh-boh-sáh-dahs) Sautéed battered frog's legs.

*Anchoas* (ahn-chóh-ahs) Anchovies.

*Andalucía* (ahn-dah-loo-sée-ah) Region in southern Spain bordering on the Atlantic and the Mediterranean. Its cuisine has a very strong Arab and Jewish influence.

*Anguila* (ahn-guée-lah) Eel.

— *a la morisca* (ah lah moh-rées-kah) Eel medallions, larded with anchovy fillets, baked in the oven with lemon juice, oil, and white wine.

— *a la valenciana* (ah lah bah-lehn-see-áh-nah) Eel simmered in paprika sauce.

*Angulas* (ahn-góo-lahs) Baby eels.

— *a la bilbaina* (ah lah beel-bah-ée-nah) Baby eels fried in olive oil.

— *a la ovetense* (ah lah oh-beh-téhn-seh) Baby eels fried with garlic and hot chili peppers.

*Anís* (ah-nées) Aniseed, anise liquor.

*Apio* (áh-pee-oh) Celery.

— *a la iruñesa* (ah lah ee-roo-nyéh-sah) Boiled celery stewed in olive oil, white wine, tomato, garlic, and parsley (from the Basque Country).

— *con salsa holandesa* (kohn sáhl-sah oh-lahn-déh sah) Boiled celery with hollandaise sauce.

**Aragón** (ah-rah-góhn) A region in northeastern Spain, formerly a kingdom. Dishes prepared with *chilindron* sauce are well-known in this area.

**Arándanos** (ah-ráhn-dah-nohs) Blueberries.

**Arenque** (ah-réhn-kehs) Herring.

— *a la nórdica* (ah lah nóhr-dee-kah) Herring simmered in a champagne sauce with fresh mint.

**Armada** (ahr-máh-dah) Semi-hard ewe's-milk cheese from León. It is bitter in taste and very flavorful.

**Aros de cebolla ocultos** (áh-rohs deh seh-bóh-yah oh-kóol-tohs) Beer-battered, deep-fried onion rings.

**Arrope cántabro** (ah-rróh-peh káhn-tah-broh) Assorted candied fruit flavored with rum.

**Arroz** (ah-rróhs) Rice.

— *a banda* (ah báhn-dah) Fishermen's rice made with fish broth and served with garlic mayonnaise.

— *a la alicantina* (ah lah ah-lee-kahn-tée-nah) Rice with a *sofrito* containing crushed sweet dry peppers, meat, and shellfish.

— *a la americana* (ah lah ah-meh-ree-káh-nah) Rice with chopped ham without saffron.

— *a la andaluza* (ah lah ahn-dah-lóo-sah) Rice with a *sofrito*, chicken, cured ham, bacon, and chorizo.

— *a la catalana* (ah lah kah-tah-láh-nah) Rice with a *sofrito*, rabbit, cured ham, sausage, and diced pork.

— *a la criolla* (ah lah kree-óh-yah) Plain boiled rice garnished with bacon strips, fried eggs, fried bananas, and tomato sauce.

— *a la cubana* (ah lah koo-báh-nah) Plain boiled rice garnished with fried eggs and bananas.

— *a la griega* (ah lah gree-éh-gah) Rice containing onion, green pepper, prunes, walnuts, and black olives. Served cold.

— *a la italiana* (ah lah ee-tah-lee-áh-nah) Rice with fresh sausage, chicken livers, white wine, grated cheese, but without saffron.

— *a la malagueña* (ah lah mah-lah-guéh-nyah) Rice with *sofrito*, clams, shrimp, asparagus, green peas, saffron, and paprika.

— *a la mallorquina* (ah lah mah-yohr-kée-nah) Rice with *sofrito*, seafood, and paprika-spread sausage (*sobrasada*).

— *a la milanesa* (ah lah mee-lah-néh-sah) Rice with ham, green peas, and grated parmesan.

— *a la primavera* (ah lah pree-mah-béh-rah) Rice with assorted vegetables.

— *a la sevillana* (ah lah seh-bee-yáh-nah) Rice with *sofrito*, fish broth, squid, angler, cured ham, and green peas and garnished with crayfish, roasted peppers, hard-boiled egg, and fried chorizo slices.

— *al curry* (ahl kóo-rree) Curried rice.

— *al horno* (ahl óhr-noh) Rice cooked in the oven.

— *blanco* (bláhn-koh) Plain boiled rice.

— *canario* (kah-náh-ree-oh) Rice garnished with fried eggs and fried bananas dredged in flour and egg-wash.

— *con alcachofas* (kohn ahl-kah-chóh-fahs) Rice with artichokes.

— *con almejas* (kohn ahl-méh-hahs) Rice with clams.

— *con azafrán* (kohn ah-sah-fráhn) Saffron rice.

— *con bacalao* (kohn bah-kah-láh-oh) Rice with salt-cod.

— *con calamares* (kohn kah-lah-máh-rehs) Rice with squid.

— *con caracoles* (kohn kah-rah-kóh-lehs) Rice with snails (escargots).

— *con cerdo* (kohn séhr-doh) Rice with diced pork.

— *con chipirones* (kohn chee-pee-róh-nehs) Rice with squid.

— *con conejo* (kohn koh-néh-hoh) Rice with rabbit.

— *con cordero* (kohn kohr-déh-roh) Rice with lamb.

— *con costra* (kohn kóhs-trah) Rice with meatballs, chicken, sausage, and chickpeas, topped with beaten eggs.

— *con jerez* (kohn heh-réhs) Rice with sherry wine.

— *con jibia* (kohn hée-bee-ah) Rice with cuttlefish.

— *con langostinos* (kohn lahn-gohs-tée-nohs) Rice with prawns.

— *con leche* (kohn léh-cheh) Rice pudding.

  – *a la asturiana* (ah lah ahs-too-ree-áh-nah) Rice pudding flavored with anise liquor.

— *con magra* (kohn máh-grah) Rice with fresh pork.

— *con mariscos* (kohn mah-rées-kohs) Rice with shellfish.

— *con mejillones* (kohn meh-hee-yóh-nehs) Rice with mussels.

— *con menudillos* (kohn meh-noo-dée-yohs) Rice with chicken giblets.

— *con pavo* (kohn páh-boh) Rice with turkey.

— *con perdiz* (kohn pehr-dées) Rice with partridge.

— *con pescado* (kohn pehs-káh-doh) Rice with fish.

— *con picadillo* (kohn pee-kah-dée-yoh) Rice with a *sofrito* containing diced pork, cured ham, and chicken livers.

— *con pichones* (kohn pee-chóh-nehs) Rice with squab.

— *con pollo* (kohn póh-yoh) Rice with chicken.

— *con rape* (kohn ráh-peh) Rice with anglerfish.

— *con riñones* (kohn ree-nyóh-nehs) Rice with veal kidneys.

— *con verduras* (kohn behr-dóo-rahs) Rice with mixed vegetables.

— *con vino* (kohn bée-noh) Rice with chicken and a *sofrito* containing white wine.

— *de Cádiz* (deh káh-dees) Rice with a *sofrito* and fish broth, seasoned with lemon juice.

— *de caril de Camarao* (deh kah-réel deh kah-mah-ráh-oh) Spiced sautéed shrimp served on a bed of rice (from Portugal).

— *en caldero* (ehn kahl-déh-roh) Rice cooked with fish broth, dried red peppers, and abundant garlic (from Murcia).

— *emperatriz* (ehm-peh-rah-trées) Rice pudding with candied fruit macerated in brandy.

— *frío en ensaladilla* (frée-oh ehn ehn-sah-lah-dée-yah) Plain

**Arroz frío en ensaladilla** (cont.) boiled rice mixed with canned tuna, pimiento, hard-boiled egg, capers, and gherkins.

— *frito* (frée-toh) Fried rice.

— *integral* (een-teh-gráhl) Brown rice.

— *jerezano* (heh-reh-sáh-noh) Rice with a *sofrito* containing sherry wine.

— *murciano* (moor-see-áh-noh) Rice with pork and garden vegetables.

— *navarro* (nah-báh-rroh) Rice with lamb (from Navarra).

— *negro* (néh-groh) Rice with squid and the squid's ink.

— *pamplonica* (pahm-ploy-née-kah) Rice with salt cod and sweet peppers (from Navarra).

— *verde con almejas* (béhr-deh kohn ahl-méh-hahs) Soupy rice with clams, green peppers, and parsley.

— *viudo* (bee-óo-doh) Rice with artichokes, red peppers, snow peas, onions, and tomatoes.

**Áspic de langostinos** (áhs-peek deh lahn-gohs-tée-nohs) Shrimp aspic.

**Asturias** (ahs-tóo-ree-ahs) Region in northwestern Spain.

**Atascaburras** (ah-tahs-kah-bóo-rrahs) Blend of boiled potatoes and shredded salt-cod folded with egg yolk and walnuts.

**Atún** (ah-tóon) Tuna fish.

— *a la barquera* (ah lah bahr-kéh-rah) Tuna baked in a thick *sofrito* containing almonds.

— *con alcaparras* (kohn ahl-kah-páh-rrahs) Fried fresh tuna steaks with capers.

— *con tomate* (kohn toh-máh-teh) Tuna steaks fried in tomato sauce.

— *en conserva* (ehn kohn-séhr-bah) Canned tuna.

— *en escabeche* (ehn ehs-kah-béh-cheh) Pickled tuna fish.

— *mechado* (meh-cháh-doh) Larded tuna in casserole.

— *pamplonica* (pahm-ploh-née-kah) Poached tuna garnished with minced onion, parsley, and hard-boiled egg.

— *provenzal* (proh-behn-sáhl) Tuna fish baked in an anchovy sauce with black olives.

**Avellanas** (ah-beh-yáh-nahs) Hazelnuts.

**Avila** (áh-bee-lah) City in Old Castile where lamb dishes are exquisitely prepared.

**Azafrán** (ah-sah-fráhn) Saffron.

## B

**Baba al ron** (báh-bah ahl rohn) Rum-soaked savarin-dough cake

**Babarúa arlequín** (bah-bah-róo-ah ahr-leh-kéen) Chilled vanilla and chocolate custard garnished with mandarine sections.

— *de café* (deh kah-féh) Chilled custard with coffee flavor.

**Bacalao** (bah-kah-láh-oh) Codfish, salted cod fish.

— *ajoarriero* (ah-hoh-ah-rree-éh-roh) Salt-cod simmered in a tomato sauce with vinegar and paprika.

— *a la manchega* (ah lah mahn-chéh-gah) Flaked salt-cod baked in a *sofrito* containing roasted peppers, topped with eggs.

— *a la navarra* (ah lah nah-báh-rrah) Boiled salt-cod dressed with a *sofrito* containing red peppers.

— *a la riojana* (ah lah ree-oh-háh-nah) Salt-cod stew with white beans and red peppers.

— *a la valenciana* (ah lah bah-lehn-se-áh-nah) Salt-cod baked with a *sofrito* containing rice, green peas, and pimiento.

— *a la vizcaina* (ah lah bees-kah-ée-nah) Salt-cod baked in a hot dried pepper and olive oil sauce garnished with sweet red peppers.

— *al pil-pil* (ahl peel-péel) Salt-cod fried with garlic and hot peppers.

— *con manzanas* (kohn mahn-sáh-nahs) Salt-cod simmered with sautéed apples.

— *de Alcántara* (deh ahl-káhn-tah-rah) Pot-roasted salt-cod with spinach.

— *en sanfaina* (ehn sahn-fáh-ee-nah) Shredded salt-cod sautéed with ratatouille.

— *pueblerino* (poo-eh-bleh-rée-noh) Casserole of shredded salt-cod mixed with puree of legumes.

*Bacalhau a Gomes de Sa* (bah-kah-láh-oo ah góh-mehs deh sah) Baked salt-cod in a sauce containing milk and boiled potatoes (from Portugal).

*Banderillas* (bahn-deh-rée-yahs) Bite-sized snacks threaded together with a toothpick.

*Barcelona* (bahr-seh-lóh-nah) Second largest city in Spain and capital of Cataluña. Barcelona's restaurants are among the best in the Peninsula.

*Barquitas* (bahr-kée-tahs) A bite-sized, stuffed boat-shaped baked

dough snack.

— *de pepino y atún* (deh peh-pée-noh ee ah-toon) Mixed cucumber, canned tuna, and mayonnaise barquettes.

*Bartolillos* (bahr-toh-lée-yohs) Fried pastries filled with custard.

*Batatas* (bah-táh-tahs) Potatoes, in Portuguese.

— *a portuguesa* (ah pohr-too-guéh-sah) Sliced sautéed potatoes (from Portugal).

*Bayas* (báh-yahs) Berries.

*Becada* (beh-káh-dah) Woodcock.

— *a la bilbaina* (ah lah beel-bah-ée-nah) Woodcock braised in broth, sherry, turnips, and a *majado* of fried bread and potato puree.

— *a la guadalupe* (ah lah goo-ah-dah-lóo-peh) Woodcock braised with a *sofrito* containing wine and the woodcock's giblets.

— *al jerez* (ahl heh-réhs) Roast woodcock basted with sherry wine.

*Bellota* (beh-yóh-tah) Acorn.

*Berberechos* (behr-beh-réh-chohs). Cockles.

*Berenjena* (beh-rehn héh-nah) Eggplant.

— *a la crema* (ah lah kréh-mah) Fried eggplant slices dredged in flour, napped with cream sauce, and browned in the oven.

— *a la eibarresa* (ah lah eh-ee-bah-rréh-sah) Baked eggplant stuffed with anchovies, bread soaked in milk, and fried tomato.

— *a la mallorquina* (ah lah mah-yohr-kée-nah) Stuffed eggplant baked with chorizo spread napped with white sauce.

— *a la parrilla* (ah lah pah-rrée-yah) Grilled eggplant dressed with a sauce made with meat broth, olive oil, parsley, bread crumbs, and lemon juice.

— *con queso* (kohn kéh-soh) Baked eggplant topped with cheese slices.

— *duquesa* (doo-kéh-sah) Eggplant stuffed with diced ham, tomato, mushrooms, and white wine.

— *fritas* (frée-tahs) Eggplant slices dredged in flour and fried in olive oil.

— *rellenas* (reh-yéh-nahs) Eggplant stuffed with broad soaked in milk, garlic sausage, and egg.

— *rebozadas* (reh-boh-sáh-dahs) Slices of eggplant, cooked ham, and cheese dipped in beaten egg, dredged in flour, and deep fried.

— *salteadas* (sahl-teh-áh-dahs) Sautéed eggplant simmered in a touch of stock with tomato.

*Berros* (béh-rrohs) Watercress.

*Berza* (béhr-sah) Green cabbage.

— *a la campesina* (ah lah kahm-peh-sée-nah) Cabbage leaves stuffed with minced pork and ham.

— *con patatas* (kohn pah-táh-tahs) Boiled cabbage and potatoes sautéed with chorizo sausage and bread slices (from the Basque Country).

*Besugo* (beh-sóo-goh) Red porgy.

— *a la madrileña* (ah lah mah-dree-léh-nyan) Baked porgy with white wine and bread crumbs.

— *al horno* (ahl óhr-noh) Baked red porgy.

— *con almendras* (kohn ahl-méhn-drahs) Sautéed red porgy in a wine sauce containing almonds.

— *con piñones* (kohn pee-nyóh-nehs) Sea bream with pine nuts.

— *donostiarra* (doh-nohs-tee-áh-rrah) Red porgy baked with lemon juice, garlic, and hot red pepper.

*Bienmesabes* (bee-ehn-meh-sáh-behs) Ground hazelnuts baked with butter, sugar, egg yolks, and cinnamon.

*Bifes de cebollada* (bée-fehs deh seh-boh-láh-dah) Beefsteak with onions (from Portugal).

*Bilbaos* (beel-báh-ohs) Ground toasted almonds mixed with flour, sugar, grated orange, and lemon.

*Bistec a la andaluza* (bees-téhk ah lah ahn-dah-lóo-sah) Grilled beefsteak garnished with baked eggplant stuffed with ham and fried tomatoes with onions.

— *con pimientos* (kohn pee-mee-éhn-tohs) Grilled beefsteak garnished with roasted sweet peppers.

*Bizcocho* (bees-kóh-choh) Cake.

— *borracho* (boh-rráh-choh) Liqueur-soaked cake.

— *de almendra* (deh ahl-méhn-drah) Almond cake.

— *de avellana* (deh ah-beh-yáh-nah) Hazelnut cake.

— *de San Lorenzo* (deh sahn loh-réhn-soh) Chestnut-puree cake.

— *de reina* (deh réh-ee-nah) Layer cake filled with stawberry jam.

*Blanco y negro* (bláhn-koh ee néh-groh) Iced coffee with vanilla ice cream.

*Blanqueta de ternera* (blahn-kéhtah deh tehr-néh-rah) Veal blanquette.

**Bocaditos de dama** (boh-kah-dée-tohs deh dáh-mah) Apricot jam filled cake with lemon icing.

**Bodega** (boh-déh-gah) Cellars where wines are matured, tavern.

**Boga** (bóh-gah) Sea bream.

— **a las finas hierbas** (ah lahs fée-nahs ee-éhr-bahs) Fried sea bream in a parsley *sofrito*.

**Bolas de Berlín** (bóh-lahs deh behr-léen) Deep-fried pâte-à-choux balls filled with quince jelly.

— **de castaña** (deh kahs-táh-nyah) Fried balls made with pureed chestnuts boiled in milk.

**Bolinhos de bacalhau** (boh-lée-nyohs deh bah-kah-láh-oo) Deep-fried salt-cod cakes, from Portugal.

**Bolitas de oro** (boh-lée-tahs deh óh-roh) Hard-boiled egg yolks with pâté and gelatin.

— **de queso** (deh kéh-soh) Fried battered cheese balls.

— **de zanahoria** (deh sah-nah-óh-ree-ah) Fried battered carrot balls.

**Bollos de aceite** (bóh-yohs deh ah-séh-ee-teh) Sweet rolls made with olive oil.

**Bolo** (bóh-loh) Cake in Portuguese.

— **de amendoras** (deh ah-méhn-doh-rahs) Almond cake, from Portugal.

**Bonito** (boh-née-toh) Bonito (striped tuna).

— **a la oriotarra** (ah lah oh-ree-oh-táh-rrah) Fried bonito steak dressed with tomato and green pepper puree.

**Boquerones** (boh-keh-róh-nehs) Small sardines.

— **en salmuera** (ehn sahl-moo-éh-rah) Small sardines pickled in salt.

— **en vinagre** (ehn bee-náh-greh) Small sardines pickled in vinegar.

**Boronitas** (boh-roh-née-tahs) Sweet cornmeal squares.

**Borrachuelos** (boh-rrah-choo-éh-lohs) Fried *choux* paste pastries flavored with anise liquor.

**Brazo gitano** (bráh-soh hee-táh-noh) Rolled cream-filled sponge cake.

**Brécol** (bréh-kohl) Broccoli.

**Broa** (bróh-ah) Cornbread (from Portugal).

**Brochetas** (broh-chéh-tahs) Brochettes.

— **de cordero** (deh kohr-déh-roh) Lamb brochettes.

**Budín** (boo-déen) Pudding.

— **a la cántabra** (ah lah káhn-tah-brah) Baked mixture of pound cake, grated toasted almonds, pineapple chunks, eggs, and brandy.

— **puertorriqueño** (poo-ehr-toh-rree-kéh-nyoh) Milk and wine-soaked pound cake mixed with raisins, toasted almonds, and cinnamon.

**Buñuelo** (boo-nyoo-éh-loh) Fritter.

— **de bacalao** (deh bah-kah-láh-oh) Salt-cod fritters.

— **de chorizo** (deh choh-rée-soh) Chorizo sausage fritters.

— **de higo** (deh ée-goh) Fig fritters.

— **de jamón** (deh hah-móhn) Prosciutto ham fritters.

— **del Ampurdán** (dehl ahm-poor-dáhn) Fritters with aniseed, coriander, and cinnamon.

— **de manzana** (deh mahn-sáh-nah) Apple fritters.

— *de queso* (deh kéh-soh) Cheese fritters.

— *de San Isidro* (deh sahn ee-sée-droh) Fritters filled with custard.

— *de San José* (deh sahn hoh-séh) Rice fritters flavored with sweet sherry wine.

**Burgos** (bóor-gohs) Fresh, ewe's-milk cheese from the province of Burgos.

**Butifarra catalana** (boo-tee-fáh-rrah kah-tah-láh-nah) Pork white sausage (from Cataluña).

## C

**Caballa** (kah-báh-yah) Mackerel.

— *a la parrilla* (ah lah pah-rrée-yah) Grilled mackerel, usually served with fried chopped tomato in olive oil.

— *a la vizcaina* (ah lah bees-kah-ée-nah) Mackerel baked with bread crumbs, garlic, parsley, paprika, and hard cider.

— *trianera* (tree-ah-néh-rah) Baked mackerel with ratatouille.

**Caballitos** (kah-bah-yée-tohs). Deep-fried battered shrimp.

**Cabello de ángel** (kah-béh-yoh deh áhn-hehl) Candied squash meat.

**Cabeza de cordero al horno** (kah-béh-sah deh kohr-déh-roh ahl óhr-noh) Roast lamb's head.

**Cabrales** (kah-bráh-lehs) Cow's blue-streaked cheese from Asturias.

**Cabrito** (kah-brée-toh) Baby goat.

— *a la castellana* (ah lah kahs-teh-yáh-nah) Sautéed diced lamb oven-baked dressed with a *majado* made with garlic, parsley, and vinegar.

— *a la extremeña* (ah lah ehks-treh-méh-nyah) Baby goat casserole with a *majado* made with its liver, garlic, pimiento, and paprika.

— *al ron* (ahl rohn) Broiled baby goat marinated in rum sauce.

**Cacahuetes** (kah-kah-oo-éh-tehs) Peanuts.

**Cachelada gallega** (kah-cheh-láh-dah gah-yéh-gah) Octopus stew with new potatoes.

**Cachelos** (kah-chéh-lohs) New potatoes (in Galicia).

— *a la castellana* (ah lah kahs-teh-yáh-nah) Diced boiled new potatoes dressed with fried garlic, paprika, and vinegar and garnished with chopped hard-boiled egg.

**Cachopo** (kah-chóh-poh) Veal cutlet fried with cheese and ham.

**Cádiz** (káh-dees) Goat's-milk cheese that is hard and mellow in taste (from the province of Cádiz).

**Café** (kah-féh) Coffee.

— *con leche* (kohn léh-cheh) Coffee with milk.

— *solo* (sóh-loh) Black coffee.

**Calabacín** (kah-lah-bah-séen) Zucchini.

**Calabacines a la marinera** (kah-lah-bah-sée-nehs ah lah mah-ree-néh-rah) Baked zucchini stuffed with a mixture of poached fish, mushrooms, onion, egg, and bread crumb.

— *a la turca* (ah lah tóor-kah) Boiled zucchini, stuffed with sautéed chicken livers, onion, tomato, and rice, sprinkled with Parmesan, and baked in the oven.

— *al horno* (ahl óhr-noh) Baked zucchini.

— *empanados* (ehm-pah-náh-dohs) Deep-fried zucchini.

— *rellenos andaluza* (reh-yéh-nohs ahn-dah-lóo-sah) Deep-fried zucchini stuffed with sautéed onion, minced pork, hard-boiled egg, and bread crumbs.

— *salteados* (sahl-teh-áh-dohs) Boiled zucchini fried with onion and garlic.

**Calamares** (kah-lah-máh-rehs) Squid.

— *a la bilbaina* (ah lah beel-bah-ée-nah) Squid simmered in a *sofrito* containing the squid's own ink.

— *a la romana* (ah lah roh-máh-nah) Deep-fried squid.

— *al jerez* (ahl heh-réhs) Squid simmered in sherry sauce.

— *con cebolla* (kohn seh-bóh-yah) Squid fried with onions.

— *encebollados* (ehn-seh-boh-yáh-dohs) Squid braised with onions.

— *en su tinta* (ehn soo téen-tah) Squid stewed in their own ink.

— *rellenos* (reh-yéh-nos) Stuffed squid.

— *rellenos menorquina* (reh-yéh-nohs meh-nohr-kée-nah) Braised squid stuffed with pine nuts, raisins, and fresh mint (from the island of Menorca).

**Caldeirada** (kahl-deh-ee-ráh-dah) Assorted-fish stew with tomato, peppers, onion, potatoes, and paprika (from Galicia).

— *a pescadora* (ah pehs-kah-dóh-rah) Seafood casserole, fisherman style (from Portugal).

**Caldereta a la menorquina** (kahl-deh-réh-tah ah lah men-nohr-kée-nah) Lobster casserole with fish fumet and a *majado* of onion, tomtato, garlic, and parsley.

— *asturiana* (ahs-too-ree-áh-nah) Seafood stew with fish fumet, brandy, green peppers, lemon juice, and cayenne pepper (from Asturias).

— *de cordero* (deh kohr-déh-roh) Lamb stew with *sofrito,* cured ham, white wine, and thyme.

— *de lomo* (deh lóh-moh) Casserole of pork medallions and artichokes stewed in meat broth and white wine.

— *de pescado* (deh pehs-káh-doh) Fish stew.

— *de rape* (deh ráh-peh) Angler-fish casserole with sliced potatoes, *sofrito,* and a *majado* with saffron, garlic, clove, almonds, hazelnuts, and parsley.

— *extremeña* (ehks-treh-méh-nyah) Cubed-lamb stew with lamb's liver, red wine, and a *majado* with garlic, black peppercorns, paprika, and vinegar.

— *de Tarazona* (deh tah-rah-sóh-nah) Rabbit, lamb, and potato casserole with a *majado* of walnuts and the rabbit's liver.

— *manchega* (mahn-chéh-gah) Lamb shoulder casserole containing a *majado* made with sautéed lamb brain, liver, and bread.

**Caldero de pastor** (kahl-déh-roh deh pahs-tóhr) Lamb and potato casserole with onion and tomato *sofrito.*

**Caldo** (káhl-doh) Broth.

— *a la francesa* (ah lah frahn-séh-sah) Clear consommé.

— *de jaramago* (deh hah-rah-máh-goh) Boiled navy beans, potatoes, salt pork, and wall rocket leaves (*jaramago*) mixed with corn meal and dressed with vinegar (from the Canary Islands).

— *de perro gaditano* (deh péh-rroh gah-dee-táh-noh) Fish soup with orange juice (from Cádiz).

— *de pescado con pimientos* (deh pehs-káh-doh kohn pee-mee-éhn-tohs) Fish broth with bell peppers and potatoes seasoned with cumin.

— *de verduras* (deh behr-dóo-rahs) Vegetable broth.

— *gallego* (gah-yéh-goh) Soup from Galicia made from beef, salt pork, white beans, potatoes, and greens.

— *navarro* (nah-báh-rroh) Chicken broth flavored with clove, cinnamon, and saffron.

— *verde* (béhr-deh) Kale and potato soup with chorizo sausage (from Portugal).

*Callos* (káh-yohs) Beef tripe.

— *a la asturiana* (ah lah ahs-too-ree-áh-nah) Tripe casserole with chickpeas and white wine.

— *a la madrileña* (ah lah mah-dree-léh-nyah) Tripe casserole with cured ham, beef feet, chorizo, morcilla sausage, paprika, and chili peppers.

— *murcianos* (moor-see-áh-nohs) Tripe stew with veal's feet, chorizo, cured ham, and chickpeas. The liquid is flavored with saffron and fresh mint.

*Camarones* (kah-mah-róh-nehs) Prawns.

— *a la andaluza* (ah lah ahn-dah-lóo-sah) Fried prawns garnished with fried tomato and garlic.

*Camerano* (kah-meh-ráh-noh) Very soft goat's-milk cheese from the Rioja.

*Canapé* (kah-nah-péh) Canapé.

— *de anchoas y pimiento* (deh ahn-chóh-ahs ee pee-mee-éhn-toh) Anchovy and pimiento canapé.

— *de atún y tomate* (deh ah-tóon ee toh-máh-teh) Canned tuna and tomato canapé.

*Canela* (kah-néh-lah) Cinnamon.

*Canelones* (kah-neh-lóh-nehs) Cannelloni.

— *con espinacas* (kohn ehs-pee-náh-kahs) Baked stuffed canneloni with spinach, anchovies and béchamel sauce.

— *con jamón* (kohn hah-móhn) Baked canneloni stuffed with minced cured ham and tomato puree.

— *con langostinos* (kohn lahn-gohs-tée-nohs) Baked canneloni stuffed with prawns in white sauce.

— *de pescado* (deh pehs-káh-doh) Baked canneloni stuffed with flaked boiled fish, mushrooms, and hard-boiled egg.

— *de pollo* (deh póh-yoh) Baked canneloni stuffed with minced chicken in tomato sauce.

— *de vigilia* (deh bee-hée-lee-ah) Baked canneloni stuffed with a paste made with fish, truffles, tomato puree, white wine and Parmesan cheese.

— *Rossini* (roh-sée-nee) Baked canneloni stuffed with a paste made with chicken livers, calf's brain and spices.

*Cangrejo* (kah-gréh-hoh) Crab.

— *de mar al jerez* (deh mahr ahl heh-réhs) Sautéed sea crab in sherry sauce.

— *de rio al vino blanco* (deh rée-oh ahl bée-noh bláhn-koh) Crawfish sautéed in white wine.

*Canja* (káhn-chah) Chicken soup with mint leaves and lemon (from Portugal).

*Canutillos* (kah-noo-tée-yohs) Custard-filled puff pastry cylinders.

*Capón* (kah-póhn) Capon.

— *a la andaluza* (ah lah ahn-dah-lóo-sah) Roast capon stuffed with raisins, pine nuts, bacon, milk-soaked bread, egg, sherry, and cinnamon.

— *al estilo de Lazcano* (ahl esh-tée-loh deh lahs-káh-noh) Oven-baked chicken stuffed with a mixture made with apples, chestnuts, bacon, milk, and hard cider (from the Basque Country).

— *asado* (ah-sah-doh) Roast capon.

— *borracho* (boh-rráh-choh) Capon sautéed in olive oil simmered in white wine.

— *picante* (pee-káhn-teh) Capon sautéed in oil with *sofrito* containing paprika and hot chili peppers.

*Caqui* (káh-kee) Persimmon.

*Caracoles* (kah-rah-kóh-lehs) Snails, escargots.

— *a la andaluza* (ah lah ahn-dah-lóo-sah) Stewed snails with *sofrito* and a *majado* made with garlic, fried almonds, and fried bread.

— *picantes* (pee-káhn-tehs) Stewed escargots with chili peppers.

*Carajillo* (kah-rah-hée-yoh) Black coffee with dash of brandy.

*Cardamomo* (kahr-dah-móh-moh) Cardamom.

*Cariñena* (kah-ree-nyéh-nah) Wine-producing area of Aragón.

*Carne* (káhr-neh) Meat.

— *a la montañesa* (ah lah mohn-tah-nyéh-sah) Cubed leg of veal stew with sautéed onion, white wine, and meat broth.

— *fiambre* (fee-áhm-breh) Cold cuts.

*Carnero* (kahr-néh-roh) Mutton.

— *a la española* (ah lah ehs-pah-nyóh-lah) Roast leg of mutton with garlic and rosemary, dressed with its own gravy, and garnished with green peas.

— *en adobo* (ehn ah-dóh-boh) Sautéed marinated mutton.

*Casadielles* (kah-sah-dee-éh-yehs) Turnovers filled with ground walnuts and cinnamon, flavored with anise liquor (from Asturias).

*Casolet* (kah-soh-léht) Dry white-bean stew with lamb, pork loin, and fresh sausage.

*Castañas* (kahs-táh-nyahs) Chestnuts.

— *en almíbar* (ehn ahl-mée-bahr) Chestnuts in vanilla syrup.

*Cataluña* (kah-tah-lóo-nyah) Region in northeastern Spain where Barcelona is the regional center. Its cuisine is well-known for its Mediterranean seafood dishes.

*Cava* (káh-bah) Spanish sparkling wine made by the Champagne method.

*Cayena* (kah-yéh-nah) Cayenne.

*Cazuela* (kah-soo-éh-lah) Casserole.

— *canaria* (kah-náh-ree-ah) Sautéed assorted fish casserole with a *sofrito* with paprika and garnished with potatoes, corn, bananas, pumpkin, and pineapple (from the Canary Islands).

— *de espárragos* (deh ehs-páh-rrah-gohs) Asparagus casserole with a *majado* made with fried garlic and bread, vinegar, and paprika, garnished with beaten egg, and browned in the oven.

— *de ternera con berenjenas* (deh tehr-néh-rah kohn beh-rehn-héh-nahs) Veal casserole with eggplant.

— *marinera* (mah-ree-néh-rah) Seafood casserole with *sofrito* and green peans.

*Cebolla* (seh-bóh-yah) Onion.

*Cebollada con almendras* (seh-bóh-yah-dah kohn ahl-méhn-drahs) Onion soup with blanched almonds.

*Cebollas rellenas* (seh-bóh-yahs reh-yéh-nahs) Baked boiled onions stuffed with minced pork, egg yolk, and seasonings.

*Cebollino* (seh-boh-yée-noh) Chives.

*Cebollitas* (seh-boh-yée-tahs) Small fresh onions.

— *al limón* (ahl lee-móhn) Chopped small fresh onions dressed with olive oil and lemon juice.

— *en vinagre* (ehn bee-náh-greh) Vinegar-pickled small fresh onions.

*Cebrero* (seh-bréh-roh) Galician cow's-milk cheese, creamy and sharp in taste.

*Cecina* (seh-sée-nah) Cured meats.

*Centollo* (sehn-tóh-yoh) Spider crab.

— *al vino blanco* (ahl bée-noh bláhn-koh) Braised spider crab in white wine.

*Cerdo* (séhr-doh) Pork.

*Cerezas* (seh-réh-sahs) Cherries.

— *infernales* (een-fehr-náh-lehs) Syrup-boiled cherries flamed with kirsch.

*Cervera* (sehr-béh-rah) Fresh white ewe's-milk cheese from Valencia.

*Ceviche al coco* (seh-bée-cheh ahl kóh-koh) Raw fish strips marinated in lemon juice and dressed with shredded coconut and whipping cream.

*Chacolí* (chah-koh-lée) White, delicate, fruity wine from the Basque Country.

*Chalotas* (chah-lóh-tahs) Shallots.

*Champán* (chahm-páhn) Common name given to sparkling wine.

*Champiñones* (chahm-pee-nyóh-nehs) Mushrooms.

— *al ajillo* (ahl ah-hée-yoh) Mushrooms sautéed with garlic.

— *a la murciana* (ah lah moor-see-áh-nah) Button mushrooms simmered with garlic, onion, diced cured ham, chorizo slices, and paprika.

— *a la polonesa* (ah lah poh-loh-néh-sah) Baked mushrooms napped with white sauce garnished with chopped hard-boiled egg.

— *al jerez* (ahl heh-réhs) Mushrooms sautéed in sherry wine.

— *con salsa holandesa* (kohn sahl-sah oh-lahn-déh-sah) Boiled mushrooms with hollandaise sauce.

— *rellenos* (reh-yéh-nohs) Meat, or seafood-stuffed mushrooms.
— *salteados* (sahl-teh-áh-dohss) Sautéed mushrooms.
**Chanfaina de ave** (chahn-fáh-ee-nah deh áh-beh) Chicken casserole with hard-boiled eggs, and a *majado* containing pig's liver, fried almonds, and roasted garlic.
**Chanquetes** (chahn-kéh-tehs) Whitebait.
— *fritos* (frée-tohs) Deep-fried whitebait dusted in flour.
**Chilindrón** (chee-leen-dróhn) Sauce made from tomato, sweet peppers, onions, garlic, and olive oil.
— *de cordero* (deh kohr-déh-roh) Lamb simmered in *chilindron* sauce.
**Chocolate** (choh-koh-láh-teh) Chocolate.
**Chorizo** (choh-rée-soh) Red pork and paprika sausage.
— *a la sidra* (ah lah sée-drah) Chorizo sausage cooked in hard cider with apple slices.
**Chuleta** (choo-léh-tah) Chop.
— *alavesa* (ah-lah-béh-sah) Grilled marinated veal chop, garnished with fried sweet red peppers.
— *de lomo a la bilbaina* (deh lóh-moh ah lah beel-bah-ée-nah) marinated beef loin chop breaded and grilled and garnished with minced garlic and parsley.
— *de ternera* (deh tehr-néh-rah) Veal chop.
- *a la castellana* (ah lah kahs-teh-yáh-nah) Fried veal chop simmered in white wine with onions and noisette potatoes.

- *a la guipuzcoana* (ah lah guee-poos-koo-áh-nah) Fried veal chop baked in meat broth, hard cider, sliced potatoes, and bouquet garni.
- *al ajo cabañil* (ahl áh-hoh kah-bah-nyéel) Fried veal chop simmered in meat broth, garlic, paprika, and vinegar.
- *a la hortelana* (ah lah ohr-teh-láh-nah) Fried veal chop garnished with sautéed onion, garlic, chopped cured ham, mushrooms, pimiento, and thyme.
- *con habas* (kohn áh-bahs) Fried veal chop garnished with a *sofrito* containing fresh fava beans.
- *villagodio* (bee-yah-góh-dee-oh) Grilled veal chop basted with olive oil.
- *zíngara* (séen-gah-rah) Fried veal chop simmered in brown sauce and garnished with thin slices of ham.
— *de cerdo a la asturiana* (deh séhr-doh ah lah ahs-too-ree-áh-nah) Sautéed pork chops and apple slices simmered in meat broth and hard cider.
- *a la madrileña* (ah lah mah-dree-léh-nyah) Marinated pork chops sautéed in olive oil.
- *a la mostaza* (ah lah mohs-táh-sah) Grilled pork chops dressed with mustard and chopped gherkins.
- *a la naranja* (ah lah nah-ráhn-hah) Pork chops in orange sauce.
- *a la portuguesa* (ah lah pohr-too-guéh-sah) Sautéed pork chops simmered in wine,

**Chuleta de cerdo a la asturiana a la portuguesa** (cont.) sautéed onion, and bouquet garni, garnished with shredded boiled cabbage.

- **al jerez** (ahl heh-réhs) Sautéed pork chops simmered in sherry and crushed almonds.
- **con ciruelas pasas** (kohn see-roo-éh-lahs páh-sahs) Browned pork chops simmered in a sauce made with prunes, red wine, sugar, and cinnamon.
- **con espinacas** (kohn ehs-pee-náh-kahs) Sautéed pork chops simmered in sherry and garnished with sautéed spinach.
- **con pimientos y jamón** (kohn pee-mee-éhn-tohs ee hah-móhn) Browned pork chops simmered in a *sofrito* containing pimiento and diced cured ham.
- **con tomate** (kohn to-máh-teh) Sautéed pork chops with tomato.
- **empanadas** (ehm-pah-náh-dahs) Fried breaded pork chops.
- **riojana** (ree-oh-háh-nah) Seared pork chops simmered with sautéed onion, garlic, tomato, and sweet red peppers.
— **de cordero a la aragonesa** (deh kohr-déh-roh ah lah ah-rah-goh-néh-sah) Fried breaded lamb chops simmered in fried tomato.
- **a la bechamel** (ah lah beh-chah-méhl) Grilled lamb cutlets wrapped in béchamel sauce.
- **al ajo cabañil** (ahl áh-hoh kah-bah-nyéel) Fried lamb cutlets dressed with a *majado* made with garlic and vinegar.

- **a la navarra** (ah lah nah-báh-rrah) Sautéed lamb cutlets simmered in a *sofrito* containing diced cured ham and chorizo sausage.
- **a la parmesana** (ah lah pahr-meh-sáh-nah) Fried lamb cutlets baked in the oven covered with potato puree blended with egg yolk, butter, and nutmeg.
- **a la parrilla** (ah lah pah-rrée-yah) Grilled lamb cutlets.
- **asadas** (ah-sáh-dahs) Grilled lamb cutlets.
- **Villarreal** (bee-yah-rreh-áhl) Baked lamb cutlets with sautéed onions in bacon fat and bouquet garni.
- **Villeroy** (beel-roo-áh) Lamb cutlets dipped in béchamel sauce, breaded and deep-fried in olive oil.

**Churrasco de ternera** (choo-rráhs-koh deh tehr-néh-rah) Veal meat baked in the oven with wine, meat broth, garlic, onion, and carrots.

**Churros** (chóo-rrohs) Deep-fried batter.

**Cilantro** (see-láhn-troh) Coriander.

**Ciruelas** (see-roo-éh-lahs) Plums.

— **pasas** (páh-sahs) Prunes.

- **rellenas** (reh-yéh-nahs) Deep-fried cured-ham-stuffed prunes.

**Clarete** (klah-réh-teh) Light red wine.

**Clavo** (kláh-boh) Clove.

**Coca de San Juan** (kóh-kah deh sahn hoo-áhn) Sweet bread containing marzipan, candied fruits, and pine nuts.

**Cochifrito** (koh-chee-frée-toh) Lamb casserole with meat broth, lemon juice, and sherry.

*Cochinillo* (koh-chee-née-yoh) Suckling pig.
— *asado* (ah-sáh-doh) Roast suckling pig.
*Cocido* (koh-sée-doh) Soup pot made from meats, vegetables, and legumes.
— *con pelotas* (kohn peh-lóh-tahs) Chickpea stew with beef, turkey, chorizo, potatoes, and green beans, garnished with meat balls made with bread, bacon, chicken livers, garlic, pine nuts, and parsley.
— *gaditano* (gah-dee-táh-noh) Veal-and-pork-meat stew with chickpeas, bacon, onion, green beans, potatoes, pumpkin, chorizo, and paprika. The stew is flavored with a *majado* made of garlic, cumin, tomato, and vinegar.
— *gallego* (gah-yéh-goh) Veal, salt pork, pig's head, and chickpea stew with cabbage and chorizo sausage (from Galicia).
— *madrileño* (mah-dree-léh-nyoh) Meat, sausage, vegetables, and chickpea stew.
— *valenciano* (bah-lehn-see-áh-noh) Veal and chickpea stew with bacon, cured ham, chorizo, potatoes, and assorted vegetables. The stew is garnished with dumplings made with poultry blood, bacon, egg, corn meal, and bread crumb.
— *zamorano* (sah-moh-ráh-noh) Chickpea and bacon stew with rice, sliced potatoes, chorizo, and *sofrito* containing paprika.
*Coco* (kóh-koh) Coconut.
*Cóctel* (kók-tehl) Cocktail.
— *de gambas* (deh gáhm-bahs) Shrimp cocktail.

*Codorniz* (koh-dohr-nées) Quail.
*Codornices a la aragonesa* (koh-dohr-née-sehs ah lah ah-rah-goh-néh-sah) Quail braised in wine with assorted vegetables.
— *a la bilbaina* (ah lah beel-bah-ée-nah) Roast quail in grape leaves flamed with brandy and served on toast.
— *a la burgalesa* (ah lah boor-gah-léh-sah) Quail braised in a broth made with the quail's giblets and white wine.
— *a la gallega* (ah lah gah-yéh-gah) Quail stewed with white beans.
— *a la riojana* (ah lah ree-oh-háh-nah) Quail simmered in a *sofrito* with wine, cured ham, and sweet green peppers.
— *a las uvas* (ah lahs óo-bahs) Roast quail dressed with a white sauce containing grapes, flamed in port wine and brandy.
— *asadas* (ah-sáh-dahs) Roast quail.
— *con jamón* (kohn hah-móhn) Quail stuffed with cured ham, braised in broth with a *majado* made of roasted almonds, garlic, and parsley.
— *con pochas* (kohn póh-chahs) Quail simmered in a *sofrito* with cured ham and chorizo sausage and garnished with cooked white beans.
*Codorníu* (koh-dohr-née-oo) Largest cava producer in the Penedés region.
*Cogollos de Tudela* (koh-góh-yohs deh too-déh-lah) Hearts of romaine lettuce with anchovy vinaigrette.

V O C A B U L A R Y

*Col* (kohl) Green cabbage.

*Coles de Bruselas* (kóh-lehs deh broo-séh-lahs) Brussels sprouts.

— *a la crema* (ah lah kréh-mah) Boiled Brussels sprouts napped with cream sauce.

— *salteadas* (sahl-teh-áh-dahs) Sautéed Brussels sprouts.

*Coles rellenas* (kóh-lehs- reh-yéh-nahs) Stuffed cabbage leaves.

*Coliflor* (koh-lee-flóhr) Cauliflower.

— *a la granadina* (ah lah grah-nah-dée-nah) Boiled cauliflower florets sautéed with bacon and onion and dressed with chicken broth containing vinegar and saffron.

— *al ajoarriero* (ahl ah-hoh-ah-rre-éh-roh) Boiled cauliflower dressed with a thin oil-garlic-vinegar sauce.

— *al estilo de Badajoz* (ahl ehs-tée-loh deh bah-dah-hóhs) Boiled cauliflower marinated in garlic and vinegar, dusted with flour, dipped in beaten egg, and deep-fried.

— *al gratén* (ahl grah-téhn) Cauliflower au gratin.

— *al horno* (ahl óhr-noh) Baked cauliflower.

— *con salsa holandesa* (kohn sáhl-sah oh-lahn-déh-sah) Boiled cauliflower with hollandaise sauce.

— *duquesa* (doo-kéh-sah) Au gratin cauliflower florets garnished with potato puree containing egg yolk and butter and dressed with béchamel sauce.

*Cominos* (koh-mée-nohs) Cumin seed.

*Compota* (kohm-póh-tah) Stewed fruit.

*Conejo* (koh-néh-hoh) Rabbit.

— *agridulce* (ah-gree-doól-seh) Sweet and sour rabbit.

— *a la alicantina* (ah lah ah-lee-kahn-tée-nah) Rabbit marinated in garlic and orange juice, fried in olive oil, and garnished with sautéed fava beans.

— *a la asturiana* (ah lah ahs-too-ree-áh-nah) Braised sautéed rabbit in a *sofrito* with added turnips, carrots, and potatoes and a *majado* with the rabbit's liver and pine nuts.

— *a la bilbaina* (ah lah beel-bah-ée-nah) Rabbit braised in stock, wine, garlic, hazelnuts, the rabbit's liver, and chocolate.

— *a la burgalesa* (ah lah boor-gah-léh-sah) Rabbit stewed in wine, meat stock, the rabbit's pureed liver, thyme, and nutmeg.

— *a la campesina* (ah lah kahm-peh-sée-nah) Rabbit marinated in a wine simmered in a *sofrito* with the liquid of the marinade and brandy.

— *a la castellana* (ah la kahs-teh-yáh-nah) Rabbit braised in a *sofrito* containing vinegar and paprika.

— *a la cazadora* (ah lah kah-sah-dóh-rah) Rabbit marinated in wine a *sofrito* containing cured ham, brandy, wine, and thyme.

— *al alioli* (ahl ah-lee-óh-lee) Grilled rabbit served with garlic mayonnaise.

— *a la montañesa* (ah lah mohn-tah-nyéh-sah) Sautéed braised rabbit in wine, mushrooms, bouquet garni, and cinnamon with a *majado* of garlic, pine nuts, and toasted almonds (from Santander).

— *a la navarra* (ah lah nah-báhrrah) Rabbit braised in wine, garlic, tomato, and rosemary.

— *a las hierbas* (ah lahs ee-éhrbahs) Rabbit braised in white wine and a *sofrito* containing thyme, oregano, and toasted almonds.

— *almogávar* (ahl-moh-gáh-bahr) Rabbit simmered in a *sofrito* with stock, wine, and a *majado* of garlic, roasted almonds, parsley, chocolate, unsweetened cake bread, and the rabbit's liver.

— *al romero* (ahl roh-méh-roh) Rabbit marinated in wine, braised in the liquid of the marinade with a *majado* of garlic, fried bread, and rosemary.

— *con castañas* (kohn kahs-táh-nyahs) Rabbit braised with a *sofrito* containing sherry, brandy, and broth, and garnished with boiled chestnuts.

— *con caracoles* (kohn cah-rah-kóh-lehs) Sautéed rabbit and snails simmered in wine, anise liquor, and meat stock with a *majado* containing saffron, garlic, pine nuts, almonds, and the rabbit's liver.

— *con chocolate* (kohn choh-koh-láh-teh) Marinated rabbit braised in the liquid of the marinade with a *majado* made of garlic, toasted almonds, pine nuts, and chocolate.

— *con tomate* (kohn toh-máh-teh) Rabbit simmered in tomato sauce.

— *en ajillo pastor* (ehn ah-hée-yoh pahs-tóhr) Rabbit sautéed with onions, simmered in wine,

brandy, saffron, thyme, and peppercorns.

— *en salmorejo* (ehn sahl-moh-réh-hoh) Marinated rabbit braised in a sauce made of hot peppers, garlic, and paprika.

— *guisado* (guee-sáh-doh) Rabbit stuffed with bread soaked in milk, bacon, veal marrow, and parsley and simmered in white wine and dressed with boiled onion puree (from the Canary Islands).

*Confitura* (kohn-fee-tóo-rah) Jam.

— *de higos* (deh ée-gohs) Fig jam.

— *de naranja* (deh nah-ráhn-hah) Orange marmalade.

*Congrio* (kóhn-gree-oh) Conger eel.

— *a la bilbilitana* (ah lah beel-bee-lee-táh-nah) Cured conger eel simmered with pine nuts, tomato sauce, and eggs.

— *en cazuela* (ehn kah-soo-éh-lah) Conger eel casserole.

*Consomé* (kohn-soh-méh) Consommé.

— *a la italiana* (ah lah ee-tah-lee-áh-nah) Consommé with pasta and grated Parmesan cheese.

— *al flan* (ahl flahn) Consommé royale.

— *al jerez* (ahl heh-réhs) Sherry consommé.

— *de ave* (deh áh-beh) Chicken consommé.

— *doble* (dóh-bleh) Double consommé.

— *madrileño* (mah-dree-léh-nyoh) Beef consommé garnished with diced tomatoes.

— *sencillo* (sehn-sée-yoh) Clear consommé.

*Coñac* (koh-nyáhk) Generic name for Spanish brandy.

*Coquillos* (koh-kée-yohs) Coconut cookies.

*Coquinas* (coh-kée-nahs) Cockles.

— *a la andaluza* (ah lah ahn-dah-lóo-sah) Cockles simmered in a spicy *sofrito*.

— *con tomate* (kohn toh-máh-teh) Boiled cockles sautéed with tomatoes and onions.

*Cordeiro a transmontana* (kohr-déh-ee-roh ah trahns-mohn-táh-nah) Rolled leg of lamb roasted with fresh mint (from Portugal).

*Cordero* (kohr-déh-roh) Lamb.

— *a la almendra* (ah lah ahl-méhn-drah) Lamb medallions baked in almond sauce.

— *a la menta* (ah lah méhn-tah) Roast saddle of lamb with mint sauce.

— *a la murciana* (ah lah moor-see-áh-nah) Baked leg of lamb with new potatoes, garlic, parsley, and pine nuts.

— *a la pastora* (ah lah pahs-tóh-rah) Marinated lamb stewed with rosemary, thyme, and meat stock, and thickened with flour.

— *a la riojana* (ah lah ree-oh-háh-nah) Roast leg of lamb basted with wine and dressed with its own gravy combined with garlic, meat stock, and vinegar.

— *a la sal* (ah lah sahl) Baked leg of lamb covered with a casing of coarse salt.

— *al chilindrón* (ahl chee-leen-dróhn) Diced lamb simmered in a *sofrito* with white wine, saffron, and dry red peppers.

— *asado a la manchega* (ah-sáh-doh ah lah mahn-chéh-gah) Roast lamb basted with white wine and dressed with its own gravy spiced with peppercorns and garlic.

- *a la segoviana* (ah lah seh-goh-bee-áh-nah) Baked leg of lamb dressed with thyme, garlic, and sherry.

- *a la vallisoletana* (ah lah bah-yee-soh-leh-táh-nah) Baked half baby lamb dressed with lard, parsley, and vinegar.

— *en salsa picante* (ehn sáhl-sah pee-káhn-teh) Baked leg of lamb dressed with piquant sauce.

— *en su jugo* (ehn soo hóo-goh) Roast lamb au jus.

*Cordiales* (kohr-dee-áh-lehs) Baked ground almonds mixed with egg, sugar, and grated lemon rind.

*Cortado* (kohr-táh-doh) Coffee with a touch of milk.

*Corvina* (kohr-bée-nah) Corbina.

— *a la andaluza* (ah lah ahn-dah-lóo-sah) Baked corbina dressed with a *sofrito* containing pimientos and sherry wine.

— *al vino blanco* (ahl bée-noh bláhn-koh) Baked corbina in white wine sauce.

*Costillas de cerdo* (kohs-tée-yahs deh séhr-doh) Pork ribs.

— *a la bejarana* (ah lah beh-hah-ráh-nah) Potato, green pepper, and pork rib stew.

— *con setas* (kohn séh-tahs) Fried pork ribs simmered in wine, sautéed mushrooms, and onions.

*Costrada* (kohs-tráh-dah) Bread, chorizo sausage, and sautéed vegetables soaked in chicken broth, topped with eggs, and baked.

*Crema* (kréh-mah) Cream.

— *a la catalana* (ah lah kah-tah-láh-nah) Crème brûlée with added cinnamon and lemon zest.

— *de cangrejos* (deh kahn-gréh-hohs) Cream of crayfish soup.

— *de champiñones* (deh chahm-pee-nyóh-nehs) Cream of mushroom soup.

— *de chocolate* (deh choh-koh-láh-teh) Chocolate cream.

— *de espárragos* (deh ehs-páh-rrah-gohs) Cream of asparagus soup.

— *de espinacas* (deh ehs-pee-náh-kahs) Cream of spinach soup.

— *de guisantes* (deh guee-sáhn-tehs) Cream of green pea soup.

— *de Málaga* (deh máh-lah-gah) Cream made with Malaga wine.

— *de naranja* (deh nah-ráhn-hah) Orange cream.

— *de San José* (deh sahn hoh-séh) Egg custard with cinnamon and lemon peel.

— *de tomate* (deh toh-máh-teh) Cream of tomato soup.

— *de yemas* (deh yéh-mahs) Chicken broth with heavy cream and egg yolks.

— *de zanahorias y nabos* (deh sah-nah-óh-ree-ahs ee náh-bohs) Cream of carrot and turnip soup.

— *florentina* (floh-rehn-tée-nah) Cream of spinach soup.

— *quemada* (keh-máh-dah) Crème brûlée.

— *solferino* (sohl-feh-rée-noh) Cream of potato and tomato soup.

*Cremat* (kreh-máht) Flamed hot black coffee spiked with brandy, rum, anisette, sugar, cinnamon stick, and lemon peel (from Cataluña).

*Croquetas* (kroh-kéh-tahs) Croquettes.

— *de gambas* (deh gáhm-bahs) Shrimp croquettes.

— *de jamón* (deh hah-móhn) Ham croquettes.

— *de merluza* (deh mehr-lóo-sah) Hake croquettes.

— *de pescado* (deh pehs-káh-doh) Fish croquettes.

*Cuajada de miel* (koo-ah-háh-dah deh mee-éhl) Curdled milk with honey.

## D

*Da serra* (dah séh-rrah) Ewe's-milk cheese from northern Portugal. It is creamy and of exquisite flavor.

*Dátil* (dáh-teel) Date.

*Delicias de queso* (deh-lée-see-ahs deh kéh-soh) Fried cheese balls.

*Dolmas* (dóhl-mahs) Simmered grape leaves stuffed with raisins, pine nuts, rice, mint, lemon, and parsley.

*Domecq* (doh-méhk) Bottler of brandy and sherry wines.

*Dorada* (doh-ráh-dah) Dorado.

— *al hinojo* (ahl ee-nóh-hoh) Baked dorado with fresh fennel.

— *de Alcántara* (deh ahl-káhn-tah-rah) Dorado stuffed with minced pike and baked in a red wine sauce.

— *gaditana* (gah-dee-táh-nah) Fried dorado in a spicy sherry sauce (from Cádiz).

— *a la sal* (ah lah sahl) Baked dorado covered with coarse salt.

— *al all-i-pebre* (ahl ahl-ee-péh-breh) Dorado baked in a garlic sauce with saffron, almonds, and parsley.

*Dulce de membrillo* (dóol-seh deh mehm-brée-yoh) Quince jelly.

VOCABULARY

# E

*Empanada* (ehm-pah-náh-dah) Pie.
— *asturiana* (ahs-too-ree-áh-nah) Chorizo pie from Asturias
— *berciana* (behr-see-áh-nah) Pork loin and chorizo pie (from León).
— *de berberechos* (deh behr-beh-réh-chohs) Cockle pie (from Galicia).
— *de espinacas* (deh ehs-pee-náh-kahs) Spinach pie.
— *de lamprea* (deh lahm-préh-ah) Lamprey fish pie.
— *de lomo* (deh lóh-moh) Pork loin pie.
— *de sardinas* (deh sahr-dée-nahs) Sardine pie.
— *gallega* (gah-yéh-gah) Marinated pork loin pie (from Galicia).
— *mallorquina* (mah-yohr-kée-nah) Lamb meat pie (from the Balearic Islands).
*Empanadilla* (ehm-pah-nah-dée-yah) Small pie.
— *de atún* (deh ah-tóon) Small canned tuna fish pie.
— *de carne* (deh káhr-neh) Small meat pie.
— *de chorizo* (deh choh-rée-soh) Small chorizo sausage pie.
— *de jamón* (deh hah-móhn) Small prosciutto ham pie.
*Endibia* (ehn-dée-bee-ah) Endive.
— *a la sartén* (ah lah sahr-téhn) Belgian endive simmered in milk with cured ham, onion, and parsley.
— *al roquefort* (ahl roh-keh-fóhrt) Endive with Roquefort cheese.
*Enebrina* (eh-neh-brée-nah) Juniper berry.
*Eneldo* (eh-néhl-doh) Dill.

*en escabeche* (ehn ehs-kah-béh-cheh) Pickled.
*Ensaimada* (ehn-sah-ee-máh-dah) Fluffy sweet roll (from Majorca).
— *de Tudela* (deh too-déh-lah) Sweet roll flavored with aniseed.
*Ensalada* (ehn-sah-láh-dah) Salad.
— *almoraina* (ahl-moh-ráh-ee-nah) Endive lettuce dressed with a pasty blend made with tomato, garlic, cumin, oil and vinegar, and black olives.
— *andaluza* (ahn-dah-lóo-sah) Blanched tomatoes and green peppers dressed with vinaigrette containing chopped hard-boiled egg.
— *bicolor* (bee-coh-lóhr) Chopped romaine, Belgian endive, red cabbage, red onion, and radishes dressed with oil and vinegar.
— *Bohemia* (boh-éh-mee-ah) Romaine lettuce with string beans, ham, and truffles folded in mayonnaise.
— *catalana* (kah-tah-láh-nah) Layered salad containing boiled potatoes, onion, peppers, olives, and canned tuna dressed with vinaigrette and garnished with hard-boiled egg.
— *césar* (séh-sahr) Caesar salad.
— *de abadejo* (deh ah-bah-deh-hoh) Poached codfish salad dressed with mustard, capers, parsley, and salt.
— *de achicoria* (deh ah-chee-kóh-ree-ah) Chicory salad.
— *de aguacate* (deh ah-goo-ah-káh-teh) Avocado salad.
- *y gambas* (ee gáhm-bahs) Avocado and shrimp salad.
— *de alcachofas* (deh ahl-kah-

chóh-fahs) Artichoke heart salad.
— *de apio* (deh áh-pee-oh) Celery salad.
— *de arroz* (deh ah-rróhs) Rice salad.
- *a la tártara* (ah lah táhr-tah-rah) Cold boiled rice combined with a mixture of cured ham, gherkins, and parsley folded in a mayonnaise/mustard sauce.
- *con frutas* (kohn fróo-tahs) Rice salad with fresh fruit.
- *marroquí* (mah-rroh-kée) Cooked browned rice mixed with banana, orange, and dates dressed with a blend of honey, oil, and pepper.
- *y anchoas* (ee ahn-chóh-ahs) Rice salad with anchovies.
— *de atún* (deh ah-tóon) Canned tuna salad.
— *de bayas* (deh báh-yahs) Mixed berry salad with pine nuts.
— *de berros* (deh béh-rrohs) Watercress salad.
— *de brécol* (deh bréh-kohl) Broccoli salad.
— *de calabacín* (deh kah-lah-bah-séen) Zucchini salad.
— *de champiñones* (deh chahm-pee-nyóh-nehs) Mushroom salad.
— *de col* (deh kohl) Cabbage salad.
— *de coles de Bruselas* (deh kóh-lehs deh broo-séh-lahs) Brussels sprouts salad.
— *de endibias y cítricos* (deh ehn-dée-bee-ahs ee sée-tree-kohs) Belgian endive salad with citrus fruit.
— *de espárragos* (deh ehs-páh-rrah-gohs) Asparagus salad.
— *de espinacas* (deh ehs-pee-náh-kahs) Spinach salad.
— *de fruta* (deh fróo-tah) Fruit salad.
- *a la madrileña* (ah lah mah-dree-léh-nyah) Fruit salad flavored with sweet sherry and rum.
— *de gambas y patatas* (deh gáhm-bahs ee pah-tah-tahs) Cooked shrimp and potato salad.
— *de garbanzos* (deh gahr-báhn-sohs) Chickpea salad.
— *de granada* (deh grah-náh-dah) Pomegranate salad.
— *de habas tiernas* (deh áh-bahs tee-éhr-nahs) Fresh fava bean salad.
— *de huevo* (deh oo-éh-boh) Hard-boiled egg salad.
— *de judías blancas* (deh hoo-dée-ahs bláhn-kahs) Navy bean salad.
— *de langosta* (deh lahn-góhs-tah) Lobster salad.
— *de lengua* (deh léhn-goo-ah) Cooked veal tongue salad.
— *de lentejas* (deh lehn-téh-hahs) Lentil salad.
— *de lombarda* (deh lohm-báhr-dah) Red cabbage salad.
— *de mango* (deh máhn-goh) Mango salad.
— *de manzana* (deh mahn-sáh-nah) Apple salad.
— *de mariscos* (deh mah-rées-kohs) Seafood salad.
— *de melocotones* (deh meh-loh-koh-tóh-nehs) Fresh peach salad.
— *de melón* (deh meh-lóhn) Melon salad.
— *de naranjas* (deh nah-ráhn-hahs) Orange salad.
— *de ostras* (deh óhs-trahs) Oyster salad.

VOCABULARY

— *de peras* (deh péh-rahs) Pear salad.

— *de pimiento y tomate* (deh pee-mee-éhn-toh ee toh-máh-teh) Roasted sweet pepper and tomato salad.

— *de plátanos* (deh pláh-tah-nohs) Banana salad.

— *de pollo* (deh póh-yoh) Chicken salad.

— *de puerros* (deh poo-éh-rrohs) Boiled leeks dressed with vinaigrette sauce.

— *de rape* (deh ráh-peh) Poached anglerfish salad.

— *de remolacha* (deh reh-moh-láh-chah) Beet salad.

— *de repollo* (deh reh-póh-yoh) Green cabbage salad.

— *de requesón* (deh reh-keh-sóhn) Cottage cheese salad.

— *de San Isidro* (deh sahn ee-sée-droh) Romaine lettuce, onion, tomato, and olives combined with canned tuna and dressed with vinaigrette.

— *de tomate y huevo* (deh toh-máh-teh ee oo-éh-boh) Tomato and hard-boiled egg salad.

— *de tomate y pepino* (deh toh-máh-teh ee peh-pée-noh) Tomato and cucumber salad.

— *de verduras* (deh behr-dóo-rahs) Vegetable salad.

— *koskera* (kohsh-kéh-rah) Shredded boiled hake and lobster medallion mixed with pimiento and olives and dressed with vinaigrette.

— *Lidia* (lée-dee-ah) Diced boiled potatoes, fruits, and walnuts dressed with a creamy mustard vinaigrette.

— *lirio del valle* (lée-ree-oh dehl báh-yeh) Celery, apple, tomato, and walnuts folded in a light mayonnaise.

— *mallorquina* (mah-yohr-kée-nah) Tomatoes sprinkled with fresh oregano and marjoram dressed with a garlicky vinaigrette.

— *manchega* (mahn-chéh-gah) De-salted salt-cod and canned tuna combined with tomatoes, onions, and olives, dressed with vinaigrette.

— *murciana* (moor-see-áh-nah) Escarole lettuce and tomatoes dressed with paprika vinaigrette.

— *piperada* (pee-peh-ráh-dah) Sweet pepper, cucumber, and tomato salad dressed with vinaigrette.

— *Raquel Méller* (rah-kéhl méh-yehr) Cucumber and tomato salad garnished with smoked herring and dressed with a vinaigrette with mustard.

— *sevillana* (seh-bee-yáh-nah) Boiled rice, pimientos, tomatoes, scallions, and green olives with vinaigrette.

— *Triana* (tree-áh-nah) Escarole lettuce, tomato, onion, and green olives dressed with vinaigrette.

— *tropical* (troh-pee-káhl) Mixed salad containing tropical fruits.

— *valenciana* (bah-lehn-see-áh-nah) Boiled potatoes and sliced oranges with onion and pimiento dressed with vinaigrette.

**Ensaladilla rusa** (ehn-sah-lah-dée-yah róo-sah) Potato, vegetable, and mayonnaise salad.

*En salmuera* (ehn sahl-moo-éh-rah) Cured in brine.

*Ensopado de borrego* (ehn-soh-páh-doh deh boh-rréh-goh) Lamb stewed with potatoes (from Portugal)

*En su tinta* (ehn soo téen-tah) Cooked in its own ink.

*Entrecote a la bordelesa* (ehn-treh-kóh-teh ah lah bohr-deh-léh-sah) Grilled beefsteak dressed with red wine sauce containing shallots and veal marrow.

— *a la mayordoma* (ah lah mah-yohr-dóh-mah) Grilled beefsteak with maître d'hôtel butter.

*Entremeses* (ehn-treh-méh-sehs) Appetizers.

— *variados* (bah-ree-áh-dohs) Selection of cold appetizers.

*En vinagre* (ehn bee-náh-greh) In vinegar.

*En vinagreta* (ehn bee-nah-gréh-tah) Dressed with vinaigrette sauce.

*Escabeche de bonito* (ehs-kah-béh-cheh deh boh-née-toh) Pickled striped tuna fish.

*Escalivada a la catalana* (ehs-kah-lee-báh-dah ah lah kah-tah-láh-nah) Baked eggplant, fennel, peppers, and onions dressed with olive oil and garnished with anchovy fillets.

*Escalope* (ehs-kah-lóh-peh) Escalope.

— *de ternera a la catalana* (deh tehr-néh-rah ah lah kah-tah-láh-nah) Fried veal escalope dressed with a sauce containing white wine and hazelnuts.

— *de ternera a la madrileña* (deh tehr-néh-rah ah lah mah-dree-leh-nyah) Fried breaded veal escalope garnished with sautéed onion and tomato sauce.

*Escalopines al limón* (ehs-kah-loh-pée-nehs ahl lee-móhn) Veal scallopini with lemon sauce.

*Escarapuche* (ehs-kah-rah-póo-cheh) Cold sautéed trout combined with chopped onion and tomato and dressed with vinegar and lemon juice.

*Escarola* (ehs-kah-róh-lah) Endive.

*Escudella a la catalana* (ehs-koo-déh-yah ah lah kah-tah-láh-nah) Cabbage, potato, and rice casserole with bacon and pasta (from Cataluña).

*Esgarrat* (ehs-gah-rráht) Sweet red pepper and shredded salt-cod salad (from the Levant).

*Espaguetis* (ehs-pah-guéh-tees) Spaghetti.

— *con almejas* (kohn ahl-méh-hahs) Spaghetti with a *sofrito* containing clams.

*Espalda* (ehs-páhl-dah) Shoulder.

— *de cordero con nabos* (deh kohr-déh-roh kohn náh-bohs) Lamb shoulder casserole with turnips.

— *de cordero rellena* (deh kohr-déh-roh reh-yéh-nah) Roast stuffed shoulder of lamb.

*Españoletas* (ehs-pah-nyoh-léh-tahs) Small brioches.

*Espárragos* (ehs-páh-rrah-gohs) Asparagus.

— *a la andaluza* (ah lah ahn-dah-lóo-sah) Simmered asparagus dressed with a blend of garlic, fried bread, paprika, and vinegar, garnished with fried croutons.

— *a la manchega* (ah lah mahn-chéh-gah) Boiled asparagus with

*Espárragos a la manchega* (cont.) a sauce made with egg yolk, cumin, and seasonings.

— *a la navarra* (ah lah nah-báh-rrah) Boiled asparagus and sautéed ham garnished with whole eggs and simmered until the eggs are set.

— *a la sevillana* (ah lah seh-bee-yáh-nah) Boiled asparagus dressed with crushed sautéed garlic and bread and garnished with hard-boiled egg.

— *Bella Elena* (béh-yah eh-léh-nah) Boiled asparagus combined with thin slices of pancake and napped with béchamel sauce.

— *con mayonesa* (kohn mah-yoh-néh-sah) Asparagus mayonnaise.

— *mimosa* (mee-móh-sah) Cooked asparagus dressed with vinaigrette, garnished with a julienne of hard-boiled egg whites, and sprinkled with the chopped yolks.

— *salteados* (sahl-teh-áh-dohs) Sautéed asparagus.

*Espetones de sardinas* (ehs-peh-tóh-nehs deh sahr-dée-nahs) Grilled sardines on a skewer.

*Espinacas* (ehs-pee-náh-kahs) Spinach.

— *a la cordobesa* (ah lah kohr-doh-béh-sah) Boiled spinach sautéed with onion, garlic, vinegar, paprika, and cinnamon.

— *a la española* (ah lah ehs-pah-nyóh-lah) Sautéed boiled spinach in olive oil and garlic.

— *al Sacromonte* (sah-kroh-móhn-teh) Boiled spinach sautéed in olive oil with almonds, garlic, vinegar, bread, and saffron (from Granada).

— *con garbanzos* (kohn gahr-báhn-sohs) Spinach and chickpea casserole.

— *con pasas y piñones* (kohn páh-sahs ee pee-nyóh-nehs) Boiled spinach sautéed with raisins and pine nuts.

*Espuma de foie-gras* (ehs-póo-mah deh foo-ah-gráh) Foie gras mousse.

*Espumoso* (ehs-poo-móh-soh) Sparkling.

*Estofado* (ehs-toh-fáh-doh) Stew.

— *a la catalana* (ah lah kah-tah-láh-nah) Beef stew with red wine, bouquet garni, new potatoes, and garlic sausage.

— *de cordero andaluza* (deh kohr-déh-roh ahn-dah-lóo-sah) Lamb stew in a flour-thickened broth with a *majado* of garlic and fresh mint.

— *de ternera* (deh tehr-néh-rah) Veal stew.

— *de toro* (deh tóh-roh) Bull meat stew.

— *de vaca aragonesa* (deh báh-kah ah-rah-goh-néh-sah) Diced beef stewed in white wine with a *sofrito* containing thyme.

— *montañesa* (mohn-tah-nyéh-sah) Cubed beef stew flavored with cocoa.

*Estragón* (ehs-trah-góhn) Tarragon.

*Expreso* (ehks-préh-soh) Espresso coffee.

*Extremadura* (eks-treh-mah-dóo-rah) Region in western Spain, bordering with Portugal. Game dishes are particularly well-prepared in this area, especially pheasant and hare.

# F

**Fabada asturiana** (fah-báh-dah ahs-too-ree-áh-nah) Dry bean stew with pig's feet, brisket of beef, chorizo, morcilla, and paprika sausage.

**Faisán** (fah-ee-sáhn) Pheasant.

— **a las uvas** (ah lahs óo-bahs) Pot-roasted pheasant with grapes.

— **con salsa de pan** (kohn sáhl-sah deh pahn) Roast phesant dressed with a sauce made of bread, milk, whipping cream, minced onion, and cayenne pepper.

— **de alcántara** (deh ahl-káhn-tah-rah) Roast pheasant in port wine with truffles.

— **en cocotte** (ehn koh-kóht) Stuffed pheasant with marrons glacés and truffles, *en cocotte*, with wine, brandy, and mushrooms.

**Faisao con Madeira** (fah-ee-sáh-oh kohn mah-déh-ee-rah) Roast pheasant with Madeira sauce (from Portugal).

**Farinatos** (fah-ree-náh-tohs) Bread-and-pork-fat sausage.

**Fariñes** (fah-rée-nyehs) Cornmeal mush with honey (from Galicia).

**Faves** (fah-behs) Fava beans, in Portuguese.

— **a portuguesa** (fáh-behs ah pohr-too-gueh-sah) Fava beans with bacon, onion, and garlic cooked in a small amount of meat broth until tender.

**Federico Paternina** (feh-deh-rée-koh pah-tehr-née-nah) Vintage wine from Rioja.

**Fiambre de atún** (fee-áhm-breh deh ah-tóon) Tuna fish galantine.

— **de ternera** (deh tehr-néh-rah) Veal galantine.

**Fideos** (fee-déh-ohs) Thin spaghetti.

— **a la cazuela** (ah lah kah-soo-éh-lah) Thin spaghetti casserole garnished with pork ribs and sausages.

— **al ajo** (ahl áh-hoh) Thin spaghetti with fried garlic and hot red peppers in olive oil, topped with Parmesan.

— **al ajoaceite** (ahl ah-hoh-ah-séh-ee-teh) Thin spaghetti with a blend of olive oil, garlic, and egg yolk.

— **campesinos** (kahm-peh-sée-nohs) Thin spaghetti with a *sofrito* containing tomato, zucchini, garlic, black olives, and parsley.

— **con almejas** (kohn ahl-méh-hahs) Thin spaghetti in a soupy stew made with fish stock and clams.

— **con moluscos** (kohn moh-lóos-kohs) Thin spaghetti in a white sauce with clams and mussels.

**Fideua de mariscos** (fee-deh-oo-áh deh mah-rées-kohs) Thin spaghetti cooked in a *sofrito* containing seafood and saffron (from Cataluña).

**Filete** (fee-léh-teh) Fillet, cutlet.

— **a caballo** (ah kah-báh-yoh) Fried veal cutlet garnished with one fried egg on a slice of french bread.

— **de ternera empanado** (deh tehr-néh-rah ehm-pah-náh-doh) Breaded veal cutlet.

— **de vaca con crema de anchoas** (deh báh-kah kohn kréh-mah deh ahn-chóh-ahs) Grilled beef fillet garnished with anchovy butter.

— **mechado con jamón** (meh-cháh-doh kohn hah-móhn)

*Filete mechado con jamón* (cont.) Roasted beef fillet larded with prosciutto ham.

— *de cerdo con queso* (deh séhr-doh kohn kéh-soh) Fried breaded pork fillets stuffed with cheese.

*Filloas* (fee-yóh-ahs) Egg pancakes (from Galicia).

*Fino* (fée-noh) Very dry sherry served chilled as an aperitif.

*Flamenquines* (flah-mehn-kée-nehs) Deep-fried pork and ham rolls.

*Flan* (flahn) Caramel custard served as a truncated cone.

— *de mariscos* (deh mah-rées-kohs) Seafood timbale.

— *de naranja* (deh nah-ráhn-hah) Caramel custard with orange juice.

*Flao* (fláh-oh) Fresh cheese torte.

*Fondos de alcachofa a la gitana* (fóhn-dohs deh ahl-kah-chóh-fah ah lah hee-táh-nah) Boiled artichoke bottoms sautéed with garlic and green pepper and dressed with a vinaigrette sauce containing tarragon.

*Frambuesas* (frahm-boo-éh-sahs) Raspberries.

*Frango* (fráhn-goh) Chicken in Portuguese.

— *a portuguesa* (ah pohr-too-guéh-sah) Chicken simmered in wine garnished with fried eggs and boiled rice (from Portugal).

— *com arroz* (cohm ah-rróhs) Chicken with rice (from Portugal).

— *na pucara* (nah póo-kah-rah) Chicken in the pot (from Portugal).

*Fresas* (fréh-sahs) Strawberries.

— *al vino tinto* (ahl bée-noh téen-toh) Macerated strawberries in red wine, cinnamon, sugar, clove, and lemon rind.

— *con anís* (kohn ah-nées) Strawberries with anise liquor.

*Fresón* (freh-sóhn) Large strawberry.

*Fresones con nata* (freh-sóh-nehs kohn náh-tah) Large strawberries with whipped cream.

*Fritada de tomates y pimientos* (free-táh-dah deh toh-máh-tehs ee pee-mee-éhn-tohs) Simmered tomatoes, sweet peppers, and onions in olive oil.

*Frito huertano* (frée-toh oo-ehr-táh-noh) Sautéed onion, eggplant, sweet pepper, tomato, and paprika, thickened with a touch of flour (from Murcia).

— *de berenjena* (deh beh-rehn-héh-nah) Deep-fried battered eggplant and salami slices.

— *de patata* (deh pah-táh-tah) Potato fritters.

*Fritura de pescado* (free-tóo-rah deh pehs-káh-doh) Fish fritter.

— *malagueña* (mah-lah-guéh-nyah) Deep-fried battered mixed fish.

## G

*Gachas* (gáh-chahs) Gruel.

— *gaditanas* (gah-dee-táh-nahs) Flour gruel with milk and anise seed (from Andalusia).

— *malagueñas* (mah-lah-guéh-nyahs) Flour gruel with potatoes and garlic (from Andalusia).

— *manchegas* (mahn-chéh-gahs) Wheat-flour gruel garnished with sautéed pork liver, bacon, potato, and chorizo (from La Mancha).

*Galicia* (gah-lée-see-ah) A maritime region in northwestern Spain, north of Portugal. Galicia's cuisine is famous for its seafood dishes and for its Celtic influence.

*Galletas* (gah-yéh-tahs) Biscuits.

*Gallina* (gah-yée-nah) Hen.

— *a la cubana* (ah lah coo-báh-nah) Poached hen in broth simmered in chicken stock with roux, egg yolk, and whipping cream.

— *a la gallega* (ah lah gah-yéh-gah) Fried chicken simmered in wine, with bouquet garni, noodles and a *sofrito* with saffron and nutmeg.

— *a la granadina* (ah lah grah-nah-dée-nah) Hen simmered in white wine, sautéed onion, and parsley, garnished with sautéed yams and bananas.

— *a la italiana* (ah la ee-tah-lee-áh-nah) Boiled hen simmered in a sauce made of onion, garlic, mushrooms, and wine.

— *al estragón* (ahl ehs-trah-góhn) Hen in tarragon sauce.

— *dorada* (doh-ráh-dah) Baked hen basted with a mixture of meat broth and sherry wine.

— *en aceite* (ehn ah-seh-ée-teh) Hen sautéed with garlic and parsley simmered in white wine, broth and thyme with a *majado* made of olive oil, almonds, and the yolk of a hard-boiled egg.

— *en pepitoria* (ehn peh-pee-tóh-ree-ah) Hen braised in chicken stock with dry sherry and a sauce made with crushed toasted almonds, fried bread, garlic, nut-

meg, and cloves.

— *en salsa* (ehn sáhl-sah) Hen simmered in a liquid made of broth, wine, vinegar, crushed tomato, and cinnamon.

*Gambas* (gáhm-bahs) Shrimp.

— *al ajillo* (ahl ah-hée-yoh) Shrimp sautéed with garlic.

— *a la plancha* (ah lah pláhn-chah) Broiled shrimp.

— *al pil-pil* (ahl peel-péel) Shrimp sautéed with hot chilis.

— *con gabardina* (kohn gah-bahr-dée-nah) Batter-fried shrimp.

— *en piperada* (ehn pee-peh-ráh-dah) Oil-simmered shrimp with tomatoes, sweet peppers, and spices.

— *Villeroy* (beel-roo-áh) bécha-mel-coated deep-fried shrimp.

*Gamonedo* (gah-moh-néh-doh) Blue-veined cheese from Asturias. It is semi-hard and milder in taste than Cabrales.

*Garbanzos* (gahr-báhn-sohs) Chick-peas.

— *a la catalana* (ah lah kah-tah-láh-nah) Chickpeas stewed with a *sofrito* containing *butifarra* sausage and garnished with chopped hard-boiled egg.

— *andaluza* (ahn-dah-lóo-sah) Chickpea casserole with beef tripe, chorizo sausage, and a *sofrito* with crushed almonds.

— *con huevos duros* (kohn oo-éh-bohs dóo-rohs) Chickpea stew with a *sofrito* containing cured ham and chorizo and a *majado* with hazelnuts and clove and garnished with hard-boiled eggs.

— *con tomate* (kohn toh-máh-teh) Chickpea casserole with a *sofrito*,

*Garbanzos con tomate* (cont.) additional fried tomato, and paprika and garnished with fried croutons.

— *refritos* (reh-frée-tohs) Chickpeas leftover from a previous stew sautéed with chorizo and pimiento.

*Garnacha* (gahr-náh-chah) Type of wine-grape.

*Gaseosa* (gah-seh-óh-sah) Sweetened bubbly water.

*Gastaika* (gahs-táh-ee-kah) Poached ray dressed with a sauce made of oil, vinegar, and hot chili peppers.

*Gazpacho* (gahs-páh-choh) Cold soup from Andalusia of blended salad vegetables (no lettuce) with oil, vinegar, and garlic.

— *alentejano* (ah-lehn-teh-háh-noh) Portuguese gazpacho containing a larger amount of bread than its Spanish counterpart.

— *extremeño* (ehks-treh-méh-nyoh) Thick gazpacho with vegetable broth (from Extremadura).

— *gaditano* (gah-dee-táh-noh) Hot gazpacho from Cádiz.

— *rojo sevillano* (róh-hoh seh-bee-yáh-noh) Gazpacho made with ripe tomatoes, sherry, and cayenne pepper.

*Gazpachuelo* (gahs-pah-choo-éh-loh) Hot fish gazpacho made with clam juice, fish, and potatoes and folded with mayonnaise.

*Gorbea* (gohr-béh-ah) Semi-hard cheese from the Basque Country. It is made of ewe's-milk and is creamy and yellowish in color.

*Granada* (grah-náh-dah) Pomegranate.

*Granadinas* (grah-nah-dée-nahs)

Ground almonds, lard, and sugar cookies.

— *de ternera a la vasca* (deh tehr-néh-rah ah lah báhs-kah) Veal grenadins simmered in the oven with a *sofrito* containing white wine, veal tongue julienne, and bouquet garni.

*Granizado* (grah-nee-sáh-doh) Iced drink.

— *de café* (deh kah-féh) Iced coffee drink.

— *de limón* (deh lee-móhn) Iced lemon drink.

*Gran reserva* (grahn reh-séhr-bah) Aged wine of guaranteed quality.

*Grazalema* (gra-sah-léh-mah) Cheese made from ewe's milk and molded in esparto grass bands; it is often cured in olive oil (from Andalusia).

*Greixonera de patas de cerdo* (greh-eek-soh-néh-rah deh páh-tahs deh séhr-doh) Baked pig's feet casserole.

*Grelos* (gréh-lohs) Spring greens, in Galicia.

— *salteados* (sahl-teh-áh-dohs) Spring greens sautéed in olive oil with garlic.

*Grosellas* (groh-séh-yahs) Red currant.

— *silvestres* (seel-béhs-trehs) Gooseberries.

*Guiberludiños* (guee-behr-loo-dée-nyohs) Sautéed wild mushrooms dressed with bread crumbs, garlic, and parsley.

*Guindas* (guéen-dahs) Cherries.

*Guindilla* (gueen-dée-yah) Hot chili pepper.

*Guisado de ternera* (guee-sáh-doh deh tehr-neh-rah) Veal ragout with white wine, bouquet garni, and nutmeg.

***Guisado de vaca al estilo de Vigo*** (guee-sáh-doh deh báh-kah ahl ehs-tée-loh deh bée-goh) Beef stew with white wine, nutmeg, and clove.

***Guisantes*** (guee-sáhn-tehs) Green peas.

— ***a la escocesa*** (ah lah ehs-koh-séh-sah) Boiled green peas with diced ham and chopped lettuce thickened with beurre manié.

— ***a la española*** (ah lah ehs-pah-nyóh-lah) Braised green peas with onions and cured ham, garnished with fresh mint.

— ***a la maña*** (ah lah máh-nyah) Green peas fried in bacon fat with diced cured ham (from Aragón).

— ***a la murciana*** (ah lah moor-see-áh-nah) Simmered sweet peas in a *sofrito* containing cured ham, chorizo slices, paprika, and a touch of flour garnished with quartered hard-boiled eggs.

— ***con lechuga*** (kohn leh-chóo-gah) Boiled green peas and lettuce sautéed with diced cured ham, garlic, and nutmeg.

— ***con salchichas*** (kohn sahl-chée-chahs) Green peas sautéed with Italian-style sausage in a tomato and onion sauce.

— ***levantina*** (leh-bahn-tée-nah) Green peas simmered in a liquid containing water, wine, sautéed onion, and garlic and garnished with pimiento strips.

***Guiso de albondigas de bacalao*** (guée-soh deh ahl-bóhn-dee-gahs deh bah-kah-láh-oh) Artichoke and green pea stew with salt-cod dumplings.

— ***de calamares y patatas*** (deh kah-lah-máh-rehs ee pah-táh-tahs) Potatoes stewed with squid.

— ***de cordero*** (deh kohr-déh-roh) Lamb stew with *sofrito* and a *majado* with garlic, parsley, and sherry wine.

— ***de gurullos con hierbabuena*** (deh goo-róo-yohs kohn ee-ehr-bah-boo-éh-nah) Chickpea stew with *sofrito*, small pieces of flour dough, and fresh mint (from Murcia).

— ***de menudos de cerdo*** (deh meh-nóo-dohs deh séhr-doh) Pork tripe casserole.

— ***de patatas*** (deh pah-táh-tahs) Fried sliced potatoes and boiled green peas with a *sofrito* containing fresh sausage stewed in meat broth and garnished with hard-boiled eggs.

— ***de pulpo con patatas*** (deh póol-poh kohn pah-táh-tahs) Octopus stew with potatoes, *sofrito*, and paprika (from Galicia).

— ***de sangre de cerdo*** (deh sáhn-greh deh séhr-doh) Pig's blood stew with a *sofrito* with paprika.

— ***de trigo*** (deh trée-goh) Stewed wheat with pig's feet, chickpeas, turnips, and a *sofrito* with paprika.

— ***de vaca al coñac*** (deh báh-kah ahl koh-nyáhk) Beef stew with brandy, cream, and paprika.

# H

***Habas*** (áh-bahs) Fava beans.

— ***a la andaluza*** (ah lah ahn-dah-lóo-sah) Sautéed fava beans and artichokes with tomato, onion, and cumin.

— *a la asturiana* (ah lah ahs-too-ree-áh- nah) Fava beans simmered in meat broth and white wine with potatoes, ham, onions, and carrots.

— *a la catalana* (ah lah kah-tah-láh-nah) Fava beans, onion, garlic, and tomato simmered in wine and brandy with chopped chorizo and herbs.

— *a la rondeña* (ah lah rohn-déh-nyah) Fava beans sautéed with cured ham, hard-boiled egg, and parsley.

— *con jamón* (kohn hah-móhn) Sautéed fava beans with cured ham.

— *con mejillones* (kohn meh-hee-yóh-nehs) Sautéed fava beans with mussels.

— *huertanas* (oo-ehr-táh-nahs) Fava beans sautéed with diced cured ham and morcilla sausage (from Murcia).

— *secas con rabo* (séh-kahs kohn ráh-boh) Stew of dried fava beans with oxtail.

*Habichuelas verdes* (ah-bee-choo-éh-lahs béhr-dehs) Green beans.

— *a la sevillana* (ah lah seh-bee-yáh-nah) Boiled green beans dressed with melted lard and vinegar.

*Helado* (eh-láh-doh) Ice cream.

— *de fresa* (deh fréh-sah) Strawberry ice cream.

*Hervido* (ehr-bée-doh) Potatoes and assorted vegetables boiled in water with lemon juice, olive oil, and a touch of paprika.

*Hígado* (ée-gah-doh) Liver.

— *de ternera con lechuga* (deh tehr-néh-rah kohn leh-chóo-gah) Fried veal liver garnished with shredded romaine lettuce and dressed with oil and vinegar.

— *encebollado* (ehn-seh-boh-yáh-doh) Sautéed veal liver and onions.

*Higos* (ée-gohs) Figs.

*Hinojo* (ee-nóh-hoh) Fennel.

*Hojaldrados de chorizo* (oh-hahl-dráh-dohs deh choh-rée-zoh) Chorizo sausage in puff pastry.

*Hojaldre* (oh-háhl-dreh) Puff pastry.

*Horchata de almendras* (ohr-cháh-tah deh ahl-méhn-drahs) Iced drink made with crushed almonds, water, sugar, and shaved ice.

*Horchata de chufa* (ohr-cháh-tah deh chóo-fah) Iced drink made with crushed sedge roots, sugar, cinnamon, and shaved ice.

*Hornazo* (ohr-náh-soh) Bread studded with chorizo, morcilla sausages, and hard-boiled eggs (in Castile); Pork, partridge, and chorizo pie (in Leon).

*Huelva* (oo-éhl-bah) Semi-hard goat's-milk cheese with a very strong flavor from the province of Huelva.

*Hueso* (oo-éh-soh) Bone.

— *de santo* (deh sáhn-toh) Marzipan paste rolls filled with candied egg yolks.

*Huevas de pescado* (oo-éh-bahs deh pehs-káh-doh) Cured fish roe.

*Huevos* (oo-éh-bohs) Eggs.

— *a la alicantina* (ah lah ah-lee-kahn-tée-nah) Potato barquettes filled with tomato puree and chopped prawns, topped with poached eggs, and napped with white sauce.

— *a la andaluza* (ah lah ahn-dah-lóo-sah) Fried eggs garnished with fried chorizo sausage and potatoes.

— *a la castellana* (ah lah kahs-teh-yáh-nah) Eggs *en cocotte* with sautéed onion and minced meat and covered with béchamel sauce.

— *a la cordobesa* (ah lah kohr-doh-béh-sah) Fried eggs garnished with sliced fried potatoes, pimiento, and sautéed chorizo.

— *a la cubana* (ah lah koo-báh-nah) Fried eggs garnished with boiled rice, fried tomato puree, and bananas.

— *a la flamenca* (ah lah flah-méhn-kah) Shirred eggs with ham, chorizo, asparagus tips, and green peas.

— *a la madrileña* (ah lah mah-dree-léh-nyah) Shirred eggs with sautéed tomato and breakfast sausage.

— *a la navarra* (ah lah nah-báh-rrah) Shirred eggs with tomato sauce, chorizo, and grated cheese.

— *a la romana* (ah lah roh-máh-nah) Shirred eggs over a bed of sautéed spinach, grated cheese, and anchovies dressed with Mornay sauce.

— *a la roncalesa* (ah lah rohn-kah-léh-sah) Baked eggs with Italian-style sausage and crumbled fried bread (from Navarra).

— *a la rusa* (ah lah róo-sah) Poached eggs on a bed of lettuce, cured ham, tomato, and diced cheese dressed with mustard sauce.

— *a la sevillana* (ah lah seh-bee-yáh-nah) Fried eggs garnished with fried cured ham, potatoes, and artichokes.

— *a la turca* (ah lah tóor-kah) Shirred eggs with chicken livers sautéed in sherry wine.

— *al estilo de Sóller* (ahl ehs-tée-loh deh soh-yehr) Fried eggs on ham dressed with a sauce made with vegetables, milk, and white wine (from the island of Majorca).

— *al plato* (ahl pláh-toh) Shirred eggs.

- *al curry* (ahl kóo-rree) Shirred eggs with lamb in a curried béchamel.

- *chiclanera* (chee-klah-néh-rah) Shirred eggs over a bed of fried garlic, almonds, and bread flavored with saffron, cumin, and cinnamon.

— *al queso azul* (ahl kéh-soh ah-sóol) Hard-boiled eggs dressed with blue cheese sauce.

— *Aurora* (ah-oo-róh-rah) Hard-boiled eggs with a béchamel sauce containing tomato puree.

— *Bella Otero* (béh-yah oh-téh-roh) Potato barquettes filled with béchamel sauce topped with soft-cooked eggs napped with the same béchamel.

— *Chiclanera* (chee-klah-néh-rah) Poached eggs over a layer of *sofrito* containing chopped ham and chorizo, napped with béchamel sauce and browned in the oven.

— *con champiñones* (kohn chahm-pee-nyóh-nehs) Shirred eggs with sautéed minced mushrooms.

— *cuajados* (koo-ah-háh-dohs) Soft-cooked eggs.

- *con espinacas* (kohn ehs-peenáh-kahs) Soft-cooked eggs over a bed of fried spinach with garlic, vinegar, and paprika.

- *con jamón* (kohn hah-móhn) Soft-cooked eggs over a slice of cured ham.

- *con tomate* (kohn toh-máh-teh) Soft-cooked eggs over tomato sauce.

- *Giralda* (hee-ráhl-dah) Soft-cooked eggs over a bed of rice mixed with chicken livers and ham, flavored with saffron (from Seville).

- *sevillana* (seh-bee-yáh-nah) Soft-cooked eggs over a bed of minced prawns, pimiento, and green peas.

— *duros* (dóo-rohs) Hard-boiled eggs.

— *empanados* (ehm-pah-náhdohs) Poached eggs covered with bread crumbs, dipped into eggwash, breaded again, then fried until golden.

— *en cama* (ehn káh-mah) Baked eggs on a bed of mashed potatoes with tomato sauce.

— *en camisa* (ehn kah-mée-sah) Baked egg yolks covered with their beaten whites and sprinkled with grated cheese.

— *en cocotera* (ehn koh-koh-téhrah) Eggs *en cocotte*.

- *con higadillos* (kohn ee-gahdée-yohs) Eggs *en cocotte* with chicken livers.

— *en salsa agria* (ehn sáhl-sah áhgree-ah) Hard-boiled eggs simmered in a sweet-sour sauce.

— *en sorpresa* (ehn sohr-préhsah) Shirred eggs with chicken livers, mushrooms, and bread crumbs.

— *escalfados* (ehs-kahl-fáh-dohs) Poached eggs.

- *a la española* (ah lah ehs-pahnyóh-lah) Poached eggs garnished with *sofrito*.

- *americana* (ah-meh-ree-káhnah) Poached eggs over a bed of rice combined with a shellfish fumet containing wine and brandy.

- *Aranjuez* (ah-rahn-hoo-éhs) Au gratin poached eggs napped with Mornay sauce garnished with asparagus.

- *Bohemia* (boh-éh-mee-ah) Foie gras-stuffed tartlettes topped with a poached egg dressed with wine sauce and baked in the oven.

- *Clamart* (clah-máhrt) Poached egg on a crouton garnished with green peas and dressed with a cream sauce containing truffles.

- *con almejas* (kohn ahl-méhhahs) Poached eggs with a white sauce containing clams.

- *con besamel* (kohn beh-sahméhl) Poached eggs dressed with béchamel sauce.

- *con gelatina* (kohn heh-lahtée-nah) Jellied poached eggs.

- *portuguesa* (pohr-too-guéhsah) Poached eggs on a crouton garnished with a tomato sauce containing mushrooms and truffles.

- *Rossini* (roh-sée-nee) Poached eggs on a tartlette stuffed with foie gras, dressed with a sauce made with Madeira wine.

— *escondidos* (ehs-kohn-dée-dohs) Scrambled eggs wrapped in ham slices and rolled in a crepe.

— *florentina* (floh-rehn-tée-nah) Poached eggs on boiled spinach puree.

— *fritos* (frée-tohs) Fried eggs.

- *a la española* (ah lah ehs-pah-nyóh-lah) Eggs fried in abundant olive oil.

- *al ajillo* (ahl ah-hée-yoh) Fried eggs with garlic, vinegar, and paprika.

- *con migas* (kohn mée-gahs) Fried eggs garnished with fried diced bread.

- *con patatas* (kohn pah-táh-tahs) Fried eggs garnished with fried potatoes.

- *con pimientos* (kohn pee-mee-éhn-tohs) Fried eggs garnished with fried green peppers.

- *en sorpresa* (ehn sohr-préh-sah) Deep-fried dough nest containing tomato sauce and one egg inside.

— *Herminia* (ehr-mée-nee-ah) Hard-boiled eggs and boiled potatoes dressed with mayonnaise sauce and garnished with sautéed green peas.

— *moscovita* (mohs-koh-bée-tah) Hard-boiled eggs on artichoke bottoms topped with anchovy fillets, napped with mayonnaise containing caviar.

— *napolitana* (nah-poh-lee-táh-nah) Fried eggs over spaghetti with tomato sauce.

— *nizarda* (nee-sáhr-dah) Potato barquettes filled with sautéed green peas and tomato, topped with a soft-cooked egg, and napped with white sauce.

— *pasados por agua* (pah-sáh-dohs pohr áh-gooah) Soft-boiled eggs.

— *presidencia* (preh-see-déhn-see-ah) Hard-boiled eggs stuffed with a mixture of the yolks and liver pâté. The eggs are placed on a bed of boiled spinach, covered with béchamel sauce, and baked briefly.

— *rellenos* (reh-yéh-nohs) Deviled eggs.

- *con anchoas* (kohn ahn-chóh-ahs) Deviled eggs with anchovies.

- *de gambas* (deh gáhm-bahs) Stuffed hard-boiled eggs with a mixture of shrimp and egg yolk.

— *revueltos* (reh-boo-éhl-tohs) Scrambled eggs.

- *al pisto* (ahl pées-toh) Scrambled eggs garnished with *pisto* (ratatouille).

- *con setas* (kohn séh-tahs) Scrambled eggs with wild mushrooms.

- *portuguesa* (pohr-too-guéh-sah) Scrambled eggs garnished with reduced tomato sauce.

- *princesa* (preen-séh-sah) Scrambled eggs with asparagus.

— *turbigo* (toor-bée-goh) Soft-cooked eggs garnished with grilled lamb kidneys and grilled tomatoes.

— *Villeroy* (beel-roo-áh) Soft-cooked eggs embedded in cold béchamel sauce dipped in egg-wash, breaded, and fried in oil.

# I

***Idiazábal*** (ee-dee-ah-sáh-bahl) Smoked ewe's-milk cheese from the Basque Country.

# J

***Jabalí*** (hah-bah-lée) Wild boar.

— ***a la cazadora*** (ah lah kah-sah-dóh-rah) Marinated wild boar medallions sautéed in olive oil and dressed with a sauce made of red wine, pine nuts, and raisins.

***Jabugo*** (hah-bóo-goh) Small town in the mountains of Andalusia, famous for its delicious cured ham.

***Jamón*** (hah-móhn) Ham.

— ***a la plancha*** (ah lah pláhn-chah) Broiled ham.

— ***al jerez*** (ahl heh-réhs) Ham stewed in sherry sauce.

— ***asado con pasas*** (ah-sáh-doh kohn páh-sahs) Roast fresh leg of pork dressed with red wine and raisin sauce.

— ***con tomate*** (kohn toh-máh-teh) Fried ham with tomatoes and sweet red peppers.

— ***de York al oporto*** (deh yohrk ahl oh-póhr-toh) Baked canned ham dressed with port wine sauce.

— ***empanado*** (ehm-pah-náh-doh) Fried breaded ham.

— ***en salsa de gitanos*** (ehn sáhl-sah deh hee-táh-nohs) Ham braised in milk and vinegar.

— ***serrano*** (seh-rráh-noh) Cured ham, prosciutto.

***Jarrete cacerola*** (hah-rréh-teh kah-seh-róh-lah) Beef shank (*jarrete*) casserole with white wine, herbs, and assorted vegetables.

***Jengibre*** (hen-hée-breh) Ginger.

***Jerez*** (heh-réhs) Fortified wine, matured in casks, that has a distinct nutty flavor and is high in alcohol content.

— ***de la Frontera*** (deh lah frohn-téh-rah) Town in the province of Cádiz, home of Spanish sherry.

— ***de los Caballeros*** (deh lohs kah-bah-yéh-rohs) Town in Extremadura, homeplace of Balboa, discoverer of the Pacific Ocean.

— ***dulce*** (dóol-seh) Sweet sherry.

— ***seco*** (séh-coh) Dry sherry.

***Jibia*** (hée-bee-ah) Cuttlefish.

***Judías*** (hoo-dée-ahs) Dry beans.

— ***a la bilbaina*** (ah lah beel-bah-ée-nah) Navy bean casserole with *sofrito*, cured ham, and green peppers.

— ***a la bretona*** (ah lah breh-tóh-nah) Navy bean casserole with sautéed onions and tomato puree.

— ***a la maconesa*** (ah lah mah-koh-néh-sah) Kidney bean casserole with bacon and a *sofrito* containing red wine.

— ***a la madrileña*** (ah lah mah-dree-léh-nyah) Navy bean stew with a *sofrito* containing chorizo and paprika.

— ***al caserío*** (ahl kah-seh-rée-oh) Navy bean casserole with *sofrito*, bacon, and red peppers.

— ***a lo tío Lucas*** (ah loh tée-oh lóo-kahs) Navy bean stew with a *sofrito* containing paprika, vinegar, cumin, clove, and parsley.

— ***con chorizo*** (kohn choh-rée-soh) Navy bean stew with chorizo.

— *con mano de cerdo* (kohn máhnoh deh séhr-doh) Navy bean stew with pig's feet.

— *con perdiz* (kohn pehr-dées) Navy bean and potato stew with partridge.

— *estofadas* (ehs-toh-fáh-dahs) Stewed dry beans.

— *pintas con cerdo* (péen-tahs kohn séhr-doh) Pinto bean stew with fresh pork.

— *verdes* (béhr-dehs) Green beans.

- *a la castellana* (ah lah kahs-teh-yáh-nah) Boiled green beans fried with pimiento, garlic, and parsley.

- *a la gallega* (ah lah gah-yéh-gah) Sautéed green beans with onion, garlic, and potatoes.

- *a la lionesa* (ah lah lee-oh-néh-sah) Boiled green beans sautéed with bacon and onions.

- *a la mayordoma* (ah lah mah-yohr-doh-mah) Boiled green beans sautéed in butter and lemon juice.

- *a la riojana* (ah lah ree-oh-háh-nah) Green beans stewed with fried pork chops, onion, garlic, and sausage.

- *con jamón* (kohn hah-móhn) Boiled green beans sautéed with cured ham.

- *en vinagreta* (ehn bee-nah-gréh-tah) Green beans vinaigrette.

- *salteadas* (sahl-teh-áh-dahs) Sautéed green beans.

*Jumilla* (hoo-mée-yah) Area in Murcia producing quite robust red wines high in alcohol content.

# L

*Lacitos* (lah-sée-tohs) Puff pastry bow rolls.

*Lacón* (lah-kóhn) Cured front leg of pig (from Galicia).

— *con grelos* (kohn gréh-lohs) Salted shoulder of pork (*lacón*) with vegetable greens (*grelos*) and dry white beans (from Galicia).

*La Mancha* (lah Máhn-chah) A barren plateau area in central Spain, the home of Cervantes' Don Quixote.

*Lamprea* (lahm-préh-ah) Lamprey fish.

— *a la gallega* (ah lah gah-yéh-gah) Lamprey casserole with wine and paprika.

*Langosta* (lahn-góhs-tah) Lobster.

— *a la americana* (ah lah ah-meh-ree-káh-nah) Lobster sautéed in brandy sauce.

— *a la catalana* (ah lah kah-tah-láh-nah) Lobster braised with almonds, garlic, hazelnuts, saffron, and chocolate.

— *a la marinera* (ah lah mah-ree-néh-rah) Lobster braised in a *sofrito* with wine and paprika.

— *al archiduque* (ahl ahr-chee-dóo-keh) Sautéed lobster in a béchamel sauce with whiskey.

— *con pollo* (kohn póh-yoh) Lobster with chicken.

— *Costa Brava* (kóhs-tah bráh-bah) Lobster shell stuffed with the lobster meat sautéed in a *sofrito* mixed with white sauce.

*Langostinos* (lahn-gohs-tée-nohs) Prawns.

— *a la rusa* (ah lah róo-sah) Prawns in aspic mayonnaise.

— *con clavo* (kohn kláh-boh) Sautéed prawns in clove-flavored marinade.

— *en salsa mahonesa* (ehn sáhl-sah mah-oh-néh-sah) Prawns in mayonnaise sauce.

— *Villeroy* (beel-roo-áh) Fried béchamel-coated prawns.

*Lasaña* (lah-sáh-nyah) Lasagna.

— *de mariscos* (deh mah-rées-kohs) Shellfish lasagna.

*Laurel* (lah-oo-réhl) Bay leaf.

*Leche* (léh-cheh) Milk.

— *frita* (frée-tah) Milk and flour squares fried in oil.

— *merengada* (meh-rehn-gáh-dah) Mixture of iced milk, egg white, cinnamon, and grated lemon rind.

*Lechón* (leh-chóhn) Suckling pig.

— *asado* (ah-sáh-doh) Roast suckling pig.

*Lechuga* (leh-chóo-gah) Lettuce.

— *al jugo* (ahl hóo-goh) Braised lettuce au jus.

— *al queso* (ahl kéh-soh) Baked boiled lettuce in chicken broth, dressed with melted butter and Parmesan cheese.

*Legumbres* (leh-góom-brehs) Vegetables.

*Lengua* (léhn-goo-ah) Tongue.

— *de cordero a la murciana* (deh kohr-déh-roh ah lah moor-see-áh-nah) Boiled lamb tongue simmered in meat stock with crushed almonds, raisins, and lemon juice and thickened with flour.

— *de gato* (deh gáh-toh) Butter, flour, and egg-white cookies, flavored with vanilla extract.

— *de ternera con ensalada* (deh tehr-néh-rah kohn ehn-sah-láh-dah) Cold boiled veal tongue gar-

nished with salad.

*Lenguado* (lehn-goo-áh-doh) Sole.

— *a la gaditana* (ah lah gah-dee-táh-nah) Milk-marinated sole fillets dusted in flour and deep-fried.

— *a la riojana* (ah lah ree-oh-háh-nah) Sautéed sole fillets with red peppers, garlic, and cayenne papper.

— *al plato* (ahl pláh-toh) Baked sole fillets in a liquid containing meat broth, white wine, olive oil, and bread crumbs.

— *al vino tinto* (ahl bée-noh téen-toh) Sole fillets simmered in red wine with onions and mushrooms.

— *al whiskey* (ahl goo-ées-kee) Grilled sole fillets egg-washed in whiskey batter.

— *Bombay* (bohm-báh-ee) Poached sole fillets with curried rice.

— *con champiñones* (kohn chahm-pee-nyóh-nehs) Sautéed sole fillets dressed with a creamy mushroom sauce.

— *con salsa de nueces* (kohn sáhl-sah deh noo-éh-sehs) Sole in walnut sauce.

— *Capri* (káh-pree) Fried sole fillet served with fried bananas on a bed of rice.

— *grenoblesa* (greh-noh-bléh-sah) Sautéed sole fillets with capers.

*Lentejas* (lehn-téh-hahs) Lentils.

— *a la burgalesa* (ah lah boor-gah-léh-sah) Lentil stew with bacon and a *sofrito* containing nutmeg.

— *a la cubana* (ah lah koo-báh-nah) Lentil stew with a *sofrito* containing nutmeg.

— *a lo pobre* (ah loh póh-breh) Lentil stew with a *sofrito* with paprika and garnished with quartered hard-boiled eggs.

— *con almejas* (kohn ahl-méh-hahs) Lentils stewed with a *sofrito* containing clams.

— *con arroz* (kohn ah-rróhs) Stewed lentils with rice and *sofrito*.

— *con chorizo y tocino* (kohn choh-rée-soh ee toh-sée-noh) Lentil stew with chorizo, salt pork, and sautéed onion.

— *con oreja de cerdo* (kohn oh-réh-hah deh séhr-doh) Lentil stew with pig's ear.

— *finas hierbas* (fée-nahs ee-éhr-bahs) Lentil casserole with a *sofrito* with cured ham, silver onions, cured ham, and bouquet garni.

— *Villalar* (bee-yah-láhr) Boiled lentils sautéed in lard with nutmeg and garnished with minced hard-boiled egg and croutons.

*León* (leh-óhn) A region in northwestern Spain, formerly a kingdom. Trout and lamb are prepared here following old recipes passed on from generation to generation. Also, a cow's-milk cheese heavy in fat from the region.

*Liadillos sevillanos* (lee-ah-dée-yohs seh-bee-yáh-nohs) Boiled stuffed cabbage leaves.

*Licor de hierbas* (lee-kóhr deh ee-éhr-bahs) Macerated leaves of mint, thyme, rosemary, savory, lemon verbena, and sage in a mixture of anise liquor and anisette, flavored with orange peel (from the island of Ibiza).

*Liebre* (lee-éh-breh) Hare.

— *a la cacereña* (ah lah kah-seh-réh-nyah) Hare marinated in red wine and braised in the liquid of the marinade with a *majado* made of garlic, clove, and nutmeg.

— *con lentejas* (kohn lehn-téh-hahs) Stewed hare with lentils.

— *en civet* (ehn see-béh) Braised hare in its own blood, red wine, bouquet garni, and herbs.

*Limón* (lee-móhn) Lemon.

*Limonada* (lee-moh-náh-dah) Water, lemon juice, sugar, lemon quarters, red wine, sugar, and cubed peaches.

*Lisa* (lée-sah) Striped mullet.

— *en amarillo* (ehn ah-mah-rée-yoh) Simmered striped mullet in a *sofrito* containing crushed fried bread, lemon juice, and saffron.

*Lombarda* (lohm-báhr-dah) Red cabbage.

— *a la San Quintín* (ah lah sahn keen-téen) Simmered red cabbage with bacon, onion, apple slices, new potatoes, and vinegar.

— *con manzanas* (kohn mahn-sáh-nahs) Boiled shredded red cabbage simmered with sliced apples, vinegar, and caraway.

— *con tocino* (kohn toh-sée-noh) Boiled red cabbage simmered in broth with added bacon.

— *de Navidad* (deh nah-bee-dáhd) Braised boiled red cabbage with apple slices.

*Lomo* (lóh-moh) Loin.

— *de cerdo adobado* (deh séhr-doh ah-doh-báh-doh) Sautéed marinated pork loin.

— *de cerdo a la andaluza* (deh séhr-doh ah lah ahn-dah-lóo-sah) Roast pork loin garnished with fried green peppers in olive oil.

— *de cerdo a la aragonesa* (deh séhr-doh ah lah ah-rah-goh-néh-sah) Marinated pork loin simmered in meat broth with sautéed onion, wine, and vinegar.

— *de cerdo a la baturra* (deh séhr-doh ah lah bah-tóo-rrah) Sautéed pork loin medallions simmered in wine, tomato puree, sautéed onion, cured ham, and green olives (from Aragón).

— *de cerdo a la miel* (deh séhr-doh ah lah mee-éhl) Roast pork loin dressed with a sauce made with red wine, vinegar, meat broth, and honey.

— *de cerdo a la vasca* (deh séhr-doh ah lah báhs-kah) Sautéed pork loin with garlic and onion simmered in milk until tender.

— *de cerdo con almejas* (deh séhr-doh kohn ahl-méh-hahs) Marinated pork loin sautéed with onions and simmered in the marinade's liquid with clams.

— *de cerdo con castañas* (deh séhr-doh kohn kahs-táh-nyahs) Roast pork loin basted with brandy and garnished with chestnut puree.

— *de cerdo con escalibada* (deh séhr-doh kohn ehs-kah-lee-báh-dah) Roast pork loin garnished with sautéed sweet red peppers and eggplant (from Catalonia).

— *de cerdo con lombarda* (deh séhr-doh kohn lohm-báhr-dah) Roast pork loin garnished with boiled red cabbage.

— *de cerdo relleno* (deh séhr-doh reh-yéh-noh) Stuffed pork loin.

— *de cerdo trufado* (deh séhr-doh troo-fáh-doh) Stuffed pork loin with truffles.

— *embuchado* (ehm-boo-cháh-doh) Cured smoked pig's loin in a sausage casing.

— *mechado Enrique IV* (meh-cháh-doh ehn-rée-keh koo-áhr-toh) Roast larded beef loin garnished with artichoke bottoms and green peas.

*Longaniza* (lohn-gah-née-sah) Thin pork sausage.

*Lubina* (loo-bée-nah) Striped bass.

— *a la greca* (ah lah gréh-kah) Poached striped bass garnished with boiled vegetables in white wine.

— *al ajillo* (ahl ah-hée-yoh) Baked striped bass dressed with fried garlic in olive oil.

— *a las hierbas* (ah lahs ee-éhr-bahs) Grilled striped bass with fresh fennel and sage.

— *a las uvas* (ah lahs óo-bahs) Baked striped bass with green grapes and white wine sauce.

— *Albufera* (ahl-boo-féh-rah) Baked striped bass in a garlic and almond sauce.

— *al hinojo* (ahl ee-nóh-hoh) Striped bass in fennel sauce.

## M

*Macarrones* (mah-kah-rróh-nehs) Macaroni.

— *a la capuchina* (ah lah kah-poo-chée-nah) Baked macaroni mixed with fried garlic, anchovies, chopped cucumbers, black olives, and capers.

— *a la española* (ah lah ehs-pah-nyóh-lah) Au gratin macaroni with onion, cured ham, and tomato puree.

— *a la italiana* (ah lah ee-tah-lee-áh-nah) Baked macaroni in a rich tomato sauce containing beef stock and Parmesan.

— *a la maltesa* (ah lah mahl-téh-sah) Baked macaroni with a mix of ground pork, ground beef, chicken livers, mushrooms, tomato sauce, and Parmesan cheese.

— *al gratén* (ahl grah-téhn) Au gratin macaroni in a tomato and cheese sauce made with butter.

— *con chorizo* (kohn choh-rée-soh) Macaroni in a thick tomato sauce containing chorizo and cured ham.

— *con espinacas* (kohn ehs-pee-náh-kahs) Macaroni in a creamy spinach sauce.

— *con frutos secos* (kohn fróo-tohs séh-kohs) Macaroni with a blend of crushed walnuts, hazelnuts, pine nuts, olive oil, milk, and Parmesan.

— *con huevos* (kohn oo-éh-bohs) Baked macaroni with egg yolks, butter, and grated cheese.

— *con mayonesa y atún* (kohn mah-yoh-néh-sah ee ah-tóon) Macaroni mixed with shredded canned tuna and mayonnaise.

— *con riñones* (kohn ree-nyóh-nehs) Macaroni with lamb kidneys sautéed in white wine.

— *con salsa americana* (kohn sáhl-sah ah-meh-ree-káh-nah) Macaroni with a blend of egg, olive oil, lemon juice, ketchup, and brandy.

— *con tomate* (kohn toh-máh-teh) Macaroni baked in tomato sauce with minced sautéed onions.

— *escondidos* (ehs-kohn-dée-dohs) Macaroni folded in a sauce consisting of sautéed onion and tomato, chorizo, and grated cheese, covered with a thin layer of pie dough, and baked.

— *saboyarda* (sah-boh-yáhr-dah) Macaroni baked in a white sauce with chopped cooked ham.

*Macedonia de frutas* (mah-seh-dóh-nee-ah deh fróo-tahs) Fruit salad.

*Madera* (mah-déh-rah) Sweet wine from the island of Madeira.

*Magdalenas* (mahg-dah-léh-nahs) Madeleines, small sponge cakes.

*Magra con tomate* (máh-grah kohn toh-máh-teh) Sautéed fresh ham with tomato.

*Mahón* (mah-óhn) Soft cow's-milk cheese with a tangy taste (from the Balearic Islands).

*Majado* (mah-háh-doh) Blend of condiments, herbs, spices, seasonings, and other ingredients used to flavor dishes in Spanish cooking. The blend is commonly prepared using a mortar and pestle.

*Málaga* (máh-lah-gah) Creamy, semi-soft cheese made with goat's milk (from Andalusia); sweet dessert wine from the Mediterranean coastal area of Málaga.

*Manchego* (mahn-chéh-goh) Ewe's-milk cheese from La Mancha, sold throughout the country.

*Manjar de monjas* (mahn-háhr de móhn-hahs) Pudding made with rice flour, milk, sugar, and cinnamon.

*Manos de cerdo* (máh-nohs deh séhr-doh) Pig's trotters.

— *a la catalana* (ah lah kah-tah-láh-nah) Boiled pig's trotters sim-

**Manos de cerdo a la catalana** (cont.) mered in wine with a *sofrito* containing pine nuts.

— **al limón** (ahl lee-móhn) Boiled pig's trotters in lemon sauce.

— **con salsa roja** (kohn sáhl-sah róh-hah) Boiled pig's trotters with red pepper sauce.

— **gratinadas** (grah-tee-náh-dahs) Boiled pig's trotters au gratin.

**Manos de cordero a la catalana** (máh-nohs deh kohr-déh-roh ah lah kah-tah-láh-nah) Boiled lamb's trotters cut into pieces, breaded, and deep-fried.

**Manos de cordero a la madrileña** (máh-nohs deh kohr-déh-roh ah lah mah-dree-léh-nyah) Boned boiled lamb's trotters dressed with a sauce made with sautéed onion, garlic, diced cured ham, and paprika and thickened with flour.

**Mantecados** (mahn-teh-káh-dohs) Lard (or butter), sugar, and flour shortbread.

— **de almendra** (deh ahl-méhn-drah) Almond shortbread.

— **de Antequera** (deh ahn-teh-kéh-rah) Almond shortbread with cinnamon.

— **manchegos** (mahn-chéh-gohs) Shortbread with orange juice and white wine (from La Mancha).

**Manzana** (man-sáh-nah) Apple.

— **asadas** (ah-sáh-dahs) Roasted apples, usually filled with powered almond and raisins.

— **rellenas** (reh-yéh-nahs) Baked apples stuffed with custard.

— **salteadas con ajonjolí** (sahl-teh-áh-dahs kohn ah-hohn-hoh-lée) Butter-sautéed rings of tart apples sprinkled with sesame seeds.

**Manzanilla** (man-sah-née-yah) Very dry, aged amber-colored sherry with a nutty flavor, usually served chilled; also, camomile tea.

**Marañuelas** (mah-rah-nyoo-éh-lahs) Cookies flavored with white wine.

**Mariscos** (mah-rées-kohs) Seafood.

**Marmitako** (mahr-mee-táh-koh) Basque fresh tuna stew with white wine and potatoes.

**Marquesa de chocolate** (mahr-kéh-sah deh choh-koh-láh-teh) Chocolate mousse with semi-sweet chocolate added.

**Marqués de Murrieta** (mahr-kéhs deh moo-rree-éh-tah) Vintage wine from Rioja.

**Marqués de Riscal** (mahr-kéhs deh rees-káhl) Vintage wine from Rioja.

**Mato** (máh-toh) Soft fresh goat's-milk cheese from Cataluña. It is often eaten with honey.

**Mazagrán** (mah-sah-gráhn) Black coffee, soda water, lemon juice, sugar, and crushed ice.

**Mazapán** (mah-sah-páhn) Marzipan.

**Medallón** (meh-dah-yóhn) Medallion.

**Medallones de cordero marengo** (meh-dah-yóh-nehs deh kohr-déh-roh mah-réhn-goh) Lamb leg medallions simmered in sherry with sautéed onions, garnished with sautéed bacon, carrots and zucchini.

**Medallones de langosta** (meh-dah-yóh-nehs deh lahn-góhs-tah) Lobster medallions with mayonnaise.

**Medallones de ternera Montpensier** (meh-dah-yóh-nehs deh tehr-néh-rah mohnt-pehn-see-éh) Fried veal medallions garnished with artichoke bottoms filled with sautéed asparagus tips.

**Medellín** (meh-deh-yéen) Town in Extremadura, homeplace of Cortes, conqueror of Mexico.

**Mediasnoches** (meh-dee-ahs-nóh-chehs) Small brioches.

**Mejillones** (meh-hee-yóh-nehs) Mussels.

— **al gratén** (ahl grah-téhn) Mussels au gratin with spinach and garlic mayonnaise.

— **en salsa picante** (ehn sahl-sah pee-kahn-teh) Mussels in mustard/mayonnaise.

— **en salsa verde** (ehn sáhl-sah béhr-deh) Mussels in green sauce.

— **en vinagreta** (ehn bee-nah-gréh-tah) Mussels in vinaigrette.

— **gratinados** (grah-tee-náh-dohs) Mussels au gratin.

— **rellenos** (reh-yéh-nohs) Mussels in béchamel with white wine, served in their own shells.

**Mejorana** (meh-hoh-ráh-nah) Marjoram.

**Melocotón** (meh-loh-koh-tóhn) Peach.

**Melocotones a la maña** (meh-loh-koh-tóh-nehs ah lah máh-nyah) Peaches marinated in red wine, sugar, and cinnamon (from Aragón).

**Melocotones al vino** (meh-loh-koh-tóh-nehs ahl bée-noh) Peaches simmered in red wine, cinnamon, and orange peel.

**Melocotones asados al vino** (meh-loh-koh-tóh-nehs ah-sáh-dohs ahl bée-noh) Peaches baked in red wine.

**Melón** (meh-lóhn) Melon.

— **con jamón** (kohn hah-móhn) Iced melon with prosciutto ham slices.

**Menestra** (meh-néhs-trah) Vegetable and meat casserole.

— **a la bilbaina** (ah lah beel-bah-ée-nah) Mixed-vegetable casserole with *sofrito* containing cured ham, white wine and chicken stock and garnished with chopped hard-boiled egg.

— **a la catalana** (ah lah kah-tah-láh-nah) Vegetable casserole with fresh sausage, cubed pork tenderloin, and white wine.

— **a la extremeña** (ah lah ehks-treh-méh-nyah) Swiss chard and potato casserole dressed with beaten egg.

— **a la murciana** (ah lah moor-see-áh-nah) Assorted vegetable casserole.

— **a la riojana** (ah lah ree-oh-háh-nah) Sautéed vegetables mixed with a *sofrito* with cured ham, baked and garnished with quartered hard-boiled eggs and pimiento strips.

— **a la rondeña** (ah lah rohn-déh-nyah) Artichoke, fava bean, and green pea casserole with *morcilla* sausage and *sofrito*.

— **a la tudelana** (ah lah too-deh-láh-nah) Artichoke and fava bean casserole with *majado* of garlic, parsley, almonds, fried bread, and saffron, garnished with sliced hard-boiled egg.

— **con jamón** (kohn hah-móhn) Ham and vegetable casserole.

— *de ternera* (deh tehr-néh-rah) Diced veal stewed with spring vegetables.

— *de verduras* (deh behr-dóo-rahs) Assorted vegetable casserole.

— *gallega* (gah-yéh-gah) Casserole of assorted vegetables sautéed with diced ham and garnished with poached eggs.

— *ribereña* (ree-beh-réh-nyah) Stew of assorted vegetables with cured ham and *sofrito*.

*Menta* (méhn-tah) Mint.

*Merengue* (meh-réhn-gueh) Meringue.

— *de fresa* (deh fréh-sah) Strawberry-flavored meringue.

*Merluza* (mehr-lóo-sah) Hake.

— *a la Alhambra* (ah lah ah-láhm-brah) Marinated hake fillets baked in a mixture of bread crumbs, parsley, and lemon juice.

— *a la asturiana* (ah lah ahs-too-ree-áh-nah) Baked hake in a hard cider sauce.

— *a la chiclanera* (ah lah chee-klah-néh-rah) Hake baked in a liquid made of oil, garlic, water-soaked bread, and vinegar.

— *a la española* (ah lah ehs-pah-nyóh-lah) Fried hake garnished with sautéed onions and sweet red peppers.

— *a la gallega* (ah lah gah-yéh-gah) Hake casserole with fish fumet and paprika.

— *a la koskera* (ah lah kohs-kéh-rah) Hake sautéed in white wine with clams and garnished with hard-boiled egg and parsley.

— *a la serrana* (ah lah seh-rráh-nah) Baked hake with cured ham and mushroom sauce.

— *a la sevillana* (ah lah seh-bee-yáh-nah) Hake simmered in a *sofrito* containing fried bread crumbs, sherry, pine seeds, almonds, and walnuts.

— *a la vasca* (ah lah báhs-kah) Hake steak casserole prepared with white wine and green peas.

— *a la vinagreta* (ah lah bee-nah-gréh-tah) Poached hake with vinaigrette sauce.

— *al jerez* (ahl heh-réhs) Hake baked with shrimp puree and sherry wine.

— *al rojo y blanco* (ahl róh-hoh ee bláhn-koh) Poached stuffed hake served with béchamel sauce and decorated with tomato sauce.

— *Bellavista* (beh-yah-bées-tah) Cold hake in aspic.

— *con ajo* (kohn áh-hoh) Poached hake with garlic sauce.

— *en blanco* (ehn bláhn-koh) Poached hake served with mayonnaise diluted in the poaching fumet.

— *en salsa lucentina* (ehn sáhl-sah loo-sehn-tée-nah) Poached hake dressed with a blend of water-soaked bread, oil, and vinegar and garnished with hard-boiled eggs.

— *en salsa verde* (ehn sáhl-sah béhr-deh) Poached hake in parsley sauce with almonds, green peas, and hard-boiled egg.

— *gratinada a la andaluza* (grah-tee-náh-dah ah lah ahn-dah-lóo-sah) Hake au gratin dressed with bread crumbs, garlic, parsley, and oil.

*Mero* (méh-roh) Grouper.

— *a la tarraconense* (ah lah tah-

rrah-koh-néhn-seh) Grilled grouper dressed with a sauce made with olive oil, almonds, hazelnuts, and hot red peppers.
— *a la valenciana* (ah lah bah-lehn-see-áh-nah) Sautéed grouper served with a thickened garlic sauce containing saffron.
— *en salsa de ostras* (ehn sáhl-sah deh óhs-trahs) Baked grouper in a *sofrito* containing chopped oysters.
**Michirones** (mee-chee-róh-nehs) Boiled dried fava beans with hot chilis (from Murcia).
— *picantes* (pee-káhn-tehs) Stewed dried fava beans in hot sauce.
**Miel** (mee-éhl) Honey.
**Migas** (mée-gahs) Water-soaked bread crumb sautéed in olive oil, often garnished with sausages.
— *a la serrana* (ah lah seh-rráh-nah) Sautéed water-soaked bread with crisp pork rinds.
— *canas* (káh-nahs) Sautéed water-soaked bread (from La Mancha).
— *de la Tierra de Barros* (deh lah tee-éh-rrah deh báh-rrohs) Sautéed water-soaked bread with bacon and dried peppers.
— *de rico* (deh rée-koh) Sautéed water-soaked bread with pork loin.
— *manchegas* (man-chéh-gahs) Sautéed water-soaked bread with diced prosciutto ham and pork rind.
**Mojama** (moh-háh-mah) Cured Mediterranean shark meat.
**Mojicones** (moh-hee-kóh-nehs) Flour snaps.

*Mojo de cerdo* (móh-hoh deh séhr-doh) Pig's lung and heart casserole with a *sofrito* with white wine and a *majado* made with oregano, thyme, cumin, vinegar, and paprika (from the Canary Islands).
**Moras** (móh-rahs) Mulberries.
**Morcilla** (mohr-sée-yah) Black sausage made with pig's blood.
**Morón** (moh-róhn) Soft, creamy cheese made from ewe's milk (from the province of Seville).
*Morteruelo manchego* (mohr-teh-roo-éh-loh mahn-chéh-goh) Minced boiled hare, hen, and pork loin with bread crumb simmered in the liquid and flavored with clove, paprika, and caraway.
**Moscatel** (mohs-kah-téhl) Sweet dessert wine.
**Mostachones** (mohs-tah-chóh-nehs) Brioche topped with chopped almonds.
**Mostaza** (mohs-táh-sah) Mustard.
*Mousse de pescado* (moos deh pehs-káh-doh) Fish mousse.
**Mújol** (móo-hohl) Mullet.
— *a la sal* (ah lah sahl) Mullet baked in a casing of coarse salt.
**Murcia** (móor-see-ah) Province in southeastern Spain.
*Muslos de gallina rellenos* (móos-lohs deh gah-yée-nah reh-yeh-nohs) Stuffed hen thighs.

## N

**Nabos** (náh-bohs) Turnips.
— *a la Badajoz* (ah lah bah-dah-hóhs) Sautée turnips with cured ham simmered in water thickened with flour and flavored with nutmeg.

*Naranja* (nah-ráhn-hah) Orange.

*Naranjada* (nah-rahn-háh-dah) Orangeade.

*Natillas* (nah-tée-yahs) Cream custard.

*Navajas* (nah-báh-hahs) Razor clams.

— *a la plancha* (ah lah pláhn-chah) Grilled fresh razor clams.

*Nidos de patata* (née-dohs deh pah-táh-tah) Deep-fried shredded potato nests filled with sautéed chopped ham, shrimp, green peas, and hard-boiled egg.

*Nueces* (noo-éh-sehs) Walnuts.

*Nuez moscada* (noo-éhs mohs-káh-dah) Nutmeg.

# Ñ

*Ñoquis* (nyóh-kees) Gnocchi.

— *al gratén* (ahl grah-téhn) Au gratin gnocchi.

— *de patatas y jamón* (deh pah-táh-tahs ee hah-móhn) Gnocchi made with mashed potatoes and cooked ham.

— *de sémola* (deh séh-moh-lah) Gnocchi made with semolina flour.

# O

*Oca* (óh-kah) Goose.

— *con peras* (kohn péh-rahs) Goose casserole with pears (from Catalonia).

*Oliagua amb escarrats* (oh-lee-áh-goo-ah ahmb ehs-kah-rráhts) Asparagus, tomato, and garlic soup (from Catalonia).

*Olla de cerdo* (óh-yah deh séhr-doh) Boiled dry beans, rice, and turnips with bacon slab, morcilla, pig's

ear, garlic, and tomato.

— *gitana con peras* (hee-táh-nah kohn péh-rahs) Chickpea stew with potatoes, green beans, pumpkin, fresh pears, and *sofrito*.

— *podrida* (poh-drée-dah) Veal, pork, mutton, poultry, duck, patridge, veal brain, and chicken liver stew with assorted vegetables and a *sofrito* (from La Mancha).

*Ollo salda* (óh-yoh sáhl-dah) Chicken consommé (from the Basque Country).

*Oloroso* (oh-loh-róh-soh) Dry dark-amber sherry.

*Omeleta de atún* (oh-meh-léh-tah deh ah-tóon) Canned-tuna omelet (from Portugal).

*Oporto* (oh-póhr-toh) Port, dessert wine from Portugal.

*Orduña* (ohr-dóo-nyah) Hard ewe's-milk cheese from the Basque Country.

*Orégano* (oh-réh-gah-noh) Oregano.

*Oreja* (oh-réh-hah) Ear.

*Orejas* (oh-réh-hahs) Fried dumplings made with brandy.

— *de cerdo a la leonesa* (deh séhr-doh ah lah leh-oh-néh-sah) Pig's-ear casserole with sautéed onion, bacon, and meat broth.

*Ostras* (óhs-trahs) Oysters.

— *al limón* (ahl lee-móhn) Oysters on the half-shell served with lemon.

*Ovos Quinta das Torres* (óh-bohs kéen-tah dahs tóh-rrehs) Fried eggs embedded in cold cheese béchamel sauce, dipped in egg-wash, breaded and deep-fried (from Portugal).

# P

**Pacharán** (pah-chah-ráhn) Sloe-berry liqueur from Navarra.

**Paella** (pah-éh-yah) Meat, seafood, and vegetable rice with *sofrito* and saffron.

— **barcelonesa** (bahr-seh-loh-néh-sah) Paella variation containing sausages.

— **huertana** (oo-ehr-táh-nah) Paella made with assorted vegetables.

— **marinera** (mah-ree-néh-rah) Seafood paella.

— **valenciana** (bah-lehn-see-áh-nah) Traditional paella made with chicken and seafood.

**Pagel** (pah-héhl) Sea bream.

— **a la jerezana** (ah lah heh-reh-sáh-nah) Baked sea bream with sherry and fennel.

— **a la playera** (ah lah plah-yéh-rah) Simmered sea bream with vegetables and saffron.

— **al vino blanco** (ahl bée-noh bláhn-koh) Baked sea bream with a thickened *sofrito* containing flour and white wine.

— **en salsa de pepinillos** (ehn sáhl-sah deh peh-pee-née-yohs) Baked sea bream with a *sofrito* containing saffron and garnished with gherkins.

**Pajas al queso** (páh-hahs ahl kéh-soh) Cheese straws.

**Palmeras** (pahl-méh-rahs) Puff pastry rolls.

**Paloma torcaz** (pah-lóh-mah tohr-káhs) Ringdove.

— **al vino tinto** (ahl bée-noh téen-toh) Braised ringdove in red wine.

**Palometa** (pah-loh-méh-tah) Yellow jack.

— **a la gaditana** (ah lah gah-dee-táh-nah) Baked yellow jack with a *sofrito* made with fish broth, thickened with flour, and garnished with sliced hard-boiled eggs.

— **con anchoas** (kohn ahn-chóh-ahs) Grilled yellow jack garnished with anchovy mayonnaise.

**Palomino** (pah-loh-mée-noh) Type of grape used to make sherry wine.

**Pan** (pahn) Bread.

— **blanco** (bláhn-koh) White bread.

— **candeal** (kahn-deh-áhl) Bread made with white flour.

— **de caridad** (deh kah-ree-dáhd) Bread made with olive oil and cumin.

— **de cebada** (deh seh-báh-dah) Barley bread.

— **de centeno** (deh sehn-téh-noh) Rye bread common in Galicia.

— **de higo** (deh ée-goh) Ground dried figs with ground almonds, hazelnuts, chocholate, cinnamon, grated lemon rind, and anise liquor.

— **de pasas** (deh páh-sahs) Raisin bread.

— **de pueblo** (deh poo-éh-bloh) Regular wheat bread.

— **de Santa Teresa** (deh sáhn-tah teh-réh-sah) French toast.

— **dulce** (dóol-seh) Sweet bread.

— **integral** (een-teh-gráhl) Whole wheat bread.

— **quemado** (keh-máh-doh) Baked sweet bread topped with egg white and sugar (from Va-lencia).

— **relleno** (reh-yéh-noh) Bread crust stuffed with minced ham,

**VOCABULARY**

*Pan relleno* (cont.)
beef tongue, roast veal, hard-boiled egg, and gherkins.

*Panecillo* (pah-neh-sée-yoh) Roll.

— *de Viena* (deh bee-éh-nah) Rolls made with milk.

*Papandúas* (pah-pahn-dóo-ahs) Simmered shredded salt-cod with flour, yeast, and saffron worked to a dough and deep-fried in small portions.

*Parrillada de pescado* (pah-rree-yáh-dah deh pehs-káh-doh) Grilled seafood.

*Pasiego* (pah-see-éh-goh) Fresh, soft cow's-milk cheese from the province of Santander.

*Pasta a la bechamel* (páhs-tah ah lah beh-chah-méhl) Pasta with béchamel sauce.

*Pasta al curry* (páhs-tah ahl kóo-rree) Pasta in curry sauce.

*Pasta con albondiguillas* (páhs-tah kohn ahl-bohn-dee-guée-yahs) Pasta with meat balls.

*Pasta con pisto* (páhs-tah kohn pées-toh) Pasta served combined with ratatouille.

*Pasteis de bacalhau* (pahs-téh-ees deh bah-kah-láh-oo) Salt-cod fritters (from Portugal).

*Pastel* (pahs-téhl) Pie, cake.

— *cordobés* (kohr-doh-béhs) Candied squash torte.

— *de alcachofas* (deh ahl-kah-chóh-fahs) Pie shell filled with boiled artichokes, butter, beaten egg, and milk set in a *bain Marie* and baked in the oven until the egg is done.

— *de arroz* (deh ah-rróhs) Diced cooked seafood folded in mayonnaise and placed between two layers of rice boiled in the seafood's fumet.

— *de carne* (deh káhr-neh) Puff pastry meat pie (from the province of Murcia).

— *de liebre* (deh lee-éh-breh) Hare pie.

— *de macarrones* (deh mah-kah-rróh-nehs) Baked macaroni with a mixture of ground beef, tomato, onion, and white wine sautéed in olive oil.

— *de perdices* (deh pehr-dée-sehs) Partridge pie.

— *de tortillas* (deh tohr-tée-yahs) Four omelets placed over each other: one mushroom, one shrimp, one potato, one mixed vegetable; all are cut like a cake and served with tomato puree.

— *vasco* (báhs-koh) Black cherry tart (from the Basque Country).

*Patatas* (pah-táh-tahs) Potatoes.

— *a la extremeña* (ah lah eks-treh-méh-nyah) Simmered potatoes, green beans, onion, tomato, and green peppers.

— *a la brava* (ah lah bráh-bah) Potatoes browned in oil dressed with a sautéed onion and garlic sauce containing tomato sauce, wine, hot pepper, and tabasco.

— *a la castellana* (ah-lah kahs-teh-yáh-nah) Sautéed potatoes sprinkled with flour and paprika cooked in a small amount of chicken broth until almost dry.

— *a la flamenca* (ah lah flah-méhn-kah) Boiled potatoes sautéed in oil and dressed with vinegar and mustard.

— *al ajo cabañil* (ahl áh-hoh kah-bah-nyéel) Sautéed sliced potatoes dressed with a blend of water, garlic, vinegar, and parsley.

— *a la judía* (ah lah hoo-dée-ah) Boiled diced potatoes cooked in wine and dressed with egg yolk, olive oil, vinegar, and mustard.

— *al all-i-oli* (ahl ahl-ee-óh-lee) Boiled potatoes with garlic mayonnaise.

— *a la leonesa* (ah lah lee-oh-néh-sah) Sautéed potatoes with onion.

— *a la malagueña* (ah lah mah-lah-guéh-nyah) Potatoes simmered in a *sofrito* containing paprika and green olives.

— *a la mallorquina* (ah lah mah-yohr-kée-nah) Baked stuffed potatoes with chorizo spread, napped with white sauce.

— *a la riojana* (ah lah ree-oh-háh-nah) Fried sliced potatoes simmered in a touch of water containing vinegar, garlic, and pepper.

— *aliñadas* (ah-lee-nyáh-dahs) Sliced boiled potatoes dressed with a blend of garlic, parsley, hard-boiled egg, oil, and vinegar.

— *a lo pobre* (ah loh póh-breh) Simmered sliced potatoes in olive oil sprinkled with minced garlic and parsley.

— *al vapor* (ahl bah-póhr) Steamed potatoes.

— *Ana* (áh-nah) Baked buttered sliced potatoes.

— *con ajo* (kohn áh-hoh) Boiled potatoes dressed with garlic mayonnaise.

— *con bacalao* (kohn bah-kah-láh-oh) Potatoes cooked in a liquid containing a *sofrito* with paprika and shredded salt-cod.

— *con chorizo* (kohn choh-rée-soh) Sliced potatoes sautéed with chorizo and bacon.

— *con huevos duros* (kohn oo-éh-bohs dóo-rohs) Sliced potatoes cooked in a *sofrito* and garnished with hard-boiled eggs.

— *con rape* (kohn ráh-peh) Potatoes and anglerfish casserole.

— *con raya* (kohn ráh-yah) Potatoes and skate casserole.

— *doradas* (doh-ráh-dahs) Steamed potatoes brushed with melted butter and baked in the oven until golden.

— *duquesa* (doo-kéh-sah) Duchess potatoes.

— *en ajopollo* (ehn ah-hoh-póh-yoh) Potatoes cooked in broth containing sautéed garlic, bread, almonds, and parsley.

— *en salsa verde* (ehn sáhl-sah béhr-deh) Potatoes in green sauce.

— *estofadas* (ehs-toh-fáh-dahs) Stewed potatoes.

— *goncourt* (gohn-kóort) Potatoes browned in oil and cooked in a touch of broth containing chopped tomatoes, thyme, and bay leaf.

— *paja* (páh-hah) Straw potatoes.

— *picantes* (pee-káhn-tehs) Sautéed boiled potatoes seasoned with paprika, chili pepper, and garlic.

— *rellenas* (reh-yéh-nahs) Stuffed potatoes.

— *salteadas* (sahl-teh-áh-dahs) Sautéed potatoes.

— *San Florentino* (sahn floh-rehn-tée-noh) Pureed potatoes with egg yolk, butter, and diced ham shaped like a pear and deep-fried in olive oil.

V O C A B U L A R Y

— *Susana* (soo-sáh-nah) Baked potatoes stuffed with béchamel sauce mixed with diced ham, chicken breast, and truffles.

*Paté de gambas* (pah-téh deh gáhm-bahs) Shrimp pâté.

*Paté del Pirineo* (pah-téh dehl pee-ree-néh-oh) Pork pâté with apples and nuts.

*Paté de mariscos* (pah-téh deh mah-rées-kohs) Seafood pâté.

*Paternina* (pah-tehr-née-nah) Vintage wine from Rioja.

*Pato* (páh-toh) Duck.

— *a la andaluza* (ah lah ahn-dah-lóo-sah) Duck stew with chickpeas.

— *a la gallega* (ah lah gah-yéh-gah) Braised duck with wine, anise liquor, turnips, carrots, onions, bouquet garni, and garlic.

— *a la maltesa* (ah lah mahl-téh-sah) Roast duck dressed with a sauce made of wine and orange juice.

— *a la montañesa* (ah lah mohn-tah-nyéh-sah) Duck braised in a *sofrito* containing sherry, stock, and paprika.

— *a la naranja* (ah lah nah-ráhn-hah) Braised duck with orange sauce.

— *a la sevillana* (ah lah seh-bee-yáh-nah) Braised duck with green olives and sherry sauce.

— *a la vasca* (ah lah báhs-kah) Duck braised in wine, stock, tarragon, thyme, and clove.

— *asado con manzanas* (ah-sáh-doh kohn mahn-sáh-nahs) Roast duck with apples.

— *con nabos* (kohn náh-bohs) Baked duck dressed with a *majado* made of sautéed turnips, onion, carrots, parsnips, and wine.

— *con aceitunas* (kohn ah-seh-ee-tóo-nahs) Braised duck in green olive sauce.

— *con salsa de alcaparras* (kohn sáhl-sah deh ahl-kah-páh-rrahs) Duck casserole with a *sofrito* containing capers, almonds, green olives, and raisins.

— *con higos* (kohn ée-gohs) Roast duck in a dried fig sauce.

— *en salsa de almendras* (ehn sáhl-sah deh ahl-méhn-drahs) Braised duck in almond sauce.

*Patorra extremeña* (pah-tóh-rrah ehs-treh-méh-nyah) Sautéed diced mutton liver, lungs, and blood simmered in meat broth with sautéed onion, paprika, and flour and garnished with beaten egg (from Extremadura).

*Pavo* (páh-boh) Turkey.

— *adobado* (ah-doh-báh-doh) Turkey marinated in wine, cloves, peppercorns, onion, and bay leaf, sautéed, and then simmered in the liquid of the marinade with tomato, cinnamon, and clove.

— *a la madrileña* (ah lah mah-dree-léh-nyah) Roast turkey basted with wine and dressed with its own pan gravy.

— *a la menorquina* (ah lah meh-nohr-kée-nah) Roast turkey stuffed with bread crumbs, butter, honey, raisins, lemon rind, egg, and cinnamon.

— *con verduras* (kohn behr-dóo-rahs) Turkey casserole with assorted vegetables.

— *en salsa de almendras* (ehn sáhl-sah deh ahl-méhn-drahs)

Sautéed turkey simmered in meat broth with a *sofrito* containing crushed almonds. The gravy is flavored with lemon juice and thickened with flour.

— *trufado* (troo-fáh-doh) Roast turkey stuffed with ground veal, ground pork loin, truffles, milk-soaked bread crumb, egg, sherry, and nutmeg.

*Pebre murciano* (péh-breh moor-see-áh-noh) Boiled shoulder of lamb with a *majado* made with boiled tomatoes and cumin (from Murcia).

*Pechuga de pollo* (peh-chóo-gah deh póh-yoh) Chicken breast.

— *a la suprema* (ah lah soo-préh-mah) Chicken breast *chaud-froid*.

— *a la naranja* (ah lah nah-ráhn-hah) Chicken breast in orange sauce.

— *con piñones* (kohn pee-nyóh-nehs) Sautéed chicken breasts simmered with onion, garlic, parsley, pine nuts and white wine.

— *rellenas* (reh-yéh-nahs) Stuffed chicken breasts.

— *Villeroy* (beel-roo-áh) Deep-fried chicken breast coated with a sauce made with roux, chicken stock, milk, and nutmeg.

*Pedroches* (peh-dróh-chehs) Piquant, semi-hard ewe's-milk cheese from La Mancha.

*Pelotas en salsa roja* (peh-lóh-tahs ehn sáhl-sah róh-hah) Meatballs in red sherry sauce.

*Penedés* (peh-neh-déhs) Catalonian region where excellent table wines and *cava* sparklers are made.

*Pepinillos en vinagre* (peh-pee-née-yohs ehn bee-náh-greh) Pickled gherkins.

*Pepino* (peh-pée-noh) Cucumber.

*Pepito de ternera* (peh-pée-toh deh tehr-néh-rah) Grilled veal steak sandwich.

*Pera* (péh-rah) Pear.

— *con vino* (kohn bée-noh) Pears poached in red wine with cinnamon.

— *de Lérida* (deh léh-ree-dah) Pears simmered in milk and folded with a mixture of the simmering liquid and beaten egg whites.

*Perdiz* (pehr-dées) Partridge.

— *a la andaluza* (ah lah ahn-dah-lóo-sah) Partridge, stuffed with its giblets, bacon, and anchovies and simmered in wine, tomato, and green peppers.

— *a la Briand* (ah lah bree-áhn) Partridge stuffed with fresh sausage meat, egg yolk, and truffles and simmered in sherry with minced onions and carrots.

— *a la catalana* (ah lah kah-tah-láh-nah) Partridge stew garnished with shredded boiled cabbage.

— *a la cortijera* (ah lah kohr-tee-héh-rah) Partridge braised in stock with boiled shredded cabbage, bacon, chopped salami, and bouquet garni.

— *a la manchega* (ah lah mahn-chéh-gah) Partridge braised in a *sofrito* with thyme, cured ham, and a touch of cinnamon.

— *a lo tío Lucas* (ah loh tée-oh lóo-kahs) Braised partridge with a *majado* made of truffles, pine nuts, onion, parsley, bread, and sherry.

— *al vino tinto* (ahl bée-noh téen-toh) Braised partridge in red wine.

— *con almendras* (kohn ahl-méhn-drahs) Braised partridge with a *majado* made of garlic, toasted almonds, parsley, and sherry wine.

— *con coles* (kohn kóh-lehs) Braised partridge with cured ham and fresh sausage and garnished with boiled Brussels sprouts.

— *en escabeche* (ehn ehs-kah-béh-cheh) Braised marinated partridge.

— *estofada* (ehs-toh-fáh-dah) Partridge stewed in wine and vinegar with vegetables and garlic.

*Perdices escabechadas* (pehr-dée-sehs ehs-kah-beh-cháh-dahs) Pickled partridges.

*Perejil* (peh-reh-héel) Parsley

*Perifollo* (peh-ree-fóh-yoh) Chervil.

*Perlas doradas* (péhr-lahs doh-ráh-dahs) Chicken stock with tapioca and egg yolks.

*Perrunillas* (peh-rroo-née-yahs) Cookies made with lard, eggs, anise liquor, and cinnamon.

*Pescadilla* (pehs-kah-dée-yah) Whiting.

— *a la alcarreña* (ah lah ahl-kah-rréh-nyah) Baked stuffed whiting with béchamel sauce.

— *a la malagueña* (ah lah mah-lah-guéh-nyah) Poached whiting dressed with a mayonnaise diluted in the poaching fumet.

— *a la mayordoma* (ah lah mah-yohr-dóh-mah) Fried whiting served with maître d'hôtel butter.

— *a la monegasca* (ah lah moh-neh-gáhs-kah) Fried whiting served with ratatouille.

— *en escabeche* (ehn ehs-kah-beh-cheh) Fried whiting marinated in vinegar flavored with saffron, cumin, ginger, and bay leaf.

*Pescado* (pehs-káh-doh) Fish.

*Pestiños de anís* (pehs-tée-nyohs deh ah-nées) Deep-fried choux paste pastries flavored with anise liquor.

*Pez espada* (pehs ehs-páh-dah) Swordfish.

— *a la plancha* (ah lah pláhn-chah) Grilled swordfish.

— *en adobo* (ehn ah-dóh-boh) Marinated swordfish.

*Pichón* (pee-chóhn) Squab.

*Pichones a la andaluza* (pee-chóh-nehs ah lah ahn-dah-lóo-sah) Squab, larded with anchovy fillets, braised in white wine with garlic and parsley.

*Pichones a la dogaresa* (pee-chóh-nehs ah lah doh-gah-réh-sah) Squab, stuffed with ground veal, egg, truffles, and nutmeg and simmered in a *sofrito* containing sherry and mushrooms.

*Pichones en chocolate* (pee-chóh-nehs ehn choh-koh-láh-teh) Braised squab with chocolate sauce.

*Pichones en compota* (pee-chóh-nehs ehn kohm-póh-tah) Squab browned in bacon fat, braised in wine and broth, and garnished with fried bread triangles.

*Pierna* (pee-éhr-nah) Leg.

— *de cerdo encebollada* (deh séhr-doh ehn-seh-boh-yáh-dah) Leg of pork simmered with onion, green peppers, tomato, paprika, clove, and oil and a *majado* of gar-

lic, paprika, and saffron.
— *de cerdo estofada* (deh séhr-doh ehs-toh-fáh-dah) Braised leg of pork.
— *de cordero a la cordobesa* (deh kohr-déh-roh ah lah kohr-doh-béh-sah) Roast leg of lamb with wine, bouquet garni, meat broth, and tomato sauce.
— *de cordero a la orensana* (deh kohr-déh-roh ah lah oh-rehn-sáh-nah) Leg of lamb roasted in meat broth and garnished with cooked navy beans (from Galicia).
— *de cordero asada* (deh kohr-déh-roh ah-sáh-dah) Roasted leg of lamb.
— *de cordero con alioli de membrillo* (deh kohr-déh-roh kohn ah-lee-óh-lee deh mehm-brée-yoh) Roast leg of lamb garnished with quince *alioli.*
— *de cordero mechada* (deh kohr-déh-roh meh-cháh-dah) Roast, larded leg of lamb.
*Pimentón* (pee-mehn-tóhn) Paprika.
*Pimienta* (pee-mee-éhn-tah) Pepper (spice).
— *blanca* (bláhn-kah) White pepper.
— *inglesa* (een-gléh-sah) Allspice.
— *negra* (néh-grah) Black pepper.
— *roja* (róh-hah) Red pepper.
*Pimientos* (pee-mee-éhn-tohs) Peppers (vegetable).
— *con huevos de codorniz* (kohn oo-éh-bohs deh koh-dohr-nées) Fried quail eggs and sweet peppers.
— *con nata* (kohn náh-tah) Grilled sweet peppers napped with whipped cream.

— *fritos* (frée-tohs) Fried sweet peppers.
— *morrones* (moh-rróh-nehs) Pimientos.
— *rellenos* (reh-yéh-nohs) Stuffed peppers.
- *de merluza* (deh mehr-lóo-sah) Peppers stuffed with boiled hake.
— *rojos* (róh-hohs) Red peppers.
— *verdes* (béhr-dehs) Green peppers.
*Pinchos morunos* (péen-chohs moh-róo-nohs) Grilled marinated miniature kabobs.
*Pintada* (peen-táh-dah) Guinea fowl.
— *al vino tinto* (ahl bée-noh téen-toh) Guinea fowl braised in red wine.
*Piña* (pée-nyah) Pineapple.
*Piñones* (pee-nyóh-nehs) Pine nuts.
*Piononos* (pee-oh-nóh-nohs) Cream rolls.
*Piperrada* (pee-peh-rráh-dah) Flat omelet with sweet peppers, onion, garlic, cured ham, and tomato (from the Basque Country).
*Pipirrana* (pee-pee-rráh-nah) Finely chopped green peppers, onions, tomatoes, and cucumbers dressed with oil and vinegar.
*Pisto* (peés-toh) Ratatouille.
— *albacetense* (ahl-bah-seh-téhn-seh) Ratatouille made with pickled bonito fish.
— *castellano* (kahs-teh-yáh-noh) Vegetables sautéed in bacon grease and simmered in chicken stock with beaten egg.
— *de Semana Santa* (deh seh-máh-nah sáhn-tah) Sautéed peppers, tomatoes, onions, and canned tuna.

— *manchego* (mahn-chéh-goh) Zucchini, tomato, green pepper, onion, and bacon ratatouille.

*Pixín a la asturiana* (peek-séen ah lah ahs-too-ree-áh-nah) Monkfish in hard cider sauce with apples.

*Plasencia* (plah-séhn-see-ah) Semihard goat's-milk cheese from Extremadura.

*Plátano* (pláh-tah-noh) Banana.

— *a la catalana* (ah lah kah-tah-láh-nah) Baked banana puree combined with sugar, ground hazelnuts, and brandy.

— *a la puertorriqueña* (ah lah poo-ehr-toh-rree-kéh-nyah) Fried bananas with wine, sugar, and cinnamon.

— *con miel y piñones* (kohn mee-éhl ee pee-nyóh-nehs) Bananas sautéed in butter mixed with honey and garnished with pine nuts.

*Pollo* (pó-yoh) Chicken.

— *a la andaluza* (ah lah ahn-dah-lóo-sah) Floured chicken fried in olive oil and simmered in broth, sherry, and *sofrito*, with a *majado* made from fried garlic, almonds, saffron, parsley, and hard-boiled egg yolk.

— *a la bilbaina* (ah lah beel-bah-ée-nah) Sautéed chicken simmered in a *sofrito* containing sweet red peppers and white wine.

— *a la bordelesa* (ah lah bohr-deh-léh-sah) Truffle-stuffed chicken *en cocotte* with onion, brandy, wine, tomato, and chicken stock, dressed with a sauce made with shallots, mushrooms, and chervil.

— *a la buena mujer* (ah lah boo-éh-nah moo-héhr) Roast chicken *en cocotte* with sherry, potatoes, silver onions, bacon, and brandy.

— *a la castellana* (ah lah kahs-teh-yáh-nah) Sautéed chicken simmered in wine, chicken broth, pureed onion, and spices.

— *a la catalana* (ah lah kah-tah-láh-nah) Sautéed chicken simmered in a *sofrito* with white wine, zucchini, and eggplant.

— *a la cerveza* (ah lah sehr-béh-sah) Chicken simmered in beer with sautéed potatoes and onions.

— *a la chilena* (ah lah chee-léh-nah) Pulled chicken meat cooked in a mixture of milk and cream and garnished with spaghetti.

— *a la española* (ah lah ehs-pah-nyóh-lah) Chicken sautéed in casserole with sautéed onion, white wine, chicken stock, basil, garlic, parsley, and pine nuts.

— *a la extremeña* (ah lah ehs-treh-méh-nyah) Sautéed chicken simmered in a sauce made of lemon rind, honey, rosemary, and white wine.

— *a la flamenca* (ah lah flah-méhn-kah) Chicken sautéed in lard with minced onion, parsley, and garlic and simmered in chicken broth and white wine, thickened with flour.

— *a la gelatina* (ah lah heh-lah-tée-nah) Chicken in aspic.

— *al ajillo* (ahl ah-hée-yoh) Fried chicken with garlic.

— *a la manchega* (ah lah mahn-chéh-gah) Sautéed chicken simmered in a *sofrito* with cured ham and fried garlic and flavored with thyme, bay leaf, and cinnamon.

— *a la molinera* (ah lah moh-lee-néh-rah) Chicken stuffed with sautéed mushrooms, chicken liver, onion, brandy, and sherry and simmered in white wine.

— *a la murciana* (ah lah moor-see-áh-nah) Chicken simmered in a *sofrito* with tomatoes, red peppers, and a touch of sugar.

— *a la navarra* (ah lah nah-báh-rrah) Chicken simmered with wild mushrooms and a *majado* made with the chicken's liver, garlic, and white wine.

— *a la pimienta* (ah lah pee-mee-éhn-tah) Pepper-seasoned fried chicken simmered in stock with chili peppers, saffron, and nutmeg and a *majado* made of garlic, parsley, toasted almonds, and pine nuts.

— *a la piña* (ah lah pée-nyah) Roast chicken with pineapple sauce.

— *a la praviana* (ah lah prah-bee-áh-nah) Sautéed chicken simmered in hard cider with sautéed cured ham, onion, garlic, paprika, and blanched shrimp and garnished with fried bread (from Asturias).

— *a la sal* (ah lah sahl) Chicken covered with a paste made with coarse salt and water and roasted in the oven.

— *a la santanderina* (ah lah sahn-tahn-deh-rée-nah) Sautéed chicken simmered in a *sofrito* with white wine and brandy.

— *a las finas hierbas* (ah lahs fée-nahs ee-éhr-bahs) Chicken casserole with bacon, parsley, potatoes, and green onions.

— *al ast* (ahl ahst) Spit-roasted chicken.

— *al café* (ahl kah-féh) Sautéed chicken with sherry and walnuts simmered in coffee and thickened with cornstarch.

— *al champán* (ahl cham-páhn) Chicken in champagne sauce.

— *al chilindrón* (ahl chee-leen-dróhn) Braised chicken in olive oil with sweet red peppers, tomatoes, onions, and diced cured ham.

— *al horno* (ahl óhr-noh) Roast chicken.

— *al pimentón* (ahl pee-mehn-tóhn) Chicken in paprika sauce.

— *al vino tinto* (ahl bée-noh téen-toh) Chicken in red wine sauce.

— *campurriano* (kahm-poo-rree-áh-noh) Chicken sautéed in bacon fat stewed in chicken stock and white wine with a *sofrito* with paprika.

— *con caracoles* (kohn kah-rah-kóh-lehs) Chicken casserole with *sofrito*, snails, and a paste made with the chicken's liver and olive oil.

— *con col* (kohn kohl) Chicken boiled in water containing olive oil, vinegar, cloves, and a *sofrito* with shredded boiled cabbage and white wine.

— *con gambas* (kohn gáhm-bahs) Sautéed chicken and shrimp simmered in wine, chicken broth, and brandy.

— *con higos* (kohn ée-gohs) Chicken simmered in a sauce made with fresh figs, white wine, olive oil, and cinnamon.

VOCABULARY

— *con jamón serrano* (kohn hah-mohn seh-rráh-noh) Chicken pieces larded with cured serrano ham sautéed with onion, tomatoes, and brandy and simmered until tender.

— *con langosta* (kohn lahn-góhs-tah) Sautéed chicken and lobster in casserole with a sauce that combines almonds, hazelnuts, saffron, and unsweetened dark chocolate.

— *con manzanas* (kohn mahn-sáh-nahs) Roast chicken with apples.

— *con naranja* (kohn nah-ráhn-hahs) Chicken à l'orange.

— *con piñones* (kohn pee-nyóh-nehs) Chicken stewed with onions, olive oil and pine nuts.

— *con pisto* (kohn pées-toh) Sautéed chicken with ratatouille.

— *con salsa de ajos* (kohn sáhl-sah deh áh-hohs) Sautéed chicken simmered in wine and saffron with a *majado* of garlic and fried bread.

— *con tomate* (kohn toh-máh-teh) Fried chicken in tomato sauce.

— *empanado* (ehm-pah-náh-doh) Deep-fried breaded chicken.

— *en chanfaina* (ehn chan-fáh-ee-nah) Sautéed chicken with onion, garlic, eggplant, peppers, tomato, white wine, and thyme.

— *hervido con bechamel* (ehr-bée-doh kohn beh-chah-méhl) Poached chicken napped with béchamel sauce.

— *jerezano* (heh-reh-sáh-noh) Bacon-larded chicken baked with carrots, onion, garlic, and parsley,

until brown. Meat broth and sherry wine are added, and the whole simmered until the chicken is done.

— *morisco* (moh-rées-koh) Sautéed chicken simmered in water with crushed almonds, onion, and raisins.

— *relleno* (reh-yéh-noh) Stuffed chicken.

— *riojano* (ree-oh-hah-noh) Sautéed chicken simmered in a *sofrito* containing sweet red peppers, hot chilis, and white wine.

— *salteado* (sahl-teh-áh-doh) Sautéed chicken.

— *vienesa* (bee-eh-néh-sah) Boiled chicken pieces breaded and fried in oil.

*Polvorones* (pohl-boh-róh-nehs) Shortbread.

— *de Écija* (deh éh-see-hah) Shortbread flavored with cinnamon and brandy.

*Pomelo* (poh-méh-loh) Grapefruit.

— *caliente con crema* (kah-lee-éhn-teh kohn kreh-mah) Grapefruit half covered with whipped cream and brown sugar and lightly broiled.

*Ponche* (póhn-cheh) Hot punch made from milk, chopped almonds, egg yolks, sugar, brandy, and vanilla extract.

— *de leche* (deh léh-cheh) Milk with beaten egg, sugar, and a dash of brandy.

— *romano* (roh-máh-noh) Iced tea with sugar, rum, lemon, orange juice, and triple sec liqueur.

*Popietas a la romana* (poh-pee-éh-tahs ah lah roh-máh-nah) Beef paupiettes stuffed with minced pork,hard-boiled egg, and minced gherkins.

***Potaje blanco*** (poh-táh-heh bláhn-koh) Navy bean, chickpea, and rice stew with a *sofrito* made with lard.

— ***de garbanzos con acelgas*** (deh gahr-bahn-sohs kohn ah-sehl-gahs) Chickpea and Swiss chard stew with a *sofrito* containing almonds and vinegar.

— ***de viernes*** (deh bee-éhr-nehs) Chickpea and spinach stew with salt-cod, *sofrito*, and paprika.

***Pote asturiano*** (póh-teh ahs-too-ree-áh-noh) Salt pork, pig's ear, *morcilla* sausage, navy beans, potatoes, and cabbage stew flavored with smoked lard.

***Pote del Cantábrico*** (dehl kahn-táh-bree-koh) Cabbage, potatoes, and dry bean stew with salted pork shoulder meat (*lacón*), chorizo, and *morcilla* sausage.

***Poti-poti de Mura*** (póh-tee póh-tee deh móo-rah) Boiled potatoes, salt-cod, tomato, and onion salad garnished with red peppers and black olives.

***Porrusalda*** (poh-rroo-sáhl-dah) Salt-cod, potato, and leek soup (from the Basque Country).

***Prueba de cerdo*** (proo-éh-bah deh séhr-doh) Fried cubed pork meat with onion, garlic, hot chilis, cayenne, thyme, and paprika (served to "test" the meat of the pig that has just been butchered).

***Puchero canario*** (poo-chéh-roh kah-náh-ree-oh) Beef brisket, chorizo, *morcilla* sausage, and chickpea stew with potatoes, sweet potatoes, pumpkin, corn, cabbage, and pears and a *majado* containing clove, saffron, and garlic.

***Puchero casero*** (poo-chéh-roh kah-séh-roh) Cabbage and potato stew with chorizo and *morcilla* sausage.

***Puchero de gallina*** (poo-chéh-roh deh gah-yée-nah) Broth-simmered hen, stuffed with bacon, cured ham, the hen's liver, garlic, parsley, tarragon, bread crumb, egg, and white wine.

***Puchero de las Hurdes*** (poo-chéh-roh deh lahs óor-dehs) Stewed rabbit with potatoes, vinegar, olive oil, and minced onion (from Extremadura).

***Puerros*** (poo-éh-rrohs) Leeks.

— ***con bechamel*** (kohn beh-chah-méhl) Baked leeks with béchamel sauce.

***Pulpo*** (póol-poh) Octopus.

— ***a la feria*** (ah lah féh-ree-ah) Sliced boiled octopus in a paprika marinade.

— ***a la gallega*** (ah lah gah-yéh-gah) Boiled octopus dressed with paprika and oil.

— ***en vinagreta*** (ehn bee-nah-gréh-tah) Boiled octopus in vinaigrette sauce.

***Puré*** (poo-réh) Puree.

— ***de patatas y zanahorias*** (deh pah-táh-tahs ee sah-nah-óh-ree-ahs) Potato and carrot puree.

— ***dorado*** (doh-ráh-doh) Navy bean and pumpkin puree.

— ***leontino*** (leh-ohn-tée-noh) Thick vegetable soup with milk.

***Puzol*** (poo-sóhl) Fresh cheese from Valencia.

## Q

*Queimada* (keh-ee-máh-dah) Hot toddy made by flaming marc liquor (from Galicia).

*Queso* (kéh-soh) Cheese.

— *con nueces* (kohn noo-éh-sehs) Cream cheese with walnuts.

— *de bola* (deh bóh-lah) Gouda-style cheese.

— *de cabra* (deh káh-brah) Goat's-milk cheese.

— *de oveja* (deh oh-béh-hah) Ewe's-milk cheese.

— *de vaca* (deh báh-kah) Cow's-milk cheese.

— *frito* (frée-toh) Fried cheese.

## R

*Rábano* (ráh-bah-noh) Radish.

*Rabo de toro* (ráh-boh deh tóh-roh) Oxtail.

— *a la andaluza* (ah lah ahn-dah-loo-sah) Oxtail stew with a *sofrito* containing cured ham and paprika.

— *a la jerezana* (ah lah heh-reh-sáh-nah) Oxtail stew with bouquet garni, meat broth, white wine, and a *sofrito* containing paprika.

*Ragout de cordero* (rah-góo deh kohr-déh-roh) Lamb ragout.

*Ragout de ternera* (rah-góo deh tehr-néh-rah) Veal ragout.

*Rancho* (ráhn-choh) Stew in Portuguese.

— *a porta nova* (ah póhr-tah nóh-bah) Chickpea stew with pork shank, beef brisket, macaroni, and *sofrito* with cumin (from Portugal).

*Rape* (ráh-peh) Anglerfish.

— *a la Costa Brava* (ah lah kóhs-tah bráh-bah) Baked angler in wine sauce flavored with saffron.

— *a la malagueña* (ah lah mah-lah-guéh-nyah) Braised angler with a *sofrito* containing fried bread and saffron.

— *con pimentón* (kohn pee-mehn-tóhn) Angler simmered in a liquid containing oil, garlic, paprika and bay leaf.

— *comodoro* (koh-moh-dóh-roh) Fried angler with mushrooms and artichokes.

— *con piñones* (kohn pee-nyóh-nehs) Sautéed angler with pine nuts.

— *Pompadour* (pohm-pah-dóor) Poached angler medallions with hollandaise sauce and garnished with tomato sauce and mushrooms.

— *marinera* (mah-ree-néh-rah) Angler casserole made with clam juice, green peas, pimiento, and paprika.

— *hawayana* (hah-oo-ah-yáh-nah) Fried angler with onion rings and grilled pineapple.

*Raspadura de limón* (rahs-pah-dóo rah deh lee-móhn) Grated lemon rind.

*Raspadura de naranja* (rahs-pah-dóo-rah deh nah-ráhn-hah) Grated orange rind.

*Ravioles* (rah-bee-óh-lehs) Ravioli.

— *con tomate* (kohn toh-máh-teh) Ravioli in tomato sauce.

— *regios* (réh-hee-ohs) Ravioli in a sauce containing foie gras, whipping cream, brandy, and Parmesan cheese.

**Redondo de ternera** (reh-dóhn-doh deh tehr-néh-rah) Veal round.

— **al horno** (ahl óhr-noh) Roasted veal round.

**Remojón** (reh-moh-hóhn) Shredded de-salted salt-cod and orange slices combined with black olives and scallions dressed with a paprika vinaigrette.

**Remolacha** (reh-moh-láh-chah) Beet.

— **aliñada** (ah-lee-nyáh-dah) Boiled beet dressed with oil and vinegar and garnished with quartered hard-boiled egg.

— **con atún** (kohn ah-tóon) Diced boiled beet mixed with canned tuna in oil and dressed with minced garlic, fresh parsley, oil, and vinegar.

**Rene Barbier** (reh-néh bahr-bee-éhr) Vintage wine from Penedés.

**Repollo** (reh-póh-yoh) Green cabbage.

— **con salsa holandesa** (kohn sáh-sah oh-lahn-déh-sah) Boiled shredded cabbage with hollandaise sauce.

— **relleno de salchicha** (reh-yéh-noh deh sahl-chée-chah) Cabbage leaf stuffed with sausage.

**Requesón** (reh-keh-sóhn) Cottage cheese.

**Reserva** (reh-séhr-bah) Aged wine of special quality.

**Respigos** (rehs-pée-gohs) Sautéed turnip greens with bacon, anchovies, and green peppers.

**Ribeiro** (ree-béh-ee-roh) Area in Galicia producing fruity wines of low alcohol content.

**Ribera del Duero** (ree-béh-rah dehl doo-éh-roh) Region where the

famous Vega Sicilia wines are made.

**Riñones** (ree-nyóh-nehs) Kidneys.

— **a la cántabra** (ah lah káhn-tah-bra) Lamb kidneys, bacon, sausage, and mushrooms on a skewer.

— **al jerez** (ahl heh-réhs) Sautéed veal kidneys in sherry sauce.

**Rioja** (ree-óh-hah) A region south of the Basque Country, famous for its excellent wines.

— **Bordón** (bohr-dóhn) Vintage wine from Rioja.

**Rissois de camarao** (ree-sóh-ehs deh kah-mah-ráh-oh) Shrimp rissolés (from Portugal).

**Rizos de jamón de York** (rée-sohs deh hah-móhn deh yóhrk) Ham rolls filled with gelatine foie gras.

**Rodaballo** (roh-dah-báh-yoh) Turbot.

— **a la andaluza** (ah lah ahn-dah-lóo-sah) Baked turbot in a fumet containing sautéed vegetables.

— **California** (kah-lee-fóhr-nee-ah) Poached turbot with brandy sauce.

— **con grelos y almejas** (kohn gréh-lohs ee ahl-méh-hahs) Cooked turbot with vegetable greens and clams (from Galicia).

— **miramar** (mee-rah-máhr) Grilled turbot seasoned with lemon juice, salt, and pepper.

**Rollitos de lenguado** (roh-yée-tohs deh lehn-goo-áh-doh) Sole, bacon, and cheese paupiettes.

**Rollos de anís** (róh-yohs deh ah-nées) Single knot sweet rolls made with *aguardiente* liquor.

**Rollos de manteca** (róh-yohs de mahn-téh-kah) Single knot sweet rolls made with lard.

V O C A B U L A R Y

*Romero* (roh-méh-roh) Rosemary.

*Roncal* (rohn-káhl) Ewe's-milk cheese with a smoky flavor (from Navarra).

*Ropa vieja* (róh-pah bee-éh-hah) Chopped leftover stewed beef sautéed with diced potatoes, onion, tomato, eggplant, and thyme.

*Rosca de arroz con salmón* (róhs-kah deh ah-rróhs kohn sahl-móhn) Béchamel sauce with shredded salmon surrounded by a white rice circle.

*Roscón de reyes* (rohs-kóhn deh réh-yehs) Large ring-shaped brioche containing minced candied fruit.

*Roscos* (róhs-kohs) Baked dough rings made of flour, lard, egg, sugar, and grated lemon rind.

— *de candelilla* (deh kahn-deh-lée-yah) Single knot sweet rolls made with honey and lemon juice.

— *de Reinosa* (deh reh-ee-nóh-sah) Single knot sweet rolls made with dry sherry.

— *de vino* (deh bée-noh) Single knot sweet rolls made with wine and flavored with aniseed.

*Rosquillas* (rohs-kée-yahs) Deep-fried rings made with a dough containing white wine and olive oil.

— *de La Mancha* (deh lah máhn-chah) Single knot sweet rolls made with lemon juice and aniseed.

*Rubio* (róo-bee-oh) Red gurnard.

— *a la casera* (ah lah kah-séh-rah) Simmered red gurnard with a *sofrito* containing lemon juice, saffron and fish fumet.

# S

*Sabayón de naranja* (sah-bah-yóhn deh nah-ráhn-hah) Orange sabayon.

*Sal* (sahl) Salt.

*Salada* (sah-láh-dah) Salad.

— *a lisbonense* (ah lees-boh-néhn-seh) Cooked Belgian endive, carrots, and beets combined with fresh tomatoes and hard-boiled egg with vinaigrette dressing (from Portugal).

— *de bacalhau* (deh bah-kah-láh-oo) Shredded de-salted salt-cod combined with green peppers and tomatoes and dressed with olive oil, lemon juice, and fresh chopped parsley (from Portugal).

— *portuguesa* (pohr-too-guéh-sah) Boston lettuce, watercress, tomato, onion, and anchovy-stuffed olives with vinaigrette dressing (from Portugal).

*Salamanca* (sah-lah-máhn-kah) City in the region of León, site of one of the first European universities.

*Salchicha* (sahl-chée-chah) Thin pork sausage.

— *al jerez* (ahl heh-réhs) Thin pork sausage in sherry wine sauce.

*Salchichón* (sahl-chee-chóhn) Thick salami sausage.

*Salmon* (sahl-móhn) Salmon.

— *ahumado* (ah-oo-máh-doh) Smoked salmon.

— *a la alicantina* (ah lah ah-lee-kahn-tée-nah) Grilled salmon steak previously marinated in olive oil, lemon juice, red peppers, and seasonings.

— *a la andaluza* (ah lah ahn-dah-lóo-sah) Salmon simmered in a liquid containing oil, vinegar, green olives, and parsley and garnished with hard-boiled eggs.

— *a la sidra* (ah lah sée-drah) Baked salmon with ham and hard cider.

**Salmonetes** (sahl-moh-néh-tehs) Red mullets.

— *a la nizarda* (ah lah nee-sáhr-dah) Fried red mullets garnished with a *sofrito* containing anchovies and gherkins.

— *en escabeche* (ehn ehs-kah-béh-cheh) Pickled red mullets.

— *fritos* (frée-tohs) Fried red mullets.

**Salmorejo** (sahl-moh-réh-hoh) Pasty combination of tomatoes, garlic, soaked bread, vinegar, and olive oil, garnished with diced cured ham and hard-boiled eggs.

**Salpicón de mariscos** (sahl-pee-kóhn deh mah-rées-kohs) Seafood salmagundi.

**Salsa** (sáhl-sah) Sauce.

— *alioli* (ah-lee-óh-lee) Garlic mayonnaise sauce.

— *al jerez* (ahl heh-réhs) Sherry sauce made with butter, shallots, flour, stock, parsley, salt, and peper.

— *amarilla* (ah-mah-rée-yah) Cold sauce made from egg, olive oil, French mustard, vinegar, salt, and pepper.

— *Aranjuez* (ah-rahn-hoo-éhs) Sauce made with asparagus, leek, carrot, rice, butter, whipping cream, egg yolk, salt, and pepper.

— *bechamel* (beh-chah-méhl) White sauce made from flour, butter, milk, nutmeg, salt, and pepper.

— *campesina* (kahm-peh-sée-nah) Sauce made with tomato, red wine, mushrooms, onion, paprika, vegetable broth, bread crumb, herbs, olive oil, and salt.

— *castellana* (kahs-teh-yáh-nah) Sauce made from crushed fried bread, garlic, egg, minced cured ham, paprika, olive oil, and salt.

— *catalana* (kah-tah-láh-nah) Sauce made from minced beef, egg, garlic, onion, pureed celery and turnip, tomato puree, parsley, fresh mint, bay leaf, olive oil, salt, and pepper.

— *chateaubriand* (chah-toh-bree-áhnd) White wine sauce with butter, shallots, mushrooms, meat juice, tarragon, lemon juice, parsley, salt, and pepper.

— *chilindrón* (chee-leen-dróhn) Tomato sauce made from sweet peppers, onions, garlic, and olive oil.

— *de aceitunas* (deh ah-seh-ee-tóo-nahs) Green olive sauce with butter, onion, flour, broth, parsley, dry white wine, and salt to taste.

— *de aguacate* (deh ah-goo-ah-káh-teh) Cold avocado sauce with onion, lemon juice, mayonnaise, tabasco, salt, and pepper.

— *de ajo* (deh áh-hoh) Cold sauce with garlic, vinegar, bread crumb, meat broth, paprika, and salt.

— *de albahaca* (deh ahl-bah-áh-kah) Fresh mint sauce with onion, dry vermouth, lemon juice, corn stearch, whipping cream,oil, salt, and pepper.

— *de alcachofas* (deh ahl-kah-chóh-fahs) Pureed artichoke bottoms with butter, milk, whipping cream, flour, salt, and pepper.

— *de alcaparras* (deh ahl-kah-páh-rrahs) White sauce with capers, butter, flour, nutmeg, milk, whipping cream, lemon juice, and salt.

— *de almejas* (deh ahl-méh-hahs) Clam sauce made with fish broth, onion, whipping cream, flour, parsley, garlic, tomato puree, saffron, olive oil, and salt.

— *de almendras* (deh ahl-méhn-drahs) Sauce made with puree of blanched almonds, tomatoes, olive oil, salt, and pepper.

— *de anchoas* (deh ahn-chóh-ahs) Sauce made with canned anchovies, butter, and cream cheese.

— *de apio* (deh áh-pee-oh) Béchamel sauce with pureed celery, onion, garlic, egg yolk, parsley, brandy, bay leaf, olive oil, salt, and pepper.

— *de arroz* (deh ah-rróhs) Sauce made with boiled rice, meat broth, butter, parsley, hard-boiled egg, and salt.

— *de atún* (deh ah-tóon) Cold sauce made with canned tuna fish, egg yolk, garlic, olive oil, vinegar and salt.

— *de azafrán* (deh ah-sah-fráhn) Sauce made with fish broth, egg yolk, whipping cream, corn starch, saffron, and salt.

— *de castañas* (de kahs-táh-nyahs) Chestnut sauce made from chestnut puree, raisins, meat broth, butter, and salt.

— *de ciruelas* (deh see-roo-éh-lahs) Sauce made from pureed plums, butter, sugar, corn starch, pine nuts, and salt.

— *de espinacas* (deh ehs-pee-náh-kahs) Boiled spinach sauce made with butter, milk, raisins, pine nuts, whipping cream, flour, salt, and pepper.

— *de gambas* (deh gáhm-bahs) Sauce made with pureed shrimp, butter, garlic, onion, tomato puree, white wine, flour, brandy, thyme, parsley, salt, and pepper.

— *de limón* (deh lee-móhn) Cold lemon sauce made with lemon juice, onion, parsley, gherkins, capers, hard-boiled egg, olive oil, and salt.

— *de marisco* (deh mah-rées-koh) Seafood sauce made from pureed seafood, butter, flour, tomato puree, whipping cream, white wine, brandy, salt, and pepper.

— *de mejillones* (deh meh-hee-yóh-nehs) Sauce made with pureed mussels, butter, egg yolk, milk, corn starch, ketchup, nutmeg, and salt.

— *de mostaza* (deh mohs-táh-sah) Mustard sauce made from butter, flour, egg yolk, stock, dry mustard, salt, and pepper.

— *de naranjas* (deh nah-ráhn-hahs) Sauce made with orange juice, onion, butter, flour, sugar, and salt.

— *de olivas* (deh oh-lée-bahs) Cold sauce made from black olives, minced onion, and cream cheese.

— *de ostras* (deh óhs-trahs) Oyster sauce made from béchamel, oyster fumet, parsley, salt, and pepper.

— *de pan* (deh pahn) Bread sauce made with milk, onion, whipping cream, butter, cayenne, and salt to taste.

- *frito* (frée-toh) Fried bread sauce made with fried bread crumbs, butter, stock, diced ham, onion, parsley, and lemon juice.

— *de pimientos* (de pee-mee-éhn-tohs) Cold sauce consisting of a blend of canned pimientos, shallots, garlic, parsley, and salt.

- *rojos* (róh-hohs) Sauce made from sweet red peppers with onion, garlic, olive oil, and salt.

— *de rábanos* (deh ráh-bah-nohs) Béchamel sauce with added pureed boiled radishes and dry mustard.

— *de remolacha* (deh reh-moh-láh-chah) Sauce made with pureed beets, meat broth, whipping cream, salt, and pepper.

— *de tomate* (deh toh-máh-teh) Tomato sauce made with sautéed fresh tomatoes, onions, garlic, paprika, and salt.

— *de vino blanco* (deh bée-noh bláhn-koh) White wine sauce with butter, egg yolks, shallots, and lemon juice.

— *española* (ehs-pah-nyóh-lah) Brown sauce made from a reduced sherry-deglazed rich stock.

— *madera* (mah-déh-rah) Madeira wine sauce made with butter, shallots, flour, stock, parsley, salt, and pepper.

— *mahonesa* (mah-oh-néh-sah) Mayonnaise sauce made from eggs, olive oil, dry mustard, lemon juice, and salt.

— *mornay* (móhr-neh) Béchamel sauce with beer, grated cheese, and cayenne.

— *moruna* (moh-róo-nah) Cold sauce made with lemon juice, olive oil, paprika, Tabasco, salt, and pepper.

— *murciana* (moor-see-áh-nah) Sauce made from tomato, toasted almonds, garlic, vinegar, paprika, parsley, mayonnaise, salt, and pepper.

— *muselina* (moo-seh-lée-nah) White wine sauce with egg yolks, butter, and lemon juice.

— *oscura* (ohs-kóo-rah) Sauce for furred game made from butter, chopped carrot, onion, flour, garlic, marjoram, meat stock, and red wine.

— *picada* (pee-káh-dah) Blend of toasted almonds, hazelnuts, saffron, herbs, and spices added to fish or meat stews.

— *primavera* (pree-mah-béh-rah) Butter sauce with flour, broth, egg yolk, salt, and pepper.

— *riojana* (ree-oh-háh-nah) *Salsa española* with sautéed onion and dry red wine added.

— *romesco* (roh-méhs-koh) Sauce from Catalonia consisting of a blend of toasted almonds, hot chili peppers, garlic, fried bread, tomatoes, olive oil, vinegar, white pepper, and salt.

— *salmorejo* (sahl-moh-réh-hoh) Cold sauce made from water, vinegar, olive oil, salt, and pepper.

— *tártara* (táhr-tah-rah) Mayonnaise sauce with chopped capers, parsley, gherkins, tarragon, dry mustard, and cayenne pepper.

VOCABULARY

— *vasca* (báhs-kah) Sauce made from fish broth, garlic, flour, asparagus puree, white wine, parsley, olive oil, and salt.

— *verde* (béhr-deh) Sauce made with parsley, olive oil, garlic, flour, ginger, milk, white wine, salt, and pepper.

— *victoria* (beek-tóh-ree-ah) Sauce for game dishes made from blackcurrant jelly, stock, orange juice, sherry, cloves, cayenne, salt, pepper, and a dash of cinnamon.

— *vinagreta* (vee-nah-gréh-tah) Vinaigrette sauce made from olive oil, vinegar, garlic, chopped parsley, salt, and pepper.

**Salsifis** (sahl-sée-fees) Salsify.

— *al gratén* (ahl grah-téhn) Au gratin salsify.

**Salvia** (sáhl-bee-ah) Sage.

**Sancocho canario** (sahn-kóh-choh kah-náh-ree-oh) Salt fish stew with potatoes, sweet potatoes, and roasted corn meal (from the Canary Islands).

**Sandía** (sahn-dée-ah) Watermelon.

**Sangre de Toro** (sáhn-greh deh tóh-roh) Vintage wine from Penedés.

**Sangría** (sahn-grée-ah) Refreshing drink generally made with red wine, brandy, fresh fruit, and soda water.

— *menorquí* (meh-nohr-kée) Red wine, water, sugar, cinnamon stick, strips of lemon, orange peel, and nutmeg (from the island of Menorca).

**San Simón** (sahn see-móhn) Smoked cow's-milk cheese from Galicia.

**Santola recheada fría** (sahn-tóh-lah reh-cheh-áh-dah frée-ah) Cold stuffed crab (from Portugal).

**Sardinas** (sahr-dée-nahs) Sardines.

— *a la navarra* (ah lah nah-báh-rrah) Baked sardines with a blend of bread crumbs, paprika, and spices.

— *a la plancha* (ah lah plán-chah) Grilled sardines.

— *a la vinagreta* (ah lah bee-nah-greh-tah) Sardines simmered in a vinaigrette sauce containing saffron and hard-boiled egg.

— *al Sacromonte* (ahl sah-kroh-móhn-teh) Sardines simmered in a liquid containing oil, onion, tomato, and paprika.

— *siciliana* (see-see-lee-áh-nah) Baked sardines stuffed with pine nuts, almonds, raisins, and bread crumbs.

**Segovia** (seh-góh-bee-ah) City in central Spain famous for its roast suckling pig.

**Sepia** (séh-pee-ah) Cuttlefish.

— *con cebolla* (kohn seh-bóh-yah) Sautéed cuttlefish with onions.

— *guisada* (guee-sáh-dah) Cuttlefish stew with potatoes.

**Sequillos** (seh-kée-yohs) Club rolls made with *aguardiente* liquor.

**Serena** (seh-réh-nah) Hard ewe's-milk cheese from Extremadura. It is creamy but bitter in flavor, although very tasty.

**Sesos** (séh-sohs) Brains.

— *de cordero rebozados* (deh kohr-déh-roh reh-boh-sáh-dohs) Breaded, fried lamb brains.

**Setas** (séh-tahs) Wild mushrooms.

— *a la casera* (ah lah kah-séh-rah) Wild mushrooms simmered with onion and sherry wine and garnished with chopped hard-boiled egg.

— *a la navarra* (ah lah nah-báh-rrah) Wild mushrooms sautéed with white wine, crushed almonds, garlic and paprika.

— *con salsa de almendras* (kohn sáhl-sah deh ahl-méhn-drahs) Wild mushrooms sautéed in butter, thickened with flour, and simmered in meat broth with crushed almonds and paprika.

— *salteadas* (sahl-teh-áh-dahs) Sautéed wild mushrooms.

*Shangurro* (shahn-góo-rroh) Stuffed crab Basque-style.

*Sidra* (see-drah) Hard cider produced in the region of Asturias.

*Sobrasada* (soh-brah-sáh-dah) Chorizo spread from the Balearic Islands.

*Sofrito* (soh-frée-toh) Basic sauce in Spanish cuisine widely used throughout the country. It consists of minced onion, garlic, tomatoes (and often sweet peppers), sautéed in olive oil with seasonings, herbs, and spices, especially saffron and paprika.

*Solera* (soh-léh-rah) Aged wine used to strengthen new vintage.

*Solomillo* (soh-loh-mée-yoh) Tenderloin.

— *a la andaluza* (ah lah ahn-dah-lóo-sah) Roast larded beef tenderloin garnished with stewed mushrooms and onions.

— *a la granadina* (ah lah grah-nah-dée-nah) Roast beef tenderloin garnished with turnips, carrots, onions, and tomatoes.

— *a la naranja* (ah lah nah-ráhn-hah) Beef tenderloin with orange sauce.

— *a la pimienta* (ah lah pee-mee-éhn-tah) Grilled beef tenderloin dressed with a sauce containing peppercorns, brandy, and whipping cream.

— *con salsa de berros* (kohn sahl-sah deh béh-rrohs) Beef tenderloin with watercress sauce.

— *de cerdo a la malagueña* (deh séhr-doh ah lah mah-lah-guéh-nyah) Roast pork tenderloin dressed with a sauce made of sautéed onion, meat broth, lemon juice, nutmeg, and flour and garnished with sliced hard-boiled egg, green peas, and cubed cured ham.

— *de cerdo al jerez* (deh séhr-doh ahl heh-réhs) Roast bacon-larded pork loin basted with meat broth and sherry wine.

— *de cerdo con aceitunas* (deh séhr-doh kohn ah-seh-ee-tóo-nahs) Roast pork tenderloin with green olive sauce.

— *de vaca al vino* (deh báh-kah ahl bée-noh) Baked beef tenderloin with wine sauce.

*Sopa* (sóh-pah) Soup.

— *a la alentejana* (ah lah ah-lehn-teh-háh-nah) Coriander and garlic soup with poached eggs (from Portugal).

— *a la castellana* (ah lah kahs-teh-yáh-nah) Almond soup Castilian-style.

— *a la malagueña* (ah lah mah-lah-guéh-nyah) Clam broth with a *sofrito* and seasoned with paprika.

— *a la marinera* (ah lah mah-ree-néh-rah) Fisherman-style soup made with shellfish.

— *a la reina andaluza* (ah lah réh-ee-nah ahn-dah-lóo-sah) Beef broth enhanced with a *sofrito* thickened with flour and garnished with diced roasted green pepper.

— *al cuarto de hora* (ahl koo-áhr-toh deh óh-rah) Seafood broth with rice and green peas.

— *asturiana* (ahs-too-ree-áh-nah) Broth made with sorrel, leeks, and corn meal to which a *sofrito* is added.

— *aterciopelada* (ah-tehr-see-oh-peh-láh-dah) Beef broth with tapioca, whipping cream, and egg yolks.

— *balear* (bah-leh-áhr) Broth made with minced beef, ham, *sofrito*, and bread soaked in red wine.

— *burgalesa* (boor-gah-léh-sah) Chicken broth enhanced with sautéed lamb meat, and crayfish.

— *catalana* (kah-tah-láh-nah) Stock enhanced with a *sofrito* made with vegetables, ham, and egg yolks (from Catalonia).

— *de ajo* (deh áh-hoh) Garlic soup.

— *a la castellana* (ah lah kahs-teh-yáh-nah) Garlic soup with bread croutons.

— *con huevos* (kohn oo-éh-bohs) Garlic soup with added egg yolks.

— *de albóndigas* (deh ahl-bóhn-dee-gahs) Meatball soup.

— *de almejas* (deh ahl-méh-hahs) Clam soup.

— *de almendras* (deh ahl-méhn-drahs) Almond soup.

— *de apio* (deh áh-pee-oh) Celery soup.

— *de Béjar* (deh béh-hahr) Chicken broth enhanced with a *sofrito* made with paprika and garnished with bread slices (from León).

— *de berros a la castellana* (deh béh-rrohs ah lah kahs-teh-yáh-nah) Watercress soup containing potatoes and whipping cream.

— *de boda* (deh bóh-dah) Chicken broth with chicken giblets and slices of bread (from León).

— *de Cádiz* (deh káh-dees) Chicken broth garnished with cured ham, sherry, and hard-boiled egg.

— *de calabacín* (deh kah-lah-bah-séen) Zucchini soup.

— *de cebolla* (deh seh-bóh-yah) Onion soup.

— *de centollo* (deh sehn-tóh-yoh) Spider crab soup.

– *a la gallega* (ah lah gah-yéh-gah) Spider crab soup containing bacon and grated cheese (from Galicia).

— *de cerezas* (deh seh-réh-sahs) Cherry soup made with wine and milk.

— *de cerveza* (deh sehr-béh-sah) Beer soup made with eggs, ham, milk, and bread slices.

— *de col* (deh kohl) Cabbage soup.

— *de coliflor* (deh koh-lee-flóhr) Cauliflower soup.

— *de congrio* (deh kóhn-gree-oh) Eel soup.

— *de gallina* (deh gah-yée-nah) Hen soup.

— *de gambas* (deh gáhm-bahs) Shrimp soup.

— *de garbanzos* (deh gahr-bahn-sohs) Chickpea soup.

— *de habas tiernas* (deh áh-bahs tee-éhr-nahs) Fresh fava bean soup.

— *de jamón* (deh hah-móhn) Ham soup.

— *de lentejas* (deh lehn-téh-hahs) Lentil soup.

— *de mariscos* (deh mah-réeskohs) Shellfish soup.

— *de mejillones* (deh meh-heeyóh-nehs) Mussel soup.

— *de menudillos* (deh men-noodée-yohs) Chicken giblet soup.

— *de mero con arroz* (deh méhroh kohn ah-rróhs) Sea bass soup with rice.

— *de ostras pontevedrense* (deh óhs-trahs pohn-teh-beh-dréhnseh) Chopped oyster soup (from Galicia).

— *de pedra* (deh péh-drah) Red kidney bean soup with vegetables and chorizo sausage (from Portugal).

— *de perdiz* (deh pehr-dées) Partridge soup with sherry wine.

— *de pescado* (deh pehs-káh-doh) Fish soup.

- *con fideos* (kohn fee-déh-ohs) Fish soup with thin spaghetti.

— *de picadillo* (de pee-kah-déeyoh) Chicken broth with diced cured ham, hard-boiled egg, and mint.

— *de pimientos* (deh pee-meeéhn-tohs) Bell pepper soup flavored with paprika.

— *de queso* (deh kéh-soh) Cheese soup.

— *de rabo de buey* (deh ráh-boh deh boo-éh-ee) Oxtail soup.

— *de rape* (deh ráh-peh) Anglerfish soup.

— *de remolacha* (deh reh-mohláh-chah) Beet soup.

— *de setas* (deh séh-tahs) Wild mushroom soup.

— *de tomate* (deh toh-máh-teh) Tomato soup.

— *de tomillo* (deh toh-mée-yoh) Thyme soup.

— *de vigilia* (deh bee-hée-lee-ah) Fish stock with a *sofrito* containing shredded boiled fish and garnished with cauliflower florets.

— *de yogur* (deh yoh-góor) Yogurt soup.

— *Donosty* (doh-nóhs-tee) Crab soup enhanced with shallots, truffles, red wine, and brandy (from the Basque Country).

— *granadina* (grah-nah-dée-nah) Bread soup with a *sofrito* flavored with saffron.

— *juliana* (hoo-lee-áh-nah) Vegetable soup with garlic.

— *leonesa* (leh-oh-néh-sah) Beaten egg, bread, and paprika soup.

— *mahonesa* (mah-oh-néh-sah) Chicken broth enhanced with sautéed bread soaked in milk and beaten eggs (from the island of Menorca).

— *mallorquina* (mah-yohr-kéenah) Cabbage soup with chorizo spread (from the Balearic Islands).

— *manchega* (mahn-chéh-gah) Chicken broth with a *sofrito* made with garlic, asparagus tips, and saffron.

— *montañesa* (mohn-tah-nyéhsah) Vegetable broth enhanced with a thick *sofrito* and macaroni.

— *oscense* (ohs-séhn-seh) Veal liver and cheese soup from Aragón.

— *payesa* (pah-yéh-sah) Cabbage and ham soup from Catalonia.

— *real* (reh-áhl) Seasoned stock garnished with cured ham, chicken, hard-boiled egg, and sherry.

— *tinerfeña* (tee-nehr-féh-nyah) Rice soup with a *sofrito* and lemon juice (from the Canary Islands).

— *torrada* (toh-rráh-dah) Chicken broth garnished with meat balls and fried bread slices.

— *gatas* (gáh-tahs) Garlic soup with beaten egg and bread.

**Sorbete** (sohr-béh-teh) Sorbet.

— *de champán* (deh chahm-páhn) Champagne sorbet.

**Soria** (sóh-ree-ah) Fresh goat's-milk cheese from Castile.

**Souffle de atún** (soo-fléh deh ah-tóon) Tuna soufflé.

**Suizos** (soo-ée-sohs) Sweet rolls.

**Suquet de pescadores** (soo-kéht deh pehs-kah-dóh-rehs) Seafood stew with *sofrito*, white wine, and a *majado* made with saffron, garlic, almonds, and parsley (from Catalonia).

**Suspiros de Murcia** (soos-pée-rohs deh móor-see-ah) Baked ground toasted almonds folded with egg white.

# T

**Tallarines** (tah-yah-rée-nehs) Noodles.

— *a la alsaciana* (ah lah ahl-sah-see-áh-nah) Baked noodles in a thick white sauce containing ham, chicken livers, truffles, and Parmesan.

— *a la boloñesa* (ah lah boh-loh-nyéh-sah) Noodles with a minced-meat tomato sauce.

— *a la carbonara* (ah lah kahr-boh-náh-rah) Noodles with egg, bacon, garlic, and butter.

— *con anchoas* (kohn ahn-chóh-ahs) Buttered noodles with a paste of crushed anchovies, garlic, parsley, and egg yolk.

**Tapas** (táh-pahs) Snacks.

**Tarta** (táhr-tah) Cake, tart.

— *al whiskey* (ahl goo-ées-kee) Frozen whiskey layer cake with vanilla ice cream.

— *de cebolla* (deh seh-bóh-yah) Pie shell filled with sautéed onion in bacon fat, eggs, milk, and seasonings.

— *de huevos* (deh oo-éh-bohs) Eggs baked over a meat or fish pie.

— *de legumbres* (deh leh-góom-brehs) Pie shell filled with a layer of spinach puree, another of chopped cooked leeks, and one of cooked potatoes. The pie is sprinkled with grated cheese and baked.

— *de manzana* (deh mahn-sáh-nah) Apple custard tart.

— *de Portomarín* (deh pohr-toh-mah-réen) Torte made with ground almonds, eggs, and syrup.

— *de Puentedeume* (deh poo-ehn-teh-déh-oo-meh) Almond and egg yolk cake.

— *de Sacromonte* (deh sah-kroh-móhn-teh) Tart made with toasted bread crumb, milk, egg, lard, and cinnamon.

— *de Santiago* (deh sahn-tee-áh-goh) Almond cake with coffee cream frosting.

**Tartaleta** (tahr-tah-léh-tah) Tartlet.

— *de arroz* (deh ah-rróhs) Tartlets filled with plain boiled rice mixed with mayonnaise and napped with tomato sauce.

— *de champiñones* (deh chahn-pee-nyóh-nehs) Mushroom-mayonnaise tartlets.

— *de riñones* (deh ree-nyóh-nehs) Tartlets of sautéed kidneys in sherry sauce.

— *de salmón* (deh sahl-móhn) Salmon tartlets.

*Tarta quemada helada* (táhr-tah keh-máh-dah eh-láh-dah) Frozen orange custard with brittle caramel.

*Té* (teh) Tea.

*Ternasco* (tehr-náhs-koh) Baby lamb.

— *asado* (ah-sáh-doh) Roast baby lamb.

*Ternera* (tehr-néh-rah) Veal.

— *a la provenzal* (ah lah proh-behn-sáhl) Veal ragout with onions and thyme.

— *a la sevillana* (ah lah seh-bee-yáh-nah) Beef tenderloin simmered with green olives, toasted almonds, sherry wine, and *sofrito*.

— *a la sidra* (ah lah sée-drah) Veal casserole with green peas, hard cider, and *sofrito*.

— *al jugo* (ahl hóo-goh) Roast veal au jus.

— *asada* (ah-sáh-dah) Roast veal.

— *con guisantes* (kohn guee-sáhn-tehs) Veal stew with green peas.

*Terrina* (teh-rrée-nah) Terrine.

— *de ahumados* (deh ah-oo-máh-dohs) Smoked fish terrine.

— *de conejo* (deh koh-néh-hoh) Rabbit terrine.

*Tetilla* (teh-tée-yah) Creamy, pear-shaped cow's-milk cheese from Galicia.

*Tila* (tée-lah) Linden tea.

*Timbal de hígado* (teem-báhl deh ée-gah-doh) Liver timbale.

*Tirabeques* (tee-rah-béh-kehs) Snow peas.

— *rellenos* (reh-yéh-nohs) Fried snow peas stuffed with a fine paste made with ground meat and cured ham.

*Tocino de cielo* (toh-sée-noh deh see-éh-loh) Egg yolk-rich caramel custard.

*Tomatada a la navarra* (toh-mah-táh-dah ah lah nah-báh-rrah) Tomatoes simmered in olive oil with cured ham, chorizo, strips of veal and sweet peppers.

*Tomate* (toh-máh-teh) Tomato.

— *a la florentina* (ah lah floh-rehn-tée-nah) Tomatoes stuffed with creamed spinach.

— *al horno* (ahl óhr-noh) Baked tomatoes.

— *rellenos* (reh-yéh-nohs) Stuffed tomatoes.

— *alicantina* (ah-lee-kahn-tée-nah) Baked tomato halves stuffed with sautéed spinach, grated orange peel, and crushed sautéed almonds.

*Tomillo* (toh-mée-yoh) Thyme.

*Tordo* (tóhr-doh) Thrush.

— *a la tudelana* (ah lah too-deh-láh-nah) Thrush, stuffed with diced cured ham and braised in wine, onion, garlic, and cloves.

— *al vino blanco* (ahl bée-noh bláhn-koh) Thrush braised in white wine.

— *fritos* (frée-tohs) Thrush fried in

***Tordo fritos*** (cont.)
olive oil and dressed with sautéed bread crumb, and parsley.

***Torrijas*** (toh-rrée-hahs) Fried milk-soaked bread flavored with cinnamon and dusted with powdered sugar.

***Torta*** (tóhr-tah) Torte, scone.

— *a la navarra* (ah lah nah-báh-rrah) Torte made with bread, milk, raisins, and cinnamon.

— *de aceite* (deh ah-seh-ée-teh) Sweet rolls made with olive oil.

— *de almendras* (deh ahl-méhn-drahs) Almond torte.

— *de bellotas* (deh beh-yóh-tahs) Acorn scone.

— *de chanchigorri* (deh chahn-chee-góh-rree) Sweet bread studded with fried pork rind.

— *de chicharrones* (deh chee-chah-rróh-nehs) Crisp pork-rind torte.

— *de manteca* (deh mahn-téh-kah) Sweet rolls made with lard and sherry wine.

— *de miel y nueces* (deh mee-éhl ee noo-éh-sehs) Honey and walnut torte.

— *de Pascua* (deh páhs-koo-ah) Sweet rolls made with lard (from Murcia).

— *de plátanos* (deh pláh-tah-nohs) Deep-fried banana dumplings.

— *de queso* (deh kéh-soh) Cheese torte.

***Tortada*** (tohr-táh-dah) Sponge cake soaked in syrup, covered with meringue (from Murcia).

***Tortells de Mallorca*** (tohr-téhys deh mah-yóhr-kah) Sweet bread containing marzipan.

***Tortilla*** (tohr-tée-yah) Omelet.

— *a la andaluza* (ah lah ahn-dah-lóo-sah) Omelet stuffed with *sofrito*.

— *a la gallega* (ah lah gah-yéh-gah) Potato omelet with chorizo sausage, diced pimiento, and a touch of paprika.

— *alicantina* (ah-lee-kahn-tée-nah) Omelet containing onion, tomato, shrimp, ham, asparagus tips, and canned tuna.

— *al queso* (ahl kéh-soh) Cheese omelet.

— *al Sacromonte* (ahl sah-kroh-móhn-teh) Omelet made with lamb's brains, cured ham, potatoes, pimiento, and green peas.

— *asturiana* (ahs-too-ree-áh-nah) Omelet containing onion, tomato, and canned tuna.

— *bretona* (breh-tóh-nah) Omelet with fried onions and mushrooms.

— *canaria* (kah-náh-ree-ah) Omelet with chopped onion, tomato, tarragon, mint, and parsley.

— *catalana* (kah-tah-láh-nah) Omelet made with canned white beans, onion, tomato, and chorizo sausage.

— *chilena* (chee-léh-nah) Folded omelet stuffed with a mixture of lamb's brains, ham, and spices.

— *coruñesa* (koh-roo-nyéh-sah) Potato omelet with bacon and paprika.

— *de angulas* (deh ahn-góo-lahs) Baby eel omelet.

— *de bacalao* (deh bah-kah-láh-oh) Salt-cod omelet.

— *de berenjena* (deh beh-rehn-héh-nah) Eggplant omelet.

— *de cebolla a la andaluza* (deh seh-bóh-yah ah lah ahn-dah-lóo-sah) Omelet made with simmered onion until it is very soft and browned.

— *de champiñones* (deh chahm-pee-nyóh-nehs) Mushroom omelet.

— *de chanquetes* (deh chahn-kéh-tehs) Omelet with fried whitebait (from Málaga).

— *de gambas* (deh gáhm-bahs) Shrimp omelet.

— *de garbanzos* (deh gahr-báhn-sohs) Canned chickpea omelet with onion and pimiento.

— *de habas* (deh áh-bahs) Fresh fava bean omelet.

— *de hierbas* (deh ee-éhr-bahs) Omelet with watercress, celery, and parsley.

— *de patatas* (deh pah-táh-tahs) Potato omelet.

— *de riñones* (deh ree-nyóh-nehs) Kidney omelet.

— *de San Juan* (deh sahn hoo-áhn) Egg dumplings made with bread, garlic, parsley, and saffron (from Andalusia).

— *española* (ehs-pah-nyóh-lah) Flat, thick potato omelet containing chopped onion.

— *francesa* (frahn-séh-sah) Plain folded omelet.

— *granadina* (grah-nah-dée-nah) Omelet with ground veal, green peas, and pimientos.

— *madrileña* (mah-dree-léh-nyah) Omelet containing sweetbreads, ham, onion, tomato, and sherry wine.

— *murciana* (moor-see-áh-nah) Omelet with mixed vegetables.

— *paisana* (pah-ee-sáh-nah) Flat omelet containing diced cured ham and a medley of vegetables.

— *rellena* (reh-yéh-nah) Stuffed folded omelet.

— *sevillana* (seh-bee-yáh-nah) Omelet with onion and red peppers garnished with sautéed mushrooms and tomatoes.

*Tortillitas de camarones* (tohr-tee-yée-tahs deh kah-mah-róh-nehs) Shrimp fritters.

*Tortitas de arroz* (tohr-tée-tahs deh ah-rróhs) Cold béchamel-battered rice cakes fried in olive oil.

*Tostón* (tohs-tóhn) Suckling pig.

— *zamorano* (sah-moh-ráh-noh) Roast suckling pig.

*Tournedos a la alsaciana* (toor-neh-dóh ah lah ahl-sah-see-áh-nah) Fried beef tournedos on toast, garnished with a creamy sauce containing green peas and onions.

– *Rossini* (roh-sée-nee) Fried beef tournedos on toast garnished with foie gras and truffles.

– *royale* (roo-ah-yáhl) Fried beef tournedos on toast garnished with green beans and dressed with a creamy tomato sauce.

*Trempó mallorquí* (trehm-póh mah-yohr-kée) Tomato, green pepper, and onion salad dressed with a vinaigrette with capers.

*Trevélez* (treh-béh-lehs) Small town in the mountains of Andalusia, famous for its delicious cured ham.

*Tronchón* (trohn-chóhn) Ewe's-milk cheese from Aragón. It is semi-hard and mild in taste.

*Trucha* (tróo-chah) Trout.

— *ahumada* (ah-oo-máh-dah) Smoked trout.

— *a la catalana* (ah lah kah-tah-láh-nah) Sautéed trout simmered in a spicy stock containing cumin.

— *a la cazuela* (ah lah kah-soo-éh-lah) Trout casserole.

— *a la judía* (ah lah hoo-dée-ah) Trout baked with onion, olive oil, and flour.

— *a la montañesa* (ah lah mohn-tah-nyéh-sah) Simmered trout in fish stock with white wine.

— *a la navarra* (ah lah nah-báh-rrah) Trout stuffed with cured ham slices and sautéed in oil.

— *al champán* (ahl chahm-páhn) Poached trout in a champagne sauce.

— *al horno* (ahl óhr-noh) Baked trout.

— *al Pirineo* (ahl pee-ree-néh-oh) Baked trout with prosciutto ham.

— *con almendras* (kohn ahl-méhn-drahs) Fried boned trout with a béchamel containing almonds.

— *en aceite* (ehn ah-séh-ee-teh) Fried trout fillets pickled in olive oil and herbs and served cold.

— *rellena jironesa* (reh-yéh-nah hee-roh-néh-sah) Trout stuffed with chopped olives, pimiento, almonds, and mushrooms and cooked *en papillote*.

*Trujillo* (troo-hée-yoh) Town in Extremadura, birthplace of Pizarro, conqueror of Peru.

*Turrón* (too-rróhn) Almond and honey nougat.

*Txangurro* (chahn-góo-rroh) Stuffed spider crab (from the Basque Country).

## U

*Ulloa* (oo-yóh-ah) Soft cheese from Galicia made with cow's milk.

*Uvas* (oó-bahs) Grapes.

## V

*Vaca guisada a la flamenca* (báh-kah guee-sáh-dah ah lah flah-méhn-kah) Beef stew with bouquet garni and bock beer.

*Vainilla* (bah-ee-née-yah) Vanilla.

*Valdepeñas* (bahl-deh-péh-nyahs) Area of La Mancha that produces a large quantity of common table wine.

*Valladolid* (bah-yah-doh-léed) City in the region of León where it is said the best Castilian Spanish is spoken.

*Vega Sicilia* (béh-gah see-sée-lee-ah) One of the best Spanish red wines (from the Ribera del Duero area).

*Venado* (beh-náh-doh) Venison.

— *con salsa de Cabrales* (kohn sáhl-sah deh kah-bráh-lehs) Roast venison with blue cheese sauce.

*Verduras* (behr-dóo-rahs) Vegetable greens.

*Vieiras* (bee-éh-ee-rahs) Galician for sea scallops.

— *de Santiago* (deh sahn-tee-áh-goh) *Coquilles St. Jacques* made with a spicy tomato and wine sauce.

— *gratinadas* (grah-tee-náh-dahs) Scallops au gratin.

*Villalón* (bee-yah-lóhn) Ewe's-milk cheese from the region of Leon. It is sold fresh and is quite mild in flavor.

*Vinagreta* (bee-nah-gréh-tah) Vinaigrette.

— *de mejillones* (deh meh-hee-yóh-nehs) Mussel vinaigrette.

*Vinhos verdes* (bée-nyohs béhr-dehs) Fruity, fresh wines from northwestern Portugal.

*Vino* (bée-noh) Wine.

— *blanco* (bláhn-koh) White wine.

— *caliente* (kah-lee-éhn-teh) Hot wine with sugar, lemon peel, cinnamon stick, and water.

— *corriente* (koh-rree-éhn-teh) Unlabled wine.

— *de la casa* (deh lah káh-sah) House wine.

— *peleón* (peh-leh-óhn) Unsophisticated wine.

— *rosado* (roh-sáh-doh) Rosé wine.

— *tinto* (téen-toh) Red wine.

*Viña* (bée-nyah) Vine.

*Viña Sol* (bée-nyah sohl) Vintage wine from Penedés.

*Viñedo* (bee-nyéh-doh) Vineyard.

## X

*Xató de Sitges* (shah-tóh deh séet-gehs) De-salted salt-cod mixed with canned tuna, anchovies, olives, and tomatoes dressed with a vinaigrette containing almonds and paprika.

## Y

*Yema* (yéh-mah) Yolk.

— *de coco* (deh kóh-koh) Candied egg yolk with grated coconut.

— *de San Leandro* (deh sahn leh-áhn-droh) Candied egg yolks.

— *de Santa Teresa* (deh sahn-tah teh-réh-sah) Candied egg yolks flavored with lemon.

## Z

*Zanahorias* (sah-nah-óh-ree-ahs) Carrots.

— *a la crema* (ah lah kréh-mah) Creamed carrots.

— *con jamón* (kohn hah-móhn) Sautéed carrots with diced cured ham.

— *salteadas* (sahl-teh-áh-dahs) Sautéed carrots.

- *con apio* (kohn ah-pee-oh) Boiled carrots and celery sautéed with garlic and cured ham.

*Zarangollo* (sah-rahn-góh-yoh) Fried zucchini and onions combined with beaten egg and simmered until the egg sets (from Murcia).

*Zancho canario* (sáhn-choh kah-náh-ree-oh) Boiled grouper and potatoes served with a sauce called *mojo colorado*, made with chili peppers, garlic, oil, cumin, and paprika.

*Zarzuela de pescado* (sahr-soo-éh-lah deh pehs-káh-doh) Seafood casserole made with shellfish fumet spiced with brandy and paprika.

— *a la vasca* (ah lah báhs-kah) Seafood casserole in a garlicky white sauce.

*Zumo de limón* (sóo-moh deh lee-móhn) Lemon juice.

*Zurracapote* (soo-rrah-kah-póh-teh) Simmered dried apricots and

**Zurracapote** (cont.)
prunes in red wine, cinnamon, and lemon peel.

**Zurrucutuna** (soo-roo-koo-tóo-nah)
Salt cod casserole with paprika and toasted bread slices.

# Dining Notes